THE BOSTON MASSACRE

MW01035432

On March 5, 1770, after being harassed for two years during their occupation of Boston, British soldiers finally lost control, firing into a mob of rioting Americans, killing several of them, including Crispus Attucks, a runaway slave and sailor, the first African American patriot killed. The aftermath of this "massacre" led to what eventually became the American Revolution. The importance of the event grew, as it was used for political purposes, to stoke the fires of rebellion in the colonists, and to show the British in the most unflattering light.

The Boston Massacre gathers together the most important primary documents pertaining to the incident, along with images, anchored together with a succinct yet thorough introduction, to give students of the Revolutionary period access to the events of the massacre as they unfolded. Included are newspaper stories, the official transcript of the trial, letters, and maps of the area, as well as consideration of how the massacre is remembered today.

Neil L. York is Mary Lou Fulton Professor of History at Brigham Young University in Utah. He is the author of *Turning the World Upside Down: The War of American Independence and the Problem of Empire.*

THE BOSTON MASSACRE
A HISTORY WITH DOCUMENTS

NEIL L. YORK

Routledge
Taylor & Francis Group

NEW YORK AND LONDON

First published 2010
by Routledge
270 Madison Avenue, New York, NY 10016

Simultaneously published in the UK
by Routledge
2 Park Square, Milton Park, Abingdon, Oxon OX14 4RN

Routledge is an imprint of the Taylor & Francis Group, an informa business

Typeset in Minion and Scala Sans
by Keystroke, Tettenhall, Wolverhampton
Printed and bound in the United States of America on acid-free paper
by Walsworth Publishing Company, Marceline, MO

Library of Congress Cataloging in Publication Data
York, Neil Longley.
The Boston Massacre : a history with documents / Neil L. York.
    p. cm.
Includes bibliographical references and index.
1. Boston Massacre, 1770. 2. Boston Massacre, 1770—Sources. I. Title.
E215.4.Y67 2010
973.3'113—dc22   2009052416

ISBN 10: 0–415–87348–7 (hbk)
ISBN 10: 0–415–87349–5 (pbk)
ISBN 10: 0–203–84909–4 (ebk)

ISBN 13: 978–0–415–87348–2 (hbk)
ISBN 13: 978–0–415–87349–9 (pbk)
ISBN 13: 978–0–203–84909–5 (ebk)

To Carole

Ever and Always

CONTENTS

ILLUSTRATIONS

CHRONOLOGY

1767	*June*	Parliament passes the Townshend Revenue Act
	November	Customs commissioners arrive in Boston
1768	*June*	*Liberty* incident in Boston
	September	Delegates from Massachusetts towns meet at extra-legal convention in Boston
	October	Arrival of the 14th and 29th regiments, from Halifax, Nova Scotia
	November	Arrival of most of the 64th and 65th regiments, from Ireland
1769	*June*	64th and 65th regiments leave Boston
	August	Governor Francis Bernard leaves Boston
1770	*February*	Incident leading to the death of Christopher Seider and arrest of Ebenezer Richardson
	March 5	The massacre; three die that night, two mortally wounded, another half-dozen wounded less seriously
	6–26	Arrest and indictment of nine soldiers and four civilians for murder
	8	Public funeral for Attucks, Caldwell, Gray, and Maverick

1770 (contd)	11	29th Regiment withdrawn to Castle Island in Boston harbor
	12–24	Depositions taken for *A Short Narrative* and *A Fair Account*
	14	14th Regiment also removed to Castle Island; Patrick Carr dies
	17	Patrick Carr buried with other four slain
	April	Richardson convicted of murdering Seider; Repeal of the Townshend Revenue Act, except the duty on tea
	June	29th Regiment leaves Castle Island for New Jersey
	September	Accused soldiers and civilians arraigned for murder
	October 24–30	Preston trial and acquittal
	November 27– December 5	Soldiers' trial; six acquitted; two (Kilroy and Montgomery) convicted of manslaughter
	December 12	Civilians' trial; all four acquitted
	14	Kilroy and Montgomery branded on their left hands
1771	April 2	James Lovell delivers the first annual massacre oration
1772	March 5	Dr. James Warren, second annual massacre oration
	August	14th Regiment leaves Castle Island for the West Indies
1773	March 5	Dr. Benjamin Church, third annual oration
	May	Parliament passes the Tea Act
	December 16	The Boston Tea Party
1774	March 5	John Hancock, fourth annual oration
1775	March 6	Dr. Joseph Warren, fifth annual oration
	April 19	Fighting at Lexington and Concord

1776	*March 5*	Peter Thacher, sixth annual oration (in Watertown)
	17	British and loyalists evacuate Boston
1777	*March 5*	Benjamin Hichborn, seventh annual oration
1778	*March 5*	Jonathan Austin, eighth annual oration
1779	*March 5*	William Tudor, ninth annual oration
1780	*March 6*	Jonathan Mason, tenth annual oration
1781	*March 5*	Thomas Dawes, eleventh annual oration
1782	*March 5*	George Richards Minot, twelfth annual oration
1783	*March 5*	Dr. Thomas Welsh, thirteenth annual oration
1887		Circle of paving stones set in State Street (formerly King Street) to mark the massacre site
1888	*November*	Massacre Monument erected on Boston Common
1906		Attucks, Caldwell, Carr, Gray, and Maverick, along with Seider, reinterred under new marker in the Granary burying ground
1951		Official designation of Boston's Freedom Trail
1960s		Circle of paving stones moved to present location, after street intersection reconfigured

PREFACE

Paul Revere's engraving of the Boston Massacre is an iconic image. I suspect that most Americans have seen it somewhere—reproduced in a book, enlarged to a poster, or even reduced to a postcard. They would no doubt recognize it if they saw it again. They most likely would not remember when they saw it first, they might not know the details of what it depicts, but they do know that it shows British soldiers firing on American civilians and that it is somehow connected with the American Revolution. A few might even know that Revere's graphic representation was done for political purposes and that there are questions about its accuracy. Beyond that they may not give it much thought.

Revere's visual image is a document from the past, just the same as a written text. Working with texts is the stock in trade of professional historians. Sadly, over the years I have seen a lack of interest in such things among my students, even among history majors—those, ironically enough, planning to teach, perhaps even write, history. Document anthologies for classroom use are less common than they once were, largely, I fear, because students dislike reading the documents inside. I have heard the groans of those who would rather not deal with Revolutionary Era writing. Most enjoy reading the Declaration of Independence but, stylistically, that text is pithy and direct—hardly typical of the age. Revolutionary Americans trying to make their case against what they considered British oppression more commonly wrote very long and sometimes turgid sentences, with many dependent clauses. Their arguments have to be read closely and patiently, not something that comes naturally to those who "twitter" their text messages.

Robin Winks, a respected historian who took an interest in mystery writers as well as actual cases of espionage, once suggested that the historian ought to be considered a type of detective. Even if his characterization resonated with historians, it probably did not among those outside the profession who see little connection between the dynamic crime scene investigators of prime-time television and stodgy scholars poring over manuscripts in archives. Since the crime-solving techniques of television detectives are all too often unerring as well as unbelievably rapid, that is probably just as well. Even so, the real-world parallels do exist, as historians, like detectives, painstakingly attempt to uncover evidence that will stand as proof in the cases they attempt to make.

With the exception of a few visiting stints elsewhere, I have taught history at the same university for over thirty years, the same university I attended as an undergraduate. The courses that I teach as a professor are similar to the courses that I took as a student, in the sense that they are more or less divided into two categories: content and methodology. It is a division typical of many university history departments. Although it is a distinction that can be pedagogically useful, it is a distinction that is also somewhat artificial, even dangerously specious. Evaluating content requires methodological skill—including the sleuthing skill of a detective—and that skill is best honed when it is applied to some specific historical problem. I find myself most comfortable discussing theoretical issues involving the nature of historical inquiry when I can tie them to a particular place in time, a particular sequence of events, a particular set of participants. More often than not that means exploring some aspect of Revolutionary American history. All but a few of the books and articles I have written are tied to that period, even those that also venture off into related aspects of British or Irish politics.

My research over the years has taken me past remnants of the Boston Massacre, whether it be in the document collections at various libraries and archives or even when walking the streets of Boston. What makes the Boston Massacre interesting in historical terms is that it played a role in the coming of the American Revolution. What makes it interesting historiographically—that is to say, what makes it helpful in learning about the nature and practice of historical research and writing—is that we know so little about it.

What follows is my attempt to bring together methodology and content, in a way appealing to those who are not yet and may never be historians, but on a sufficiently sophisticated level that it will not seem too elementary for those who are already in the profession. My introductory essay is intended to lay the groundwork for a wide range of possible readers, from students taking a historical methodology course to others in a U.S. history survey to still others in a specialized course on Revolutionary America to those who themselves teach such courses.

Although I pose explicit questions here and there, most often I leave the questions implicit. Nothing kills an engaged reading and creative thinking faster than a fixed set of questions, as if those questions and no others should be asked. Some of the documentary excerpts are quite brief; a few are rather long. In some instances I made editorial emendations, but nothing that changed the essence of the text. The record is fragmentary enough and I did not want to fragment it further by excising this passage or that from a document.

The difficulties associated with reconstructing the Boston Massacre are common enough to all historians, whatever their chosen field of study. The event itself is gone; only fragments remain, in an artifact here, a written source there. Gaps in the historical record are inescapable, whether documentation is rich and thick or thin and poor. In some ways the differences that separate historians are merely echoes of what divided those they study—over who did what, and how, and most especially why. I gathered the documents printed here with that connection in mind. They exemplify the disputes leading to imperial crisis; they also show the difficulty of attempting to recapture a moment now gone, never to occur again.

Given the incomplete, hit-or-miss nature of the historical record—given, indeed, the fallibility of those who compiled that record as well as those who later seek to interpret it—historical truths are by definition relative. The real past departed with the people who lived it. We can, as the noted historian Fred Anderson put it, "speak of" those people but we cannot "speak for" them. This is a creed that history professors preach to their students and yet it is a creed they sometimes violate when they engage in their own work. I wince when I encounter a review by a historian that calls some book "definitive." I have a similar reaction to well-intentioned acknowledgments where, after others are thanked, a historian states that whatever errors remain in the book are his or hers alone. Because there can be no last word, there can be no definitive account. Likewise, errors are endemic to the enterprise; they can be minimized but they cannot be wholly eliminated.

One final comment: the reader should imagine the word "massacre" in parentheses virtually wherever I use it in the pages that follow. Boston "Massacre," written repeatedly, strikes me as both tedious and tendentious. The bloody affair involving soldiers and civilians in Boston on the evening of March 5, 1770, was—and was not—a massacre. That it could and could not be, simultaneously, is merely one reason to study this famous event, now a signpost on the road to Revolutionary America. Contradiction, irony, even paradox are inescapable in any examination of the historical past, and markedly so here.

ACKNOWLEDGMENTS

My fascination with Boston dates back many years, to when I was a boy from California visiting grandparents in Massachusetts. Much as I enjoyed seeing the Red Sox at Fenway, I enjoyed even more being in a city where people crossed the street seemingly wherever and whenever they chose. Even today, for me, no trip to Boston is complete without a fair amount of jaywalking—latent revolutionary tendencies brought to the surface.

Those trips have become more or less annual over the last decade, and each time I have met insightful, kindhearted people who have helped with my research. My most recent visit, for this book, brought me into contact with John Bell, "proprietor" of a uniquely informative blog, "Boston 1775." There is no better example of how the Internet can be used to explore the past, including aspects of the massacre. John put me in touch with Charlie Bahne, author of a widely read guide to the Freedom Trail, which barely scratches the surface of what Charlie knows about Revolutionary Boston. Others who proved indispensable were Adele Barbato of the Bostonian Society, Anne Bentley of the Massachusetts Historical Society, and Sean Casey, Ron Grim, and Christine Murphy of the Boston Public Library. Recent trips usually include comparing historical notes with Professor Dan Coquillette, who splits his time between the law schools at Boston College and Harvard. That did not happen this past year but Dan's essays had already guided me through the legal world of the men involved with the massacre trials. Closer to home, I benefited immensely from conversations with Professor Eric Hinderaker of the University of Utah, who is completing his own book on the massacre.

This book exists because Kimberly Guinta of Routledge invited me to write it. Matthew Kopel, her editorial colleague there, ably saw the manuscript through to production. Philip Parr, Belinda Wakefield, and Maggie Lindsey-Jones and her team at Keystroke took it from there. Most travel costs and reproduction fees for the illustrations were covered by funds provided generously to me as a Mary Lou Fulton Professor in my college. David Magleby has been a most supportive college dean, with this book and others. Department chair Shawn Miller and department secretary Julie Radle have likewise smoothed my way.

To all of the good folks above and others unnamed here who lent their assistance—dozens, at the very least—I offer profound thanks. It is the convention in acknowledgments like this to absolve from blame for the final result any who offered aid. If only it were that simple.

PART I

CONTEXT

INTRODUCTION
With Blood "Running Like Water"

"The 5th of March 1770, ought to be an eternal warning to this nation," advised John Adams, because "on that night the foundation of American independence was laid."[1] Adams was referring to the Boston Massacre, some sixteen years after the fact. He had not witnessed the event but less than an hour later he passed by the spot where it occurred. Sharing the concern of those who wanted reason and justice, not passion and mob violence, to prevail, he agreed to represent nine British soldiers charged with murdering five innocent civilians there. That he and his fellow lawyers for the defense were largely successful—seven acquittals and two convictions, those convictions for manslaughter, not murder—was a source of lasting pride to him. "Judgment of Death against those Soldiers would have been as foul a Stain upon this Country as the Execution of the Quakers or Witches, anciently," he reminisced; therefore, "as the Evidence was, the Verdict was exactly right." Even so, in the very next sentence he also wrote: "This however is no reason why the Town should not call the Action of that Night a Massacre."[2]

Adams's apparent inconsistency—calling the event a massacre and yet contending that the soldiers who did the killing were not guilty of murder—says much about this confused moment in time. By law there had been no massacre; rather, there had been an unfortunate incident, pitting soldiers against civilians. But most Bostonians called it a massacre before the soldiers were prosecuted and it remained just that in their minds after the trials ended, legal outcome notwithstanding. To this day law bows to opinion on the matter. Whatever sense of justice—or injustice—that popular memory has formed about the massacre has less to do with what transpired in the courtroom than with the informal trial that occurred outside it.

Although memory of the massacre has been shaped and reshaped over the past two centuries, for most Americans it still assumes a form that John Adams would recognize and most likely find *generally* acceptable. Adams lived a very long time—ninety-one years—so he had many opportunities to comment on the Revolutionary America that he helped make. Looking back as the citizen of an independent republic rather than as a subject of the British crown, he singled out turning points that led to that change in identity. Thus his settling on the massacre as the foundation for future independence. But then again he pointed to other events for the same reason, one a decade earlier, when "the child independence was born," or much earlier still, when Massachusetts was first colonized.[3] This shifting about was not because Adams's recollections were unusually faulty or his memory unnaturally selective. Adams had entered politics to defend American rights in the British empire and, before 1775, he did not intend to leave that empire to form a new nation. With the advantage of hindsight he thought he could see how one led inexorably to the other, for him and for thousands more who joined him as revolutionaries.

Adams once claimed that the massacre was more important to the American revolutionary movement than the fighting at Lexington and Concord, Burgoyne's defeat, or Cornwallis's surrender.[4] Whether it truly was or not is debatable, at best. Nevertheless, there was indeed a direct link between the events of March 5, 1770 and July 4, 1776, which some astute observers in Britain and the colonies had foreseen and yet seemed unable to prevent.

IMPERIAL AUTHORITY AND PROVINCIAL AUTONOMY

Boston's massacre is a perfect example of how difficult it can be to distinguish cause from effect. The massacre became both simultaneously, as the effect of prior events and the cause of others that would follow. Likewise the massacre resulted from developments peculiar to Boston and developments that could be traced elsewhere in the British empire, as colonies and mother country clashed over nagging questions—of responsibility and right, of liberty and authority, of supremacy and subordination. These questions had been raised from the earliest days of settlement, though they were addressed sporadically and rarely answered to anyone's lasting satisfaction. Added to these issues were concerns less obviously political, pitting merchants wanting to expand their overseas trade network against imperial authorities trying to contain their activities. Equally as real, if less tangible, was the problem of colonists living in societies of their own making, with transatlantic attachments that, for many, weakened with time.

Eighteenth-century Britain lay claim to an overseas empire produced by a consistent underlying logic, but it had not been built according to a careful blueprint. That logic had been neatly expressed by Richard Hakluyt and other promoters a generation before Boston, founded in 1630, even existed.[5] In their minds overseas empire was a matter of necessity, not choice, if the then still lowly England wanted to survive in a perennial balance of power competition that pitted one ambitious nation against another. Colonies stimulated trade, trade generated wealth, wealth produced power, and power enabled a nation to dominate its rivals—with Spain's rise to international prominence as proof. For that to happen in England the men behind imperial expansion believed that exports should exceed imports to preserve what they considered a favorable balance of trade. The resulting profits would fill public and private coffers, enabling investors to expand their operations and generate even more wealth, while also enabling government to field troops and launch fleets to protect and expand the nation's investments.

The mercantilistic notion that underlay empire-building—the idea that colonies existed to benefit their mother country and that the wealth they produced should work to the mother country's advantage—appears simple enough but it did not, in and of itself, dictate any prescribed set of policies. Hakluyt contended that Elizabethan England, just venturing out into the Atlantic, ought to have a blue water navy to protect the merchant vessels carrying trade goods between mother country and colonies, with competitors being kept from sharing the wealth and power carried on that transoceanic highway. How that objective was to be reached through actual policy proved complicated. Hakluyt's vision of England as master of overseas empire was necessarily vague. It was one thing to say that every colony ought to complement the general view; it was quite another to adapt each colony to its particular circumstances while keeping that general view in sight.

From the beginning some colonies fit into the imperial patchwork better than others. All of the colonies founded on the mainland of North America that joined Massachusetts in revolting against the empire in 1775, from Virginia as the first settled in 1607 to Georgia as the last in 1733, had one thing in common: charters from the crown stating the conditions under which they were to be developed. Virtually every one of those charters guaranteed colonists the "rights of Englishmen." They did not, however, necessarily stipulate what those rights were. Nor did London treat those charters as fundamental law, the equivalent of constitutions. They were granted by the crown and could be vacated through a legal proceeding or simply be set aside—instances of both occurred over the decades. Though some colonies were guaranteed a representative assembly, even those with that guarantee did not have specified what sort of legislation fell within provincial purview and what remained the domain of crown and Parliament. All too often colonial assemblies ended up in an adversarial relationship with Whitehall and Westminster. But that was the result of reality coming into conflict with the ideal, because the original expectation among English expansionists was that colonial governors, assemblies, and courts would work in concert, not at cross-purposes, with imperial authorities in London.

Free trade promises extended to the earliest adventurers for English overseas empire like John Cabot were retracted once that empire took on real importance and the New World began to assume a larger role in English strategic thinking. What became the navigation system—acts of Parliament intended to control the flow of trade goods within the empire —first emerged during the Cromwellian interregnum in the 1650s.[6] A further elaboration came with restoration of the monarchy when Charles II took the throne in 1660, showing that, on a most basic level, Cavalier and Roundhead had not been so far apart in their imperial designs. Nor did the Glorious Revolution of 1688–1689 change things much when James II was turned out in favor of his daughter Mary and her Dutch husband, William. They ended the failed experiment in imperial reorganization that had come just a few years before with the Dominion of New England—never to be attempted again—but they did not reject the mercantilistic thinking that underlay it.[7] Even as they allowed the Dominion to be dismantled they revamped the administrative agencies set up to act as watchdogs over colonial affairs. With their concurrence, Parliament added to navigation acts that already restricted trade to English (broadened to include colonial) vessels and expanded the list of enumerated articles—goods that had to come from within the system or be banned.[8]

Smuggling ran rampant through the now far-flung empire, even in England itself, so imperial administrators felt pressured to tighten enforcement and reduce the revenue, both public and private, lost to illicit trade.[9] Hence by century's end the customs inspectors that patrolled colonial docks and searched colonial warehouses as officers of the Treasury in London, and vice-admiralty judges who heard smuggling cases in the colonies as an extension of the Admiralty court system in England.

Vice-admiralty courts in the colonies underscored the Catch-22 of imperial enforcement: allowing trade to follow its own course meant that money seeped out to commercial rivals and potential enemies like France or Spain; attempts to force trade into certain channels might curtail the smuggling, but at a substantial political as well as financial loss. Vice-admiralty justices were royal appointees who acted as judge and jury combined in the trials of accused smugglers. They shared jurisdiction with common-law courts in the colonies, where local juries decided innocence or guilt, in some instances in trials presided over by judges who were elected by the freemen of the colony. Because convictions for smuggling were rare in those common-law courts, customs collectors and inspectors took cases to the vice-admiralty courts whenever they could. The number of convictions did increase and revenue brought from the auction of confiscated ships and cargoes helped defray the increased costs of imperial administration brought by the new posts, but smuggling continued apace and local resentment burned deep. What to London might have appeared an unavoidable adjustment to local circumstance—bringing lawbreakers to justice—could, in colonial eyes, have been seen as an attempt to circumvent legal custom—the sanctity of a jury trial—in order to achieve the desired political and financial outcome.[10]

Even in colonies like Rhode Island, where all the highest offices were elective, governors and judges were supposed to be representatives of the crown as well as the people, symbols of imperial power as well as of provincial authority. It was a dual identity that could be difficult to maintain in time of crisis. The same was true even in colonies like Massachusetts where, since the replacement charter granted in 1691, the governor was a crown appointee. He was nonetheless expected to serve the people of the colony as well as the monarch who appointed him. The inherent challenge of serving two masters became especially daunting when imperial and provincial interests, in theory convergent, in practice diverged.

SOLDIERS AMONG CIVILIANS

The history of the British empire proves that appearances can be deceiving. Just when the empire seemed to be growing stronger it could actually be weakening from within. Such was the case in 1763, after Britain had finally beaten France in the fourth of a series of wars dating back to 1689. In the first three conflicts North America was a military sideshow. The most important fighting began and ended in Europe, and European considerations came first in the negotiations leading to peace. The last conflict, remembered as the French and Indian War on this side of the Atlantic, would be different. North American concerns were at the diplomatic and military core, determining when and how the fighting would be conducted and what would be needed to end it.

British army and naval forces had been stationed in the colonies during all three of the earlier conflicts. They were deployed on a much larger scale this time around. Relations with the colonists were often strained, allies at odds with each other occasionally illustrating the old adage about familiarity breeding contempt. British naval officers who felt that they were acting within the law when they sent out press gangs to "recruit" sailors along the colonial waterfront found that locals were convinced they did not. On occasion the locals even drove the "recruiters" back to their ships. British army officers who thought they were within their rights in issuing commands to the local militia and requisitioning supplies from local provisioners found that they too ran afoul of accepted practice. Supplies could be slow in coming or not provided at all. General Jeffrey Amherst, commander of the combined British and colonial forces, was typical of the regular army officer who disliked working with provincial leaders, who, from his perspective, put colony over empire. Theirs was hardly a smooth working relationship. Likewise for his predecessors in the early stages of the war.

With the fall of New France and the French eliminated as the primary enemy to the north and west after 1763, colonies and mother country only had each other left to blame for whatever problems of empire might remain. As a French diplomat observed to an English friend:

> You are happy in the cession of Canada: we, perhaps, ought to think ourselves happy that you have acquired it. Delivered from a neighbour whom they have always feared, your other colonies will soon discover, that they stand no longer in need of your protection. You will call on them to contribute toward supporting the burthen which they have helped to bring on you, they will answer you by shaking off all dependence.[11]

It was a perceptive, even prophetic, observation. Before being relieved of command Amherst had recommended that a sizeable contingent of regulars be kept on in the colonies, primarily for "frontier" duty in an arc from the Ohio country through Canada to Nova Scotia, but also in case they were needed closer to the seaboard "to retain the Inhabitants of our antient Provinces in a State of Constitutional Dependance upon Great Britain."[12] That no troops would be so deployed for another five years—and then to Boston, thus setting the scene for the massacre—is less important than the fact that such use had been contemplated before the postwar surge of legislation that prompted it even passed Parliament.

Colonists who resented the presence of professional soldiers among them came by that feeling honestly, the result of experience reinforcing inheritance. Cromwell's "New Model Army" during the Civil War notwithstanding, England had had no true standing army until after the restoration of the monarchy. The 1689 Bill of Rights would proclaim "That the raising or keeping a standing army within the kingdom in time of peace, unless it be with consent of parliament, is against law."[13] Even then the army's existence was problematical, legal in the sense that the crown asked for it and Parliament funded it, but perhaps unconstitutional because it went against ancient custom.[14]

Cromwell had sent soldiers briefly to Virginia in the 1650s and regulars were in the expedition that seized New Netherland from the Dutch in the 1660s. Nonetheless the first redcoats in the mainland colonies long enough to get a taste of the suspicions that could lead to resentment did not arrive until January 1677. They had been sent out to quell civil unrest among white settlers, not separate Indians from whites on the frontier. Those troops—a full regiment, with artillery—had been dispatched by London once it received word of Bacon's rebellion. By the time they arrived in Virginia, Bacon was dead and order had been restored. Virginians met Colonel Herbert Jeffreys and his men with that combination of "hostility or indifference" that would mark local reaction virtually every time the colonists found regulars stationed among them.

Just over two decades later, in April 1689, the hostility was even more pronounced, this time in Massachusetts. There irate Bostonians seized and imprisoned officials of the Dominion of New England in a "bloodless coup."[15] Those officials included not only the governor, Edmund Andros, but officers in the army and Royal Navy, and officials in the customs service. Disaffected town and province leaders had formed a council of safety to take charge, Boston's militia had mustered to the beat of their drum, and ultimately Andros and the others chose to surrender peaceably rather than resist. Upon hearing of what had happened in Boston, dissident New Yorkers did the same with imperial officials posted there. Like their Boston counterparts, they claimed to be acting in the names of William and Mary, the new monarchs. Neither could be sure of London's reaction. The rebellious colonists knew that William and Mary had landed in England and that James II abdicated his throne on their approach. They could not yet know if William and Mary had established their legitimacy, nor could they know what the new monarchs would do with the Dominion of New England.

Fortunately for peace within the empire, William and Mary did not reestablish the Dominion. Interestingly enough, the end of the Dominion did not spell an end to the careers of men who held office in it. Andros would return as governor of Virginia. His lieutenant governor in the Dominion, Francis Nicholson, would also hold that post, as well as the governorship of Maryland. Customs official Edward Randolph also returned, with a promotion, to the new post of surveyor general of the customs. Andros and Nicholson were both professional soldiers but that did not prevent their holding civilian posts in the empire—indeed, Jeffreys had temporarily acted as governor of Virginia during his stay.

So, when Massachusetts patriots complained in 1774 that General Thomas Gage had been made their governor while he still acted as commander-in-chief of British army forces in North America, what they protested as a dangerous innovation was in fact a revival of an old tradition. After all, Andros's full title in the Dominion had been governor, captain-general, and vice-admiral. Andros's civilian successor under a Massachusetts freed from the Dominion had the same ceremonial title bestowed on him. The empire had never been solely a commercial entity, with trade as its only concern; it had also been an extension of English (and after 1707, with the union of the English and Scottish parliaments, British) power, so there were times over the decades when colonies bore aspects of garrison government.[16] Soldiers and sailors came and went; military officers held significant posts; the navigation system had its strategic as well as its trade component.

That the Royal Navy and eventually the army would be asked to help guarantee the integrity of that system in response to widespread smuggling should not be all that surprising.[17] "We observe with concern that through Neglect, Connivance and Fraud," complained the Treasury in October 1763, that "not only the Revenue is impaired, but the Commerce of the Colonies is diverted from its natural Course and the salutary Provisions of many wise Laws to secure it to the Mother Country are in great Measure defeated."[18] Legislation commencing the next year to tighten enforcement essentially activated what had long lain dormant. Many colonists would contend that smuggling had restored trade to, not diverted it from, its "natural Course." Accordingly, they did not think the navigation laws "wise" at all. The stage for transatlantic confrontation was being set.

The resulting legislation—which included the controversial Stamp Act of 1765—was not, as some historians would have it, intended to pay off the national debt. No one charged with running the empire was that naive. The debt had effectively doubled because of the French and Indian War, from some £75 million to roughly £140 million. Prewar income from all sources had been approximately £10 million per year. Annual spending had ranged close to £8 million. Combined with £5 million in annual interest on the debt, that put total yearly expenses at £13 million, which meant that unless crown and Parliament found new sources of revenue, Britain would spin into an endless cycle of deficit spending. Imperial authorities designed new laws to increase revenue through the navigation system so that intake could keep better pace with outflow. Since colonists on the mainland of North America were the most direct beneficiaries of French expulsion, *and* since they were taxed locally at a considerably lower rate than Britons, crown and Parliament determined that they ought to carry a larger share of the financial burden. Total cost for keeping troops in the colonies—which at projected full strength (never achieved) would number ten thousand men in twenty regiments, was estimated to be roughly £400,000 per year. George Grenville and the solid parliamentary majority backing his program hoped that new laws like the Sugar and Stamp acts would be combined with tighter enforcement of older laws long on the books to produce about half that amount.[19] Even that was too much for those who felt that London went about its fundraising programs unconstitutionally, even tyrannically.

But in London the prevailing view was that the navigation system could not continue as before. Costs, primarily in the form of salaries for customs agents and vice-admiralty judges, had already grown to exceed revenue by four to one—meaning that, ironically, a supposed source of income was actually a financial drain. Even without the new military expenditures, costs would rise again as new customs agents took up their posts and new vice-admiralty courts were formed, those courts empowered to prosecute violations of the Stamp Act as well as infractions of more traditional navigation acts. Estimates of losses due to congenital colonial smuggling ran into tens of thousands of pounds every year. Included in those losses was trade with the French, the ostensible enemy. Not surprisingly imperial accountants supported parliamentary attempts at behavior modification, if those changes could alter the revenue-to-spending ratio and improve the bottom line.

What looked perfectly logical and fiscally responsible in London did not appear so logical or responsible on the far side of the Atlantic. From a financial standpoint most Americans took their own experience with taxes as their frame of reference, not tax rates in Britain. They based their sense of equity on provincial, not imperial, conditions. Nor did it help that the increased taxes were for spending they did not endorse, whether it be for troops on the frontier who could be used to enforce a new policy that checked farther westward expansion or civilian officials on the seaboard who were sent out to collect taxes on trade goods. Besides, higher taxes are rarely popular at any time; they were particularly galling in the wake of a postwar economic downturn. Moreover, keen colonial observers knew that Whitehall and Westminster had a political agenda behind the financial plan: a desire to remind them of their subordinate place in the empire.

The likelihood that troops would be dispatched increased with opposition to a spate of new acts passed by Parliament in 1767, known collectively as the Townshend Program. Colonial belief in a reciprocal empire, where the restrictions of the navigation system were justified as working for the greater good of the whole, had always been tenuous. Shaken during the Stamp Act crisis, that belief was shaken again with the Townshend Program.[20] In yet another of those ironies that marked the coming revolution, this new program, named for Chancellor of the Exchequer Charles Townshend, was

Figure 1 A private in the 29th Regiment, c. 1770, as depicted by the noted artist Don Troiani. His uniform mixes elements of a pre-1768 warrant with changes made after the regiment arrived in Boston. The red regimental coat, lined in yellow, dates from before the change; his white woolen waistcoat and breeches date from after. The socket-style bayonet in his belt scabbard, with a seventeen-inch, triangular blade, was designed for the standard Brown Bess musket in his hands. This so-called "land pattern" version was just under five feet long and weighed nearly 10 pounds. The private wears an older-style cocked hat. That the eight enlisted men arrested with Preston were members of the 29th's grenadier company does not necessarily mean that they wore their foot-high bearskin caps on the night of March 5, 1770. As Mr. Troiani notes, they did not always wear those caps for routine duties and Paul Revere—who, after all, knew the troops and their uniforms well—shows them in tricorns in his engraving. Painting by Don Troiani, www.historicalimagebank. com.

implemented during the ministry of William Pitt, long thought by colonists to be a defender of their rights. But Pitt, now Earl of Chatham, had disengaged himself from parliamentary affairs and Townshend held sway. Pitt and Townshend, like virtually every public man in Britain, believed that the colonies were subordinate components of empire and that Parliament was supreme within that setting. They supported the navigation system and were convinced the colonies needed to carry more of the financial weight of empire. Nonetheless Pitt and a few others like him believed that Parliament did not have the authority to tax the colonists directly. Albeit Townshend and a comfortable majority disagreed with Pitt over the question of authority, a fair number could accept the need to placate the colonists for practical purposes.

Parliament had asserted itself in the Stamp Act crisis with the Declaratory Act of March 1766, which stated that it had the authority to legislate for the colonies "in all cases whatsoever."[21] Nowhere is the word "tax" used—by intention, not oversight. The Declaratory Act, like so much else that became law for the empire, had a dual purpose: to dominate and conciliate simultaneously, to confront crisis and yet at the same time avoid it. Its pairing with repeal of the Stamp Act had not been a coincidence. Even though most British politicians disliked American protests and disagreed with American assertions of right, they wanted the empire to function smoothly and if that meant finding some point at which business—public and private—could be pursued without increased political friction, so much the better. Townshend's legislative program ought to be understood in that context and not be explained away as the manifestation of one man's quirkiness or even duplicity. Even Townshend's desire to create a civil list to pay the salaries of governors and some other imperial officials from the increased revenues, thus freeing them from dependence on colonial legislatures, had antecedents going back decades. All of the components to Townshend's program passed handily through the Lords and the Commons, to be endorsed by George III.

Boston as Focal Point

Townshend, like Grenville before him, knew full well that there was no good reason to pass legislation if it were not accompanied by stricter enforcement: hence our need to view the individual acts that he advocated as part of a legislative package. A new revenue statute covering tea, paper, glass, lead, and painters' colors imported into the colonies stood at the center. Supporting legislation surrounded it, one an act that strengthened the vice-admiralty system, reorganizing existing courts and adding new ones with both original and appellate jurisdiction. Another act created an American-based board of customs that would be composed of five commissioners sent out from London to reside in Boston, where they would coordinate the efforts of customs officials posted throughout the colonies.[22] "The oppressions the officers of the Revenue labour under in America have lately grown to such an enormous height," Henry Hulton, one of the commissioners, sighed, "that it is become impossible for them to do their duty, not only from the outrage of Mobs, but for fear also of vexatious Suits, Verdicts, & Judgments in the Provincial Courts, and even of Criminal Prosecutions."[23]

Sending Hulton and his four colleagues would not change any of that. Just the opposite; their presence only added to the general resentment, and that in colonies that still had their own legislatures and common-law courts and therefore their own notions of what was legal and just. Many of the people they served saw smuggling as a fair response to oppressive legislation imposed from afar. They were particularly aggrieved that tea had been included among the five newly taxed imports in order to prop up the financially troubled East India Company. Nor did it help that Townshend—like many of his parliamentary colleagues—was an investor in that company. That he was is no proof of corruption; rather, it is just one indicator of the difficulty of separating private interest from public good. What is incontestable is that, in the grand scheme of things and in London, the fate of the East India Company mattered more than the preferences of some disgruntled colonists on the mainland of North America.

Smuggling increased along with efforts to curtail it—a volatile, potentially dangerous, situation. Resentment spilled over with the *Liberty* incident of June 1768. Wealthy Boston merchant John Hancock owned the *Liberty*; in the eyes of customs officials Hancock was nothing more than a successful smuggler, whose rise in local and provincial politics proved all the more irritating. They looked for an excuse to go after him and the master of the *Liberty* provided it by unloading his cargo before he received proper clearance. Customs officials ordered that the *Liberty* be seized. As Hancock's vessel was towed away from the dock by a British warship, a crowd set upon the customs officials, who were foolish enough to linger too long at the scene. Beaten, frightened, those officials fled to Castle William, on an island in the harbor. They entreated Governor Francis Bernard to request that troops be dispatched to restore the peace and enable them to perform their duties.[24]

Like the eventual massacre, the *Liberty* incident became both cause and effect. It resulted from pent-up hostility pitting imperial officials against local residents and it led to even more serious confrontations. Although the hostility had been growing with each new postwar act of Parliament intended to raise revenue and control trade, that hostility went back at least to the war itself, when soldiers, sailors, and imperial officials bumped up against uncooperative civilians. Those aggravations cannot be written off as some sort of temperament peculiar to Boston. New Yorkers had shown a similar tendency with the small number of troops stationed among them, just as a function of their town being the army headquarters for North America. There were the usual brawls, of course. More serious in its implications, New York's legislature had refused to provide for the troops as directed by the 1765 Quartering Act that had been introduced as part of Grenville's program. So recalcitrant were they that the governor, Henry Moore, ended the session and sent the legislators home.[25]

Wisely or not, Parliament mixed in the affair by endorsing Moore's actions and stipulating that the legislature not be reconvened until compliance could be secured. It thereby deepened local resentment and generated sympathetic responses elsewhere in the colonies. John Dickinson, the wealthy lawyer and landowner who cast himself as a simple "Pennsylvania Farmer" in a dozen widely reprinted "letters," presented the New York dispute as part of a larger constitutional crisis in the empire. He contended that any act of Parliament requiring a colony to house or otherwise provide for regular troops within its borders was a form of taxation and therefore unjustifiable—as unjustifiable, he added, as the entire vice-admiralty system because it encroached on the common law. Parliament's suspending act he condemned as a blow to constitutional liberty. Even though Moore had the authority to prorogue the legislature, Parliament, Dickinson contended, had no authority to interfere in the dispute.

Dickinson blended these complaints with his condemnation of Townshend's new duties as unconstitutional, a "most dangerous innovation,"[26] because they were intended to raise revenue, not simply regulate trade. That made what Townshend did every bit as bad as what Grenville had attempted with his Stamp Act. To acquiesce in such an abuse of authority, Dickinson told readers, would be tantamount to voluntarily becoming slaves. As Dickinson saw it, the constitutionality or unconstitutionality of any parliamentary act depended on the intentions behind it. By arguing intent, Dickinson went well beyond the taxation versus legislation distinction that some on both sides of the Atlantic had made, moving into a realm where elusive answers to hard questions could become utterly impossible to find.

Two considerations ought to be kept in mind here. First, Dickinson's linkage of the otherwise unconnected lent itself to conspiratorial fears: among colonists who imputed the worst motives to imperial administrators and parliamentary leaders, and among a growing number of Britons who viewed colonial dissent in the same light.[27] Dickinson is often labeled a conservative and he later dragged his feet when it came to declaring independence. Even so, despite his call for conciliation on both sides and despite his disdain for "inflammatory measures" by either, he also warned that "whoever seriously considers the matter must perceive that a dreadful stroke is aimed at the liberty of these colonies."[28] That was hardly the language to check the spread of conspiracy theories.

Second, Dickinson's view was at once formative and reflective, playing a part, notably, in the Massachusetts legislature's February 1768 resolution on rights in the empire that was circulated to other colonial assemblies, hoping that they would endorse them. That in turn prompted the Earl of Hillsborough, first in the new office of secretary of state for American affairs, to instruct governors not to countenance such resolutions and to prorogue those legislatures who did. Bernard took that tack with the Massachusetts General Court when the lower house refused to rescind its letter. To the general public, the men behind the letter were already heroes; Bernard turned them into political martyrs.[29]

Hillsborough and others in key positions of power in London had started talking about using troops to quell colonial disturbances months before they learned of the *Liberty* affair—because of what Dickinson wrote to such popular acclaim, because of what transpired in the Massachusetts lower house, because of warnings from Governor Bernard and General Gage to Whitehall that it would lose what little control it had left if it did not act decisively, because of the repeated attempts to intimidate imperial officials, because of countless small incidents that were now having a larger cumulative effect. And because in so many minds Boston had been at the center of civil disobedience since the Stamp Act crisis, because Boston had had a reputation for being a problem child in the imperial family since the first generation of Puritan divines who founded it, Whitehall decided that the troops would go there, not to Philadelphia, the home of John Dickinson, nor to New York City, where the local legislators had thumbed their noses at the army.[30] It would prove to be a singularly poor choice.

Governor Bernard disingenuously distanced himself from that decision.[31] Anticipating how violent local reaction could be to the news that troops were coming, he was emphatic that he had not requested that they be sent. While technically that may have been true, it was not true in any meaningful sense. Bernard, more than perhaps anyone else in the colonies, had given credence to the notion that Massachusetts was becoming ungovernable because Boston was a law unto itself, and until Boston was controlled, no imperial official could do the king's bidding or uphold acts of Parliament.[32] Bernard wanted the troops close by; he just did not want to be blamed for their being sent. He fooled no one among his political opponents in Boston.

And yet Bernard's fears for the future of imperial authority were not groundless. When the Boston town meeting heard that troops were on the way it called upon other Massachusetts towns to send delegates to a special convention—in Boston itself, right under Bernard's nose. Over two hundred delegates from nearly one hundred towns throughout the province came

Figure 2 (opposite) Paul Revere's engraving of the troops landing at the long wharf in Boston on October 1, 1768. King Street started where the wharf ended, and led to the town house. Faneuil Hall is the second prominent structure to the right. Hancock's dock, with buildings on it and ships around it, is also to the right. Christian Remick designed the scene and then colored it on paper after Revere did the engraving work on a copper plate. Revere printed the engraving after—and because of—the massacre, although he had had something like it in the works before then, and Remick had first done his drawing as early as the previous October. Courtesy of the American Antiquarian Society.

A VIEW OF PART OF THE TOWN OF BOSTON IN NEW ENGLAND AND BRITISH SHIPS OF WAR LANDING THEIR TROOPS! 1768

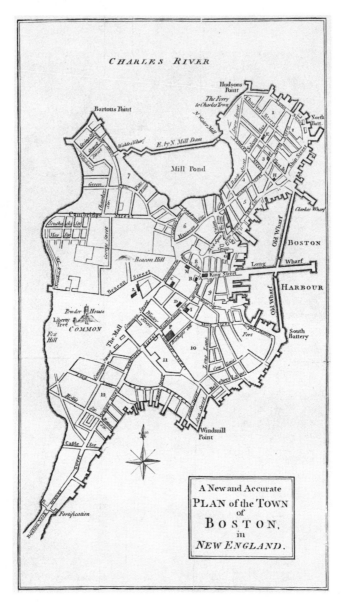

Figure 3 Boston, c. 1774, by John Hinton. A great advantage of this map is that important structures are easy to find on it. The town house is marked (A) on King Street, as the thoroughfare extends from the long wharf. Faneuil Hall is also identifiable (G), as are the court house and jail (M). Dock Square is just to the left of Faneuil Hall; Murray's barracks sat between Dock Square and Hanover Street. John Adams lived on Queen Street, just past the town house; Edes and Gill printed the Boston Gazette just a few doors farther along from Adams (near the 8). Hutchinson's house was in north Boston (near the H). King's Chapel, Boston's Anglican church, is at C; the Old South congregational meeting house is at I, with the congregational First Church or

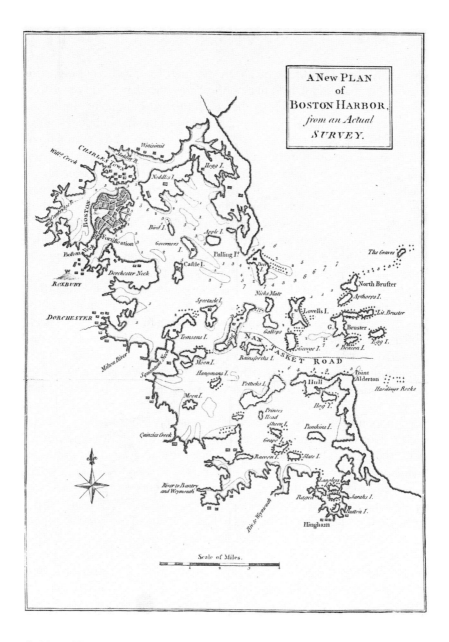

"Old Brick" meeting house at B. Both sections of the "Old Wharf" shown on the map were apparently no longer standing in 1770. The Liberty Tree is placed incorrectly on the Common; it was actually down near the intersection of Newberry (Newbury) and Essex streets (whereas the "Great Elm" was indeed on the Common). The great disadvantage of this map is that it gives no sense of the hustle and bustle of the town, with many people crammed into a small amount of space where streets are here drawn so neatly. Map reproduction courtesy of the Norman B. Leventhal Map Center of the Boston Public Library.

that September. They broke no law by meeting. Their gathering was extra-legal rather than illegal, held in a political gray area that would prove to be essential to what evolved into the revolutionary movement. Individual delegates reaffirmed their rights and condemned the stationing of regulars among them. Some resolved to stop the troops from landing, even if it cost their lives. Formally the convention did not resolve to do much of anything. The first troops arrived as it adjourned—two regiments from nearby Halifax, Nova Scotia, with another two from Ireland soon to follow. Perhaps with discretion being the better part of valor, the people of Boston chose to do nothing; perhaps the reality of facing regular troops, supported by the guns of the Royal Navy, sank in; perhaps there were those who understood that they could better cast themselves as victims, and the imperial authorities as victimizers, if they could be seen as taking the high moral ground. So, on October 1, 1768, the regulars came ashore at the long wharf and paraded up King Street, colors flying and drums beating, past sullen, mostly silent, and—for the moment—unresisting townsfolk.

The Quartering Act, passed in 1765, was still in effect and what had bothered New Yorkers would also irritate Bostonians, but on a larger scale because many more troops were involved and they were posted there for a different reason.[33] The act did not oblige private residents to house soldiers in their homes or in any building on their property then in use. There had been those in Parliament who wanted to include private dwellings, but they were outvoted by others who disliked the implications for Britain—and any perceived assault on the 1689 Bill of Rights—even if they did not ordinarily sympathize with colonial protests. But the act was still problematic because it put pressure on both local and provincial officials to accommodate soldiers in their midst at a time when they saw no need for their presence—indeed, when their presence seemed to be a violation of fundamental rights. The owners of unoccupied private buildings would be compensated for their use and reimbursed for various expenses incurred in providing for the troops, but imperial authorities expected the province to absorb those costs as a public expense. The province would reimburse private parties, but would itself receive no reimbursement from London. Warehouse owners who did not want to rent to the army, even if the premises were unoccupied, local constables who were expected to assist in the process, even members of the general population who were not directly involved, could join the ranks of the disgruntled.

Violence in the wake of the regulars' arrival in Boston did not surprise Benjamin Franklin when it finally erupted. He had not always guessed right when it came to colonial reaction to imperial policy—failing to anticipate, for example, the vehement adverse response to the Stamp Act—but he well understood the deep-seated antipathy to professional soldiers. Residing in London and called upon to testify before the House of Commons in February 1766 as an expert witness, Franklin had predicted that British troops sent to pacify American civilians would "not find a rebellion; they may indeed make one."[34] Franklin spoke with the Stamp Act in mind, knowing that a frustrated Grenville had contemplated sending soldiers to enforce it. Angered by the protest against his program, at that point Grenville was confident that the regulars would serve as both symbolic and real proof of parliamentary supremacy and British sovereignty. He later changed his mind. Not convinced that Townshend had chosen the right legislative course, he did not think the timing for a show of force was right in 1768. Perhaps Franklin's words had found their mark.

The men of the 14th and 29th regiments who marched proudly up the long wharf found themselves in a town that was essentially self-governing, virtually autonomous from provincial or imperial control. Sixteen thousand people were crowded onto part of a peninsula that sprouted above a narrow neck jutting from the mainland. Boston's east side in particular could be a bustling, jostling place—a seaport with busy docks, wharves, warehouses, and shops. The town meeting ran local affairs, with freemen voting for those who would represent them in the lower house of the General Court, various town officers, and, most importantly, the selectmen who acted as an executive committee on town business. Many of those who rose to power in the province did so first through the town, Samuel Adams perhaps foremost among them. Political caucuses like the Loyal Nine and political action groups like the Sons of Liberty played a role in shaping Revolutionary Boston, though none rivaled the town meeting in importance.[35] Merchants, wealthy and middling, dockworkers, even apprentices formed their own ad hoc groups as well, which only compounded the problems of social control in the event of a political dispute. Imperial officials found this situation difficult to accept and yet they made no significant attempt to change it until 1774. By then it was far too late.

Lieutenant Colonel William Dalrymple, commander of the newly arrived troops, got his first taste of town power almost immediately. Governor Bernard wanted the troops billeted in the town proper. Town leaders, pointing to the wording of the 1765 Quartering Act, objected that all available barracks should be filled first and there were hundreds of empty beds at Castle William—over two miles away across the harbor but technically within the town's limits. The governor's Council, which doubled as the upper house of the General Court, concurred with the town. That it, the lower house, and the town meeting routinely agreed on political issues was part and parcel of the imperial dispute. When Bernard arrived as governor in 1760 the Council sided with him as often as it went against him. An Englishman, he had already spent years in the colonies as governor of

Figure 4 Charles Coleman's twentieth-century painting of the Old State House and State Street, when they were still the town house and King Street. Coleman's rendition of the surrounding buildings and their facades may not be terribly accurate, but, from the angle that he took, it shows proportions nicely, notably the size of people in relation to structures, and the distance from the custom house, on the right, to the town house at the center. The First Church or "Old Brick" meeting house is to the left rear; the cupola of the court house and jail are visible to the right, opposite. Courtesy of the Bostonian Society/Old State House Museum.

New Jersey. With the Stamp Act crisis and subsequent events, he found himself losing the Council's support. Instead, on questions pitting provincial over imperial preferences the General Court presented a more united front, with the town's backing—and vice versa. It had not always been that way but disputes with London drove them closer together. Bernard became so alienated and isolated that he had been looking to put Massachusetts behind him ever since.

It did not help that Bernard told Dalrymple he could bivouac at least some of his troops in the town house[36] on King Street and nearby Faneuil Hall—temporarily, anyway—until more permanent accommodations could be located. Given the wording of the Quartering Act, there was never a question of imposing them on private homeowners or the owners of other buildings without compensation. Bernard thought that Dalrymple could also put some of his men in the manufactory house, built at public expense over a decade before to teach the textiles trade to the poor. That experiment in job-training had ended but there were still some tenants who paid rent and others who exercised squatter's rights. Bernard wanted them all evicted; town officials countered that the building belonged to the town, not the province, and they disagreed with his plan. A sheriff and deputies that Bernard sent to clear the building were pushed back by those inside. Soldiers sent by Dalrymple surrounded the building but did not otherwise interfere. Crowds jeered and taunted them. The impasse lasted a couple of weeks, until other arrangements had been made. This was not an auspicious beginning.

It took over a month but Dalrymple moved the men in the town house and Faneuil Hall to other quarters. He also got those camping in tents on the Common indoors before the onset of winter—and in time to house the 64th and 65th regiments when they arrived from Ireland in November as well. But his troops were not in formal cantonment. They were scattered about town, in rented space, the enlisted men in converted warehouses, the officers usually with better accommodations in boarding houses as well as private residences. This was not a situation conducive to effective control or proper discipline.

Initially Dalrymple was more concerned with desertion than he was with the snide remarks and irritating behavior of the locals. He had to post a guard on the Neck, not to control civilian traffic, but to catch deserters, who would disappear into the countryside if they could. Confrontations erupted between soldiers and civilians: fist fights, lawsuits, the usual fare—not unexpected when nearly two thousand regulars lived in close proximity to people who were ambivalent at best about their presence among them. Not every Bostonian objected to the troops' presence, not least because of the cash they brought into the local economy. But enough townsmen were aggravated that relations were never smooth and there was a constant campaign in the press to have the troops removed.[37] Some off-duty soldiers sought part-time civilian jobs to supplement their pay. That put them in competition with local workers, which may have made those workers sympathetic to political and constitutional arguments that otherwise held little appeal. "Here Americans you may behold some of the first fruits springing up from that root of bitterness a standing army," one piece harangued readers. "Troops are quartered upon us in a time of peace, on pretence of preserving order in a town that was as orderly before their arrival as any one large town in the whole extent of his Majesty's dominions."[38] The lower house of the General Court protested formally that "the experience of ages is sufficient to convince, that the military power is ever dangerous, and subversive of free constitutions."[39]

THE MASSACRE

The direst predictions did not come true, so within six months London decided that the 64th and 65th regiments could be better used back in Ireland. Bernard (soon to depart town himself), the customs commissioners, other imperial officials, and even some well-heeled locals did not want any of them to leave, however—despite the fact that the soldiers had very little to do, besides guarding a few buildings and policing each other. They were not an army of occupation and there was no martial law. They did not even displace the local constables. They were not to be called out unless there was a public disturbance of some sort and then only at the request of a local official.

The rules had been established in a Riot Act passed by the General Court in 1751, which was adapted from the 1714 Riot Act for England still in force there. Once any group of a dozen or more men "arm'd with clubs or other weapons" or a group of fifty or more unarmed men had "riotously or tumultuously assembled," they could be ordered to disperse. In both statutes the authorized officials included justices of the peace and sheriffs; in the Massachusetts version a militia officer could do so as well. Citing "our sovereign lord the king" as authority, that official could command "all persons assembled, immediately to disperse themselves, and peaceably to depart to their habitations, or to their lawful business." The crowd had one hour from that point to disperse. If it had not dispersed by then, deadly force could be used by those who in effect were deputized by the official in charge—which implicitly could include regular soldiers. If any in the crowd were killed, those who slew them would be "indemnified and held guiltless."[40]

But then there was this pressing question: how likely was it that any town official would use the Riot Act to empower the soldiers to act as policemen? The act had not been used to protect the customs commissioners during the *Liberty* riot, before the troops landed. Then the town militia would have been mobilized to disperse the crowd—and no doubt some of the militiamen were themselves part of that very crowd. Bernard and other imperial officials knew that it was as unlikely—even if for different reasons—that any local official would call on the regulars for help but, as they saw it, it was better to have the soldiers around than not there at all. They *might* cause the unruly to think twice before starting trouble; then again, their very presence could be the cause of trouble. If nothing else, soldiers—like other men—had the right of self-defense and could kill in order to save their own lives. Before the night of March 5, 1770 that last extremity had never been reached—not even close to it, really.

What is notable is that bringing regular troops to Boston had not changed the balance of power within the town. Customs collectors were still often afraid to do their jobs and Bernard could not promise them effective protection. The soldiers themselves often felt victimized, since local justices of the peace rarely found in their favor when they took their civil disputes with Bostonians to court or found themselves the subject of minor criminal prosecutions.[41] Thus, rather than think of Boston as an occupied town, with a mental image of soldiers on every street corner, it would be more accurate to think of those who were supposedly in control as increasingly powerless and themselves under siege. Imperial authority was all but impotent and the price of trying to change that dynamic might well have been higher than anyone was willing to pay.

Hutchinson and the others may have decided to avoid a disturbance of the public peace. Perhaps in a sense they hid behind the law, choosing to accept the social circumstances rather than try to use the law to alter them. In effect they accommodated themselves to a situation they wished they could change but feared they could not. It was not the first time; nor would it be the last, as the aftermath to the massacre shows.

Even though customs officials did not collect the Townshend duties zealously, the law was on the books and Townshend had called for the creation of a civil list to pay the salaries of imperial officials from its proceeds. He therefore managed to link colonial political and economic issues, which stoked deepening resentment and growing fear that worse lay ahead. It was in this heightened state of anxiety that Ebenezer Richardson became a lightning rod for local fury. Richardson, a minor employee of and sometime informant for the customs service, fired into a crowd that gathered around his house, thereby killing Christopher Seider, a boy of eleven or twelve. The incident occurred in February 1770, with a trial scheduled for April. Seider became a martyr to many in town, an incarnation of the innocent suffering at the hands of lawless power—a tenuous connection, but no less real for it. Protesters against unpopular imperial policies turned his funeral into a grand spectacle that only served to keep people on edge.[42]

Meanwhile, the recurring affrays between soldiers and civilians took on more symbolic importance as tensions heightened in the town. On Friday, March 2, an off-duty soldier from the 29th Regiment got into a fight at John Gray's ropewalk. When he returned from his barracks with some friends to try to even the score, they too were pummeled and chased off. Tempers simmered over the weekend and flared the following Monday, March 5. Some who were involved in the fisticuffs at the ropewalk would meet again with more deadly consequences later that day.[43]

What happened was a point of contention then and remains so now. Any account that smooths over contradictions and fills in gaps defeats the purpose of revisiting the massacre. The gaps and contradictions are indispensable reminders of the difficulty of reconstructing the past from a fragmentary record—a universal problem in historical explanation rather than something unique to the massacre.[44]

What can be said without much danger of controversy is that what happened on King Street that evening was part of a larger disturbance that began hours before. Soldiers and civilians in search of trouble found it and there were dozens of confrontations involving just one or two on either side, or a cluster from both. No firearms and only occasionally edged weapons were used in these earlier incidents. Most used cudgels and canes, staves and fists. Men roamed about, crowds formed then dissolved, with eruptions first on one street or adjoining alleyway, then another.

In the midst of all of this a lone sentry stood guard outside the custom house on King Street. It was by then a cold, moonlit night, with a solid coat of snow on the ground and icicles hanging from the eaves of the buildings lining both sides of the street. The sentry apparently exchanged insults with a passing apprentice, sharp words related to a purportedly unpaid bill owed by a British officer to another apprentice—on such small personal disputes could larger political events turn in the tension-filled town. The sentry struck the apprentice with the butt of his musket. Other young men clustered about and taunted the sentry; a crowd began to gather, including adult Bostonians drawn by the commotion. The sentry called for help from the main guard that was within sight up the street, across from the town house.

Officer of the day Captain Thomas Preston could see what was brewing from the main guard station, just fifty paces or so away. He formed a relief party, with bayonets fixed but guns not loaded, pushed through the growing crowd to the sentry, but then could not get back out. They formed a rough semicircle, with the custom house at their backs. The crowd pressed in, the soldiers loaded their muskets, shoving and shouting increased, one shot rang out, then others in a ragged volley. Civilians fell in the snow. The soldiers reloaded and stood their ground as the dead and wounded were carried off, and most of the crowd scattered.

Crispus Attucks, Samuel Gray, and James Caldwell all perished on King Street. Samuel Maverick died a few hours later after being carried to his mother's home. Patrick Carr, who was shot through the hip and had part of his spine torn away, lingered, most painfully, until March 14. A half-dozen more were wounded, some quite seriously.[45]

As men who had been in the crowd removed the killed and wounded from the bloody scene, lingering townsfolk warned Preston that enraged locals numbering in the thousands would converge on King Street to exact their revenge. He knew before he set forth with his relief party that troops could not perform any police functions unless authorized by the proper civilian authorities. He also believed that the danger faced by the sentry overrode those considerations if threats had indeed been made against his life. In his subsequent trial, much would hinge on whether he could prove after the fact that the sentry's life had truly been in mortal peril and that, once he and his men arrived, their peril was as great.

Common law encompassed the right of self-defense but taking a life —committing either a "justifiable" or an "excusable" homicide—could be difficult either to justify or to excuse, doubly so for soldiers who had gone among civilians.[46] Preston successfully took the sentry, Private Hugh White, under his protection, though by going to White he precipitated the clash that left three civilians dead and more than twice that number wounded, two of them mortally. He and his men were, by contrast, virtually unscathed.

Even though deciding against leaving a reinforced detail outside the custom house, Preston had no intention of fleeing back to the main guard station and closing the door behind him. He marched his party back up the street, ordered more soldiers out and formed them in ranks, muskets loaded and primed, bayonets fixed, facing out between the main guard and the town house. He had mustered most of the 29th Regiment, billeted not far away on Brattle Street. The 14th Regiment remained in other barracks but under arms. Preston notified Dalrymple, commander of the 14th Regiment and overall commander of the regulars in Boston, of his dispositions, as well as Lieutenant Colonel Maurice Carr, his immediate superior. He could guess that the threat that thousands were gathering to kill him and every man with him was just so much bluster, borne of the fear and frustration of the moment. But he also knew that there could be hundreds coming for him, that they would probably be armed with muskets and pistols—not just the canes and clubs of the earlier crowd—and that what was already an ugly incident could become decidedly uglier if seven hundred scattered regulars, with no clear line of defense, were pitted against Bostonians and neighboring townsmen.

But aside from some scuffling here and there, no further incident occurred. Summoned from his home in the north end, Lieutenant Governor Hutchinson, filling in for the departed (and never to return) Bernard, rushed to the scene. He managed to calm the threatening crowd, then persuaded the soldiers to return to barracks and the crowd to disperse when he promised that the soldiers involved would be identified, arrested, and subjected to provincial law.

Preston surrendered himself some time after midnight. Eight soldiers identified as having been with him (the sentry White included) turned themselves in the next morning. Perhaps one hundred townsmen milled about in the wee hours before dawn as local magistrates interviewed Preston and a few who claimed to be eyewitnesses. The rest of the townsfolk had gone home, possibly even to bed. In other words, a modicum of trust remained.[47] No doubt it had been a near thing—a *very* near thing. But it appears that for every British soldier itching for a fight or every local tough looking to let slip the dogs of war, there were even more looking for an excuse not to shed any more blood. That sentiment would only grow stronger between the massacre and the trials.

THE TRIALS

Hutchinson convened his council—eight members attending—the morning after the massacre, the first of what would be two meetings that day. William Dalrymple and Maurice Carr joined them for the second meeting, as did Captain Benjamin Caldwell of HMS *Rose*, the only warship then in the harbor. At the same moment that they met in the town house the selectmen convened a town meeting in Faneuil Hall. The town demanded that all of the troops—both the 14th and the 29th regiments—be removed from the town proper to Castle William. Indicative of a confused chain of command, Hutchinson replied that he could not order the troops out. Dalrymple at first wanted his men to be confined to barracks, at most; eventually he consented to the demands of the town, backed by Hutchinson's own council.[48]

Within less than a week the 29th Regiment had departed for the castle and the 14th followed in short order. The day after the council meeting town selectmen again called upon Hutchinson, this time in their capacity as militia officers: Colonel Joshua Henshaw, Colonel Joseph Jackson, and Major John Ruddock. They wanted him to authorize them to form a militia watch to secure the town and prevent any further disturbances while the regulars prepared to transfer to the castle. Convinced that they did not need Hutchinson's permission to patrol their own town, they had already formed an impromptu watch the night before.[49]

Hutchinson probably felt as much pressure from this courtesy call as he did in dealing with the British military. Dalrymple and Carr had gone along to preserve the public peace. They did not believe Preston guilty of anything prosecutable and were convinced that the townsmen were using the incident as a pretext to get the troops out of the province altogether. Hutchinson told his visitors to do as they thought best, but unofficially, as town leaders, not militia officers. He did not want it said in London that he had raised the militia to show the king's soldiers the way out of the king's province. Presumably he calmed Dalrymple, who for the next several days had to look at musket-toting townsmen patrolling the streets while his men paced in their barracks. When the last troops left for the castle—at a fairly leisurely pace, unmarred by any incident—the patrols ended, as if to underscore the town meeting's claim that the troops had been the source of trouble, not the means to end it. Peace had been restored; it would not be broken again any time soon.

Hutchinson still feared for the worst. "Our people are as infatuated as they were in the times of the Witchcraft," he lamented.[50] "I have only the Shadow of Power," he complained to Hillsborough; "the authority of government is gone in all matters wherein the Controversy between the Kingdom and the Colonies is concerned."[51] Preston had not helped matters. Upon his arrest he had spoken well of the town. After a little time in jail he spoke more harshly in an account that he sent privately to London, only for it to find its way back to the Boston press.[52] Gage, who initially approved complete withdrawal to the castle, changed his mind and urged Dalyrmple to delay transferring the 14th Regiment as long as he could, then returned to his original stance. He could shrug his shoulders, telling himself it was too late to do anything differently—whether it was the soldiers being removed from town or Preston and the eight soldiers being held in jail. Preston and the others, the general realized, were beyond his reach once they surrendered themselves to civilian authorities. Besides, they may well have broken Massachusetts law so they could justifiably face a trial before the province's Superior Court.[53]

Hutchinson bought Preston and the enlisted men some breathing space by seeing to it that any forthcoming trial was postponed, hoping that, with time, calmer heads would prevail. Thus a judicial term ended in June with no trial. So too the term scheduled to begin in August. Preston was not arraigned until September and finally tried in October. Still anticipating disaster, Hutchinson had made arrangements with imperial authorities to intercede should Preston—or the others—be found guilty. Ready to use the excuse that the king's pleasure ought to be known before anyone was executed, Hutchinson could hand down a reprieve and await a royal pardon, then try to slip the condemned out of the province altogether.[54]

Hillsborough, the American secretary, admonished Hutchinson to do all of this "in a prudent and constitutional" manner and not add to the "phrenzy" that the king's men thought gripped Boston.[55] Whether he would have been able to do so is moot. The point is that he did not even have to make the attempt. During the months between the incident and the trials a rough type of justice was already being worked out, though what seems obvious now was hardly apparent then.

It was not apparent then because the coroner's inquests had been completed, indictments had been issued, and a full-blown war of words had erupted between those who felt the soldiers were guilty of murder and those who believed they had acted in self-defense. The inquests determined that the five dead fell from bullets fired by soldiers of the 29th Regiment. The most irate of them ruled that the victims had been slain "wilfully and feloniously" and another stipulated that the killing had occurred at Preston's order.[56]

The first four to die were interred together at town expense on March 8 in the Old Granary burying ground, all eulogized as "unhappy Victims" of a "bloody Massacre." Shops throughout Boston and neighboring towns closed and church bells tolled for the late Thursday afternoon proceedings. Each body rode in its own hearse, those in the procession so numerous that they walked six abreast, the "principal Gentry" following behind in carriages. One observer guessed that some ten thousand participated as mourners or onlookers.[57] The four deceased had become martyrs in the cause of freedom, victims of the tyranny of standing armies. Patrick Carr, who died on the 14th, ultimately joined them, literally in their crypt and figuratively in the local memory. The town fittingly gave the Irishman his own procession on St. Patrick's Day.[58]

Both funeral cortèges passed through King Street, within hearing distance of the town jail where Preston and the eight enlisted men awaited their fate. They were joined, but briefly, by four civilians once the Suffolk County grand jury began looking into the case after it convened on March 13, as depositions were being taken. Some alleged that muskets had been fired from the custom house as well as from the street, and that these four men were in the custom house at the time of the incident. Roughly two weeks later the grand jury handed down its indictment, naming the thirteen men then in custody. All were accused of "not having the Fear of God before their eyes, but being moved and seduced by the Instigation of the devil and their own wicked arts," so that "with force and arms feloniously" they "wilfully and of their malice aforethought" committed murder.[59] Potentially, if one were found guilty, all could be convicted as accomplices and face the same sentence. If it was for murder, they could be hanged.

The stage had been set for retributive justice, swift and sure. But the legal outcome would be neither swift nor sure. As months passed with still no trial, all of the parties to the larger dispute stood by their initial reactions. In this interim a press battle ensued that widened the rhetorical divide. Few at the time could have predicted that, paradoxically, the press battle would help defuse tensions by acting as a court of public opinion that operated independently from a court of law. Already convinced that they knew what had happened on King Street, townsmen were more concerned that nothing

Figure 5 (opposite) Paul Revere's famous engraving of the massacre. It is actually one of three produced within a few months of the event. Henry Pelham's came first, then Revere's, then one by clockmaker Jonathan Mulliken of Newburyport. Mulliken appears to have based his engraving on Revere's, and Revere based his on Pelham's, although

The BLOODY MASSACRE perpetrated in King—↓—Street BOSTON on March 5th 1770 by a party of the 29th REGt

UnhappyBoston! see thy Sons deplore.
Thy hallow'd Walks besmear'd with guiltless Gore.
While faithlessP—n and his savageBands.
With murd'rousRancourstretch their bloodyHands;
Like fierceBarbarians grinning o'er their Prey.
Approve the Carnage,and enjoy the Day.

If scalding drops from Rage from AnguishWrung
If speechless Sorrows lab'ring for a Tongue.
Or if a weeping World can ought appease
The plaintive Ghosts of Victims such as these;
The Patriot's copious Tears for each are shed.
A glorious Tribute which embalms the Dead.

But know,Fate summons to that awful Goal.
where JUSTICE strips the Murd'rer of his Soul:
Should venalC—ts the scandal of the Land.
Snatch the relentless Villain from her Hand.
Keen Execrations on this Plate inscrib'd.
Shall reach aJUDGE who never can be brib'd.

Engrav'd Printed & Sold by Paul Revere Boston

The unhappy Sufferers were Messrs. Saml Gray. Saml Maverick, Jamcs Caldwell, Crispus Attucks & Patrk Carr
Killed Six wounded; two of them (Christr Monk & John Clark) Mortally

Revere sold his to the public first. Pelham was an artist as well as an engraver, and had shown Revere his depiction of the massacre. Irate when Revere produced a version based on it, he composed a caustic note to the silversmith. Whether he actually sent it—and Revere's response, if he did—is not clear. Revere had been the subject of a portrait by Pelham's half-brother, John Singleton Copley, some months before. Revere added "Butcher's Hall" above the custom house sign and had a gun barrel firing out one of the windows. There are other, minor, differences as well between the Revere and Pelham engravings. All three images featured a dog in the foreground, perhaps following the eighteenth-century artistic convention of the cur as mute witness. All three also compressed the action, showing civilians removing bodies as the soldiers are firing—which, of course, was not the case. Christian Remick is thought to have been the colorist for Revere's version, the red blood of the victims matching the red coats of the soldiers. Courtesy of the American Antiquarian Society.

in court contradict their opinion that a crime had been committed than they were with seeing someone executed for it.

Within two weeks of printing its first version of the "massacre" (on March 12) the *Boston Gazette* description was joined in a broadside to Paul Revere's now famous engraving. It shows troops taking deliberate aim on unarmed men, an officer behind them, sword raised, giving the command to fire. In the background a gun barrel protrudes from an upstairs window of the custom house, enveloped in smoke by the general discharge and adding to the carnage below.[60]

As if the *Boston Gazette* account and Revere's engraving were not disturbing enough to Hutchinson, town leaders, acting on their own, had justices of the peace take depositions that they collated and printed as *A Short Narrative of The horrid Massacre.*[61] This account would stand as the town's brief before the bar of public opinion and soon became more important than any argument eventually made in court. Designed to shape popular opinion, it did as intended, much to Hutchinson's dismay. "I should have attempted to suppress the proceeding if there was any sort of authority to back or join me but there is none," he grumbled self-pityingly.[62] Hutchinson believed that he had had little choice but to endorse what the town had initiated—the taking of depositions, *not* the tenor of what the deponents said, although he worried that readers of the *Short Narrative* would not make the distinction. Everywhere the *Short Narrative* went it included his endorsement: "I do hereby certify" that the depositions were executed in "full faith and credit" and that they should therefore have standing "both in Court and without"—words that must have made him wince every time he saw them.[63] Just as Dalrymple grumbled about removing the troops and then removed them, Hutchinson groused about endorsing the depositions and then endorsed them. Political realism and a desire to avoid further bloodshed trumped insistence on rightful authority or proper order.

Benjamin Edes and John Gill, publishers of the *Boston Gazette*, printed *A Short Narrative* at town expense. The town meeting resolved not to circulate it locally—for the time being, that is—so that potential jurors for "the unhappy Persons now in Custody for Trial" would not be subjected to "undue Bias."[64] Town leaders probably mixed a genuine sense of fairness with a concern that *A Short Narrative* not be the cause of a change of venue, should defense lawyers contend that the local jury pool had been tainted. What is more, the real battle for public opinion was not going to take place in Boston, where the town meeting's view could be expected to prevail, but in the Massachusetts countryside and elsewhere in the colonies and even on the far side of the Atlantic. While town leaders held most copies of *A Short Narrative* in reserve, they sent nearly forty to London with the hope of influencing imperial policy, starting with removal of the troops altogether from the province and a reconsideration of recent changes in the navigation system brought as part of the Townshend Program. Appending a letter to the Duke of Richmond, considered a friend to their cause, town leaders condemned the "execrable deed" and insisted "that a full and just representation of it should be made to persons of character, in order to frustrate the designs of certain men" who have been "plotting the ruin of our constitution and liberties."[65]

They no doubt thought Hutchinson one of those plotters. Town-appointed justices of the peace took the last deposition for *A Short Narrative* on March 24 and the pamphlet did not go to press until the end of the month. Naturally none of this could be done in secret, so Hutchinson moved quickly and had a justice of the peace more sympathetic to his cause gather another set of depositions. He rushed them off to London in the care of customs commissioner John Robinson. But Hutchinson lost whatever advantage he might have gained by his quick action because *A Fair Account* was not actually in print until copies of *A Short Narrative* had arrived in London. As in the *Short Narrative*, a long introduction designed to shape readers' impressions preceded the depositions. [66] The *Fair Account* provided little detail on what supposedly happened on King Street, its cause-and-effect associations being every bit as loose as those in the *Short Narrative*.

Tempers showed on both sides. Before *A Fair Account* even appeared in print the Boston town meeting felt compelled to issue *Additional Observations* to bolster *A Short Narrative*.[67] It took an even harsher tone. No additional blood had been shed, however. The sniping remained verbal, the rhetorical battle acting as a surrogate for physical confrontation. Protesting Bostonians charged that they were being tyrannized; imperial officials countered that they were being victimized. Both pointed to the massacre as proof of their assertions, but with a lessening sense of urgency. No soldiers remained in the town proper; no mobs roamed the streets. Time was enabling them to solidify their opposing views, but without much pressure to prove which, if either, was right. The test would be whether what happened in court disrupted the process.

All of this occurred over the summer and into the fall, to the eve of Preston's trial. During these months Preston and the eight enlisted men remained in jail. The four civilians had been allowed to post bonds on the promise of returning for trial.[68] Town leaders did not wage a sustained campaign to keep the civilians' names or those of the soldiers in the press and before the public eye. They did not need to use such tactics to achieve their ends. Not only had the soldiers gone to Castle William and been shown to be subject to local law, the 29th Regiment had been removed to New Jersey and it was evident that the 14th Regiment would not be returning to town. In their absence customs collectors were again too intimidated to pursue their jobs vigorously.

When Preston and the other soldiers were finally arraigned and prepared for trial, Boston remained calm. Not so the enlisted men. Learning that they would be tried separately from—and after—Preston, three of them petitioned the Superior Court to have their trials joined. "We only desire to Open the truth before our Captains face for it is very hard he being a Gentleman should have more chance for to save his life than we poor men that is Obliged to obey his command," they pled.[69] Quite perceptively they feared that if he were cleared of the charge of ordering them to fire, they would have to bear responsibility for the lives lost on King Street. Their request denied, they must have awaited trial with great trepidation, trepidation that only increased with Preston's acquittal and the delay in trying the four civilians—which they had no reason to think would work to their advantage.

But virtually no one demanded a blood atonement. The soldiers' trial began in late November and went as smoothly and uneventfully as Preston's the month before. There was no convincing proof that Preston had ordered anyone to fire at any time. On the contrary, the preponderance of evidence seemed to prove that he had done what he could to avoid any bloodshed, even at risk to his own life, by stepping between his men and the crowd. "The behaviour of the People was remarkably decent during the whole Trial," a surprised and relieved Hutchinson wrote to Hillsborough after Preston was set free, and "in general they are satisfied with his acquittal." That made Hutchinson optimistic for the enlisted men, too. "From the Evidence which appeared upon Capt Preston's Trial there is room to expect that, at most, they can be found Guilty of Manslaughter only and some of the Court seems to think it a justifiable homicide."[70] Hutchinson hoped for too much on the matter of justifiable homicide; he guessed more accurately on the question of manslaughter.

Almost immediately after his arrest Preston had asked Josiah Quincy Jr. to represent him and the enlisted men. Apparently Quincy agreed to do it if John Adams would join him, which Adams did. Both men had become involved in politics through the town meeting and were much more likely to side with the town against Hutchinson should there be a dispute between imperial authority and local power, including stationing soldiers among civilians. Quincy made sure that Preston knew this. And yet both these men of Boston were also committed to the idea of justice, which meant that what was determined by law should stand apart from and be above what is preferred politically—which was Preston's source of hope. Quincy's father warned him that he was afraid taking the case would destroy his political career. The soldiers, Quincy responded, were entitled "by the laws of God and man" to "counsel and aid." He was determined to do his duty and in this circumstance it was to assure that Preston and the other soldiers received a fair trial.[71] Adams was committed to the same ideals. Recall that years later he wrote: "as the Evidence was, the Verdict was exactly right."[72] The prosecution would have to prove its case. Presumption of innocence and the rules of evidence required it.

Robert Treat Paine, hired by the town, and acting solicitor general Samuel Quincy, Josiah Jr.'s older brother, served as prosecutors in the soldiers' trial. Of the thirty-two witnesses they called, only eleven had given depositions printed in the *Short Narrative*—now circulating freely around Boston—and those eleven were hardly the most inflammatory. They offered relatively mild criticism of the soldiers, as did the testimony of the others brought forward for the first time in the trial. Seven months had passed and still no witness could say unequivocally that he saw this soldier shoot that civilian; rather, courtroom testimony for the prosecution asserted little more than that the eight accused had been on King Street that night and that the provocations they received were not life-threatening. Those testimonies more or less complemented Samuel Quincy's opening argument, which sounded almost apologetic for trying anyone over the "melancholy event"— pointedly *not* the "horrid massacre"—carefully chosen words for a difficult-to-argue case.[73]

In his summation before the defense called its witnesses, Samuel Quincy concentrated on Private Matthew Kilroy, arguing that witnesses established he had shot Samuel Gray. Actually, they did not; Quincy made inferential leaps in his argument, possibly because he felt that he needed to establish one individual's guilt before contending that all involved were equally guilty. Evidence proving that another private, Hugh Montgomery, shot Attucks was even shakier. Proof that anyone in particular could be held responsible for a fatal shot was almost non-existent, except for the fact that five men died from gunshot wounds and only the soldiers had fired weapons that night on King Street. But Quincy, who—unlike his younger brother— was not all that sympathetic to the town meeting view of things, had his prosecutorial duty to perform, so perform it he did. "Here Gentlemen," Quincy stressed with Kilroy, "if any there can be, is evidence . . . of a heart desperately wicked, and bent upon mischief, the true characteristic of a wilful malicious murderer." All who acted with him, whatever their motives may have been, were equally responsible. It only remained for the jurors to determine "what species of homicide" had been committed. Still, except for his diatribe against Kilroy, Samuel Quincy had not been all that hard on the soldiers nor had he connected any but Kilroy and Montgomery to the deaths of the five victims.[74] Whether by personal preference, weak evidence, or even a combination of the two, he left the defense a wide opening.

Figure 6 Alonzo Chappel's version of the massacre, first printed in John Frederick Schroeder's Life and Times of Washington *(1857). It was a quite familiar image for over a century; it is much less so now. Chappel was already a successful portraitist when he painted the massacre but was just beginning a career of doing images that could be turned into engravings for books and magazines, something he would continue for the next thirty years. In his depiction of the massacre he seemed less interested in the event itself than the dramatic arrangement of the elements in his scene, from the grenadier at the center-right and town house to the rear, juxtaposed with the action occurring to each side. The mixing of the historical with the artistic can also be seen in F. Luis Mora's rendition, first used in Woodrow Wilson's U.S. history as it was serialized in* Harper's Monthly Magazine *in 1901, which seems to be an homage to Francisco Goya's firing squad and victims in* The Third of May 1808.*

Josiah Quincy Jr. tried to push through it. He and John Adams, joined by Sampson Salter Blowers, relied more on witnesses speaking publicly for the first time than on depositions from the *Fair Account* or on witnesses from Preston's trial repeating or adding to their testimony there. Contrary to the bitter allegations in the *Short Narrative* or the more measured charges leveled by the prosecution in court, the defense wanted to show that the soldiers had been attacked by a mob that intended them mortal harm. Had they committed homicides? Yes, but they did so in self-defense, making their actions justifiable or excusable; certainly they could be convicted of nothing worse than manslaughter. Under the circumstances, first Quincy and then Adams emphasized in their closing arguments, murder convictions were unthinkable. "If any reasonable man, in the situation of one of these soldiers, would have had reason to believe in the time of it, that people came with an intention to kill him," Adams stressed to the jurors, "whether you have this satisfaction now, or not in your own minds, they were justifiable, at least excusable in firing."[75]

Jurors returned with verdicts that, consciously or not, followed the recommendation of Edmund Trowbridge in his instructions to them. One of the four judges presiding on the bench, for this trial as for Preston's, Trowbridge advised them that, in effect, an all-or-nothing principle could be applied: if one was innocent, all could be innocent; if one was guilty, all might be guilty. If the soldiers had truly struggled to save their lives, they could be found innocent. If, in that struggle, a civilian was slain who had no part in it—Samuel Maverick, for example—they were still not guilty. If, by contrast, they were not in mortal peril and one had taken deliberate aim and killed a civilian anyway, then they could all be convicted, regardless of how the other civilians died and the individual soldiers' roles in those deaths. Moreover, there were other alternatives: all could be convicted of manslaughter or some could be found guilty while others could be acquitted altogether. Concurring with the prosecution, Trowbridge suggested that the evidence showed Montgomery had fired first and killed Crispus Attucks, and that Kilroy had slain Samuel Gray. But he steered the jury toward manslaughter and away from murder.[76]

And so the jurors decided. At first Hutchinson did not see how they could acquit six and convict two on a reduced charge. "The Jury must be excused for not fully comprehending the law of Evidence," Hutchinson wrote to Hillsborough, because "as far as I have received it here was no room for distinction between them." But then on second thought he decided that the men of Suffolk County had done well. "These are pretty good distinctions for an American jury," he concluded.[77]

Manslaughter was a felony, a capital offense, but executions for it had become exceedingly rare. Pleading benefit of the clergy, an archaic concept perpetuated for just such ticklish legal situations, Montgomery and Kilroy were released after each was, following English practice, "burnt with a hot iron in the brawn of the left thumb."[78] Had they been wrongly convicted? Perhaps, but both were probably relieved soon to put Boston behind them. Gaps in the courtroom testimony notwithstanding, there is little doubt that they fired their muskets and it is likely that their bullets hit someone, possibly the very two men they were convicted of shooting.

Trowbridge's instructions may not have been judicious in the strictly legal sense but they provided the perfect solution politically. There was more involved here than the age-old problem of balancing what the law requires with what justice demands. Pleased as Hutchinson's opponents were with

Figure 7 Howard Pyle's illustration of the massacre, done for Thomas Wentworth Higginson's essay "The British Yoke," which appeared in the August 1883 issue of Harper's New Monthly Magazine. *Higginson traced the origins of the American Revolution back to the first generation of Massachusetts settlers, juxtaposing their desire for freedom with England's attempt to control them. Imperial policy, Higginson contended, was driven more by ignorance than malice, a failure to see that colonial pride in the transatlantic connection could easily turn to resentment if Americans believed they were being treated badly. Higginson devoted but part of one sentence to the massacre; Pyle, on his way to becoming one of the great book and magazine illustrators of his day, gave it added emphasis. His soldiers seem to underscore the hauteur that lay behind British acts, as they looked disdainfully on the mob they had driven back. Technically, Pyle got much wrong, from the street's layout to the British uniforms; psychologically, he probably got it right for his readers: British villains, American victims.*

the result of their fight for public opinion, someone needed to be guilty of something in order for that victory to be sustained. Contending that all of the accused went free because of some sort of vast conspiracy orchestrated from London or closer to home by Hutchinson would have worn thin quickly, particularly because it was known that Joseph Mayo, jury foreman, was sympathetic to the town's view.[79] This is not to say that the jurors consciously contrived their verdict to produce the desired result. Nevertheless, judges, counsel, and jurors looked for a way out of this political minefield. Montgomery and Kilroy became casualties as they threaded their way through it, but at least they survived the ordeal—unlike the five slain on King Street.[80]

During the trial Josiah Quincy Jr. had wanted to exonerate the soldiers by indicting the town. Adams demurred and the defense steered a more moderate course. Quincy had not agreed to represent Preston or the soldiers before talking to town leaders, who could assure him that serving as a defense counsel would not jeopardize his standing with them or the larger community.[81] They could make those assurances not just because of their ability to distinguish what happened in court from what happened in politics or their understanding of how an adversarial legal system works but because they did not need murder convictions. Imperial reformer and former governor Thomas Pownall had advised them many months before that it would be wise to show mercy while in pursuit of justice—that their purposes would be better served by leniency than by insisting upon their pound of flesh.[82] They most likely realized that he was right.

Hutchinson thought the acquittals "deprived" his opponents of the great advantage convictions would have given them for promoting their political "cause."[83] Actually, Hutchinson's move to delay the trials may have saved the soldiers' lives—in itself no small achievement—but that delay did not cost his opponents politically because they were winning the battle for public opinion, and the trial outcomes did not set them back in the least. In mid-summer town leaders had written Benjamin Franklin that "it affords good satisfaction" to know that, locally, the *Short Narrative* "of the horrid massacre" was having "the desired effect."[84]

What happened in court became increasingly anticlimactic, so that by the third trial very few people paid much attention to the legal proceedings anyway. The soldiers were gone; the town had returned to business as usual, which meant that illicit overseas trade kept pace with legal enterprise. "The people of the Province seemed to be tired of controversy, and in general, wish to see an end to it," concluded Hutchinson.[85] If so that was probably as much because of overall satisfaction as it was growing boredom. For his part, Hutchinson was neither bored nor satisfied: he continued to lose power and his opponents continued to gain. London did nothing to reverse the

Figure 8 A century-old postcard, which is a reproduction of the massacre scene that John Bufford issued as a chromolithograph in 1857, based on a drawing done by William Champney the year before. It is perhaps the first to show Attucks and others fighting back; it is not the first to show Attucks as an African-American. That was done for William Cooper Nell's Colored Patriots of the American Revolution *(1855). Nell, himself African-American and a Boston abolitionist, wrote that Attucks "had been foremost in resisting, and was first slain." Even so, the illustration, printed as the frontispiece, did not depict Attucks or other civilians as fighting back. Rather, they look stunned as Preston, sword raised, orders his men to fire on them. Attucks is in the foreground, already hit, a white civilian doing what he can to assist him. Nell pressed to have a monument built to the memory of Attucks as martyr to the patriot cause. He failed, though the town did start celebrating a Crispus Attucks Day a few years after Nell published his book. The image in Nell's* Colored Patriots *is rarely reproduced but over the years Bufford's image and variations on it—such as Constantino Brumidi's fresco in the U.S. Capitol—have become almost as familiar as Paul Revere's engraving. Even if Bufford's picture captures the chaos of the moment, it also compounds the inaccuracies.*

flow. Although the Privy Council expressed concern that Massachusetts was spiraling out of control, it recommended to the king that Parliament determine what needed to be done. As crown and Council deferred to Parliament, in Parliament the Lords deferred to the Commons. And the Commons decided overwhelmingly not to use the massacre as an excuse to investigate Boston's affairs.[86]

Preston's trial had taken a week; that of the eight soldiers ran nearly three days longer. The case of the accused civilians was dispensed with in a single morning, on December 12. Jurors did not even leave their seats before tendering their verdict. Virtually the entire case against the four hinged on the testimony of a servant to one of the accused. The servant's claim that he and his master, Edward Manwaring, were in the custom house and that both of them had fired shots—he two, Manwaring one—was contested by others who insisted that Manwaring and the servant were nowhere near the custom house on the night of March 5. Neither, they insisted, was John Munroe, one of the other accused. The remaining two on trial, Thomas Greenwood and Hammond Green, had been there at some point but no one, not even the servant, alleged that they had fired at the crowd. With the servant having been suspect from the beginning and with nothing to corroborate his tale, Samuel Quincy, acting for the crown, "gave up the cause." It was not a case he had wanted to prosecute; it was not a case town leaders any longer had much interest in pursuing. The jury acquitted Manwaring and the others. Manwaring's servant would later be convicted of perjury, publicly whipped, and transported out of the colonies.[87]

Had he, like Montgomery and Kilroy, become a scapegoat? Perhaps, but not as likely. Hutchinson suspected that town leaders had coached him. We may never know for sure. But with his discrediting all investigation into shots being fired from the custom house ended, even though that was a distinct issue, separable from the question of the four civilians' innocence or guilt. A half-dozen of those whose depositions appeared in *A Short Narrative* claimed that they saw muzzle flashes from the custom house or at the very least heard gunfire from a point above street level. The accuracy or inaccuracy of that part of Revere's representation was destined never to be examined in court. Neither Hutchinson nor his opponents saw any benefit to digging deeper.

Aftermath

None of the trials had established many solid facts. Fortunately for public order, Bostonians did not follow those proceedings very closely anyway. There was no consensus as to how many shots were fired or by how many guns. Even the number of men Preston reportedly took with him in the relief party varied, depending on the source. Some earlier accounts put the number at twelve, others at half that, and others still at somewhere between the two. That eight soldiers were arrested and tried does not in itself prove conclusively that those eight and no others had been involved. After all, Revere's engraving shows only seven in line, with Preston behind them. Witnesses could agree that Montgomery fell, but was it before he fired, or after? And did he fall because he slipped, because he was hit by something thrown at him, because Crispus Attucks struck him, or had a piece of ice fallen on him from the roof of the custom house? Questions of motivation and provocation were contingent on just such crucial distinctions, none of which was made.

Not only was—and is—there some question as to what really happened on King Street; there are questions about what was said in court many months later.[88] Virtually no one at the time demanded that those questions be answered. People had moved on, probably with minds unchanged, imperial apologists standing by the soldiers, imperial critics siding with the slain. On that level nothing had been resolved. Hutchinson had his truth, which the trials did not uphold. Town leaders held to a different truth but they too saw another version prevail in court. They ignored verdicts that did not sustain the charges made in *A Short Narrative* and town records referred to the incident as a massacre, regardless of court findings.[89] Using the pen name "Vindex," Samuel Adams wrote a series of essays for the *Boston Gazette* to keep the *Short Narrative* view alive. He was countered by "Philanthrop," who defended what had been done in court.[90] The odds were against "Philanthrop," however. Each year for over a decade thereafter Bostonians would be reminded in the annual massacre oration sponsored by the town meeting that innocent blood had been spilled.[91]

Even in 1775, on the eve of Lexington and Concord, with troops now back in the town, imperial authorities thought it best to let the harangues continue, since any attempt to silence the speakers might have produced a confrontation—and more deaths, more martyrs? So the get-tough policies symbolized by the Coercive Acts of the year before did not bring a complete end to the politics of avoidance, if getting tough meant trying to change local minds about what really happened on King Street.

Although it would be a stretch to attribute Solomon-like wisdom to either the judges or jurors in any of the three trials, the jurors tendered verdicts and the judges pronounced sentences that sparked no riots in Boston or retaliatory policies in London. Those who considered the soldiers guilty went away placated even if not entirely satisfied. Those who believed that the soldiers had been wronged could also feel some small measure of satisfaction. In one sense that was just as well because the evidence presented in court did little to establish what really happened and those looking too hard for the truth would have gone away feeling that the legal process had failed—that the truth was lost, not found.

But in another sense the solution to one problem brought with it complications of a more troubling sort, leading ultimately to another problem that was more insoluble. The explicit concern in court—discovering who shot whom and whether those who died had been murdered or killed in self-defense—had been mixed with a deeper implicit concern: could imperial differences be put aside and a sense of transatlantic community restored? Finding a politically if not legally satisfactory answer to the first question did not necessarily mean that the second question had been answered as well. During his 1766 testimony in the House of Commons, Benjamin Franklin, after he had warned about the danger of using troops to pacify the colonists, was asked if the colonists could be counted on to help Britain should a new war erupt in Europe. He responded with an even more subtle warning.

> I do think they would as far as their circumstances would permit. They consider themselves as a part of the British empire, and as having one common interest with it; they may be looked on here as foreigners, but they do not consider themselves as such. They are zealous for the honour and prosperity of this nation, and, while they are well used, will always be ready to support it, as far as their little power goes.[92]

Figure 9 Larry Rivers's Boston Massacre, *painted for the New England Merchants National Bank of Boston in 1968. The segment above was part of a larger acrylic and oil piece on canvas that was nearly twenty feet long by some fourteen feet wide. Charles Bahne remembers it being displayed so that the soldiers could be seen through windows at the Bank's 28 State Street address as if they were firing out toward the site of the massacre. There is another building on the spot now and the mural is no longer there. Rivers, a Pop Art pioneer, had already won acclaim for* Washington Crossing the Delaware *over a decade before. Of the massacre piece, he wrote in his autobiography that he created "a visual mixture of British soldiers shooting some complaining British-Americans who turn out to be Vietnamese and civil rights activists."[93] Courtesy of the Larry Rivers Foundation and Visual Artists and Galleries Association (VAGA).*

In other words, American loyalty to the British empire was conditional and qualified. That did not, ipso facto, make it disingenuous. Britain had only itself to blame for the disenchanted colonists who believed that they had the right to be treated well—and as *they* defined "well treated." From the beginning there had been talk of reciprocity, of mutual benefit in an empire of liberty, even with its mercantilistic base and navigation system. Yet the empire was not set up to manage doubts about those claims when they arose among too many within it—not because it was so oppressive, so tyrannical, but because it was built ad hoc, because as it evolved so much was left to chance, to policies too ill-considered and too inconsistently applied.

After the massacre and trials imperial administrators continued to fear that the disobedient and disloyal had taken over Boston. Most townsmen resented any attempt by London to impose its will. Basic disagreements over provincial autonomy and imperial authority only worsened. The odd mix of confrontation and avoidance would proceed apace for another four years, with on-again and off-again enforcement of imperial policy provoking local resistance that could turn violent, even as those resisters professed their loyalty to the crown and devotion to the empire. The politics of avoidance that had proved successful in the short run exacerbated disputes over the long haul because no true reconciliation had been achieved. What worked in the aftermath of the massacre could not have worked in the aftermath of a more serious bloodletting at Lexington and Concord.

In National Memory

Talk of erecting some sort of monument at town expense to commemorate the massacre started even before then. One of the stumbling blocks to settling on a suitable memorial was deciding the place of the five slain in it. Adams, in his efforts to exonerate the soldiers during their trial, did his best to impugn the integrity of at least two of the slain: Patrick Carr and Crispus Attucks. He could accept that Samuel Maverick and possibly James Caldwell were innocent victims, but not Carr and Attucks. In casting aspersions on them he dabbled in class bias (they were working men), dropped an ethnic slur (Carr, the Irish "teague") and, most prominently, as we would now say, he "played the race card" (against Attucks, one of the disreputable "molattoes," part of "a rabble of Negroes"). Attucks in particular suffered in Adams's closing argument, upon "whose mad behaviour, in all probability, the dreadful carnage of that night, is chiefly to be ascribed."[94] Carr, in his own way, had an even more important role in Adams's case for the defense, something of which Adams reminded jurors during the closing. One of his key witnesses had been Dr. John Jeffries, a well-respected physician who treated Carr as he lingered for nine days before dying. Jeffries testified that Carr had in effect offered a deathbed confession, forgiving the soldiers for what they had done because they had been driven to it by the mob. Carr, as Jeffries reported, said "that he had seen soldiers often fire on the people in *Ireland*, but had never seen them bear half so much before they fired in his life."[95]

This may indeed have been telling testimony, but it tells us something about Adams as well as Carr, about attitudes that went beyond the particulars of this case. Adams had never been comfortable with mobs and never would be. Admittedly, he argued as a lawyer in this instance and what he said about Attucks and Carr in the courtroom may have stayed there, where it served its purpose. His job as attorney was to defend his clients, not the reputations of Crispus Attucks and Patrick Carr. Even so, like other Revolutionary Era leaders, he distinguished between lawless mobs and law-abiding citizens who organized themselves in protest—such as in Boston's town meeting. In Adams's view, mobs, alas, were what formed when thinking people surrendered to passion.[96] "Mobs will never do to govern States or command Armies," he intoned.[97] Looking back on 1770, he feared that the "explosion" that was the "massacre . . . had been intentionally wrought up by designing Men who knew what they were aiming at better than the instrument they employed."[98] Adams and men like him would not even consider equating the mob with a posse comitatus.

Adams had worried that if Boston were perceived as being too radical, too violent, it would stand alone in its fight for rights in the empire. If people in the Massachusetts countryside, if residents of other colonies, if potential sympathizers in Britain became convinced that Boston had indeed become as dangerous as its detractors claimed, then his cause was lost—ultimately even in Boston itself, he feared. Boston, after all, did not speak with a single voice; the town meeting did not represent everyone. Part of the process that would occur as a Revolutionary mentality was formed, and a nation born, included a winnowing that identified certain ideas as valid, others as not, certain behaviors as acceptable, others as not. Adams and other future Revolutionaries did not take it for granted that the prevailing shared assumption would be that all true Bostonians stood by Samuel Adams against Thomas Hutchinson, or that, when the fighting started, all good Americans took arms against the king's troops rather than rallied to their defense. It was a state of mind that had to be cultivated. Revolutions, after all, do no not just happen; they are made.

John Adams's aversion to mobs faded in the Boston that eventually erected a Massacre Monument. That it was referred to informally as the Crispus Attucks Memorial says much about what had changed to make that possible. The monument was not erected on Boston Common until 1888, where it still stands—little noticed as it now seems to be. Attucks's mixed ancestry and working-class status, liabilities in earlier years, became boons in post-Civil War, post-Reconstruction Boston.[99] At the same time that the state of Massachusetts, which provided the money, and the city of Boston, which provided the land, united for the twenty-five-foot obelisk on the Common, plans were made to reinter the bodies of the five slain.[100] They would be joined with Christopher Seider under the same gravestone in a more prominent place in the Old Granary, the burial site they now share —the five as "Victims of the Boston Massacre," Seider (there rendered Snider) as the "innocent, first victim" in the American struggle for freedom.[101] The Old Granary burial site is a stopping point along Boston's Freedom Trail, where Americans in search of their heritage are encouraged to find the past through heroic commemoration. Likewise for the circle of paving stones with a star in the center placed in State Street—once King Street—to mark the massacre site.

Many Americans now understand that Paul Revere's engraving of the massacre is a representation of the event, not the event itself, and that it was done for political purposes—to protest the presence of soldiers among civilians.[102] And yet it is still the most famous of the illustrations ever done and elements of it turn up in later renditions. For most of us, Revere's depiction and those it inspired somehow capture the truth of the moment, not in detail, but in essence. There had been a massacre, after all, just as John Adams contended.

But did it play the decisive role that Adams believed it had in bringing on a revolution? A "yes" seems in order, but how emphatic can that "yes" be? Historian Jeremy Black's advice is helpful here. A prolific and wide-ranging author, Professor Black often urges his readers to keep the "contingent" and "counterfactual" in mind.[103] The contingent emphasizes dependence and interdependence—a this-because-of-that causational approach that recognizes the tenuousness of most interpretations, an acceptance that, with most things of historical consequence, simple explanations are for the simple-minded. The counterfactual emphasizes "what if" and "what might have been." Imagining alternative outcomes—while avoiding flights of fancy—can be an effective way of reconsidering what actually did happen, and why. It can also act as a check on treating contingent developments as if they led to inevitable outcomes.

The sophisticated argument offered by Benjamin Labaree in his study of the Boston Tea Party stands as a fine example of historical writing that considers the contingent. Professor Labaree contended that the Tea Party changed history, that it, more than any other single event, was the catalyst of revolution. "In three short hours on a cold December night in 1773," he wrote, "a small band of men precipitated a reaction that led with little pause to the Declaration of Independence."[104] Crown and Parliament retaliated with the Coercive Acts and sent troops back into Boston. Protesting colonists developed shadow governments culminating in the Continental Congress. The combination led down the road to Lexington. And yet Labaree also emphasized that if there had been no Tea Party, there still may have been a revolution because the Tea Party was both cause and effect, a reflection of imperial discord and a source of it as well. The sequence leading from protest to rebellion to revolution would have been different without the Tea Party— and the parliamentary legislation that precipitated it—but the result could have been essentially the same.

No one has attempted a causational argument for the Boston Massacre along the lines that Professor Labaree made for the Tea Party; and, indeed, such an argument would be most difficult to sustain. There is no sequence of events dating from 1770 to rival or even match those subsequent to the Tea Party—no hardening of British policy, no dramatic escalation of colonial protest. But those long, unsolved problems of empire that helped precipitate the massacre remained unsolved to the end, problems both illustrated and exacerbated on March 5. Events in Boston reinforced prevailing views on both sides of the Atlantic, views that were difficult at best to reconcile with the imperial reality of that moment. If John Adams believed that the Boston Massacre helped produce the American Revolution, then it did—at least for him, and perhaps hundreds, even thousands of others. In that sense, Adams had constructed his own reality, his own understanding of cause-and-effect relationships. And so do we all.

PART II

DOCUMENTS

AMERICAN RIGHTS ASSERTED[1]

The resolutions passed by the Massachusetts House of Representatives on February 11, 1768 are printed below. They are often included in documentary anthologies for the Revolutionary Era as a classic assertion of American rights. Those rights, as the colonists construed them, came from God and through nature, as extended by the English constitution and reaffirmed in colonial charters. They provided the foundation for a position that the Massachusetts House had warned it would take in petitions to the crown and leading Members of Parliament just the month before. When pressured by Governor Bernard to rescind its resolutions, as directed by London (see Document 2), the Massachusetts House instead reaffirmed them by an even larger margin than when they were originally passed. A later generation of Massachusetts politicians would celebrate those who reaffirmed the resolutions as the "Glorious 92."[2]

The claims about rights and representation made by the Massachusetts House were not unique to it; nor was the willingness to go against a royally appointed governor in making them. What happened in Massachusetts had in fact been anticipated by a similar occurrence three years before in Virginia. At some point between 1764 and 1776 virtually every colonial legislature would have some sort of confrontation with imperial authority, whether through the person of the royally appointed governor or through some other connection to imperial authority in colonies where the governor was elected by the people (such as Rhode Island and Connecticut) or appointed by a proprietor (Pennsylvania and Maryland). What is notable in all of this is the breakdown of what was supposed to be a mutually advantageous arrangement.

Disputes over imperial policies in the 1760s compounded the difficulties. In Massachusetts the 1768 House resolutions were supported most vigorously by representatives from Boston and coastal communities. Only gradually did inland towns consistently join with Boston in common cause—a circumstance that some in London foresaw and yet, once again ironically, by their actions precipitated.

Note the combination of the explicit and implicit in these resolutions, yet another similarity with resolutions coming out of other colonial legislatures. The men of the Massachusetts House wrote as supplicants, asking that their voices be heard, and yet they also wrote as men certain of their rights, men who believed that all who served in government, even the king himself, were answerable to the people. But who were the people, how obliged was government to do what they expected, and what recourse did they have if London ignored the House resolutions? Answers to these questions proved all too elusive.

* * *

Sir,

The House of Representatives of this Province have taken into their serious consideration the great difficulties that must accrue to themselves and their constituents by the operation of several acts of Parliament imposing duties and taxes on the American colonies.

As it is a subject in which every colony is deeply interested, they have no reason to doubt but your House is duly impressed with its importance, and that such constitutional measures will be come into as are proper. It seems to be necessary, that all possible care should be taken, that the representations of the several assemblies, upon so delicate a point, should harmonize with each other: the House, therefore hope that this letter will be candidly considered in no other light than as expressing a disposition freely to communicate their mind to a sister colony, upon a common concern, in the same manner as they would be glad to receive the sentiments of your or any other House of Assembly on the continent.

The House have humbly represented to the Ministry their own sentiments: That his Majesty's high Court of Parliament is the supreme legislative power over the whole empire: That in all free States the constitution is fixed; and as the supreme legislative derives its power and authority from the constitution, it cannot overlap the bounds of it, without destroying its own foundation: That the constitution ascertains and limits both sovereignty and allegiance, and therefore his Majesty's American subjects, who acknowledge themselves bound by the ties of allegiance, have an equitable claim, to the full enjoyment of the fundamental rules of the British constitution: That it is an essential unalterable right in nature, ingrafted into the British constitution, as a fundamental law, and ever held sacred and irrevokable by the subjects within the realm, that what a man hath honestly acquired is absolutely his own, which he may freely give, but cannot be taken from him without his consent: That the American subjects may therefore, exclusive of any consideration of charter rights, with a decent firmness, adapted to the character of free men and subjects, assert this natural, constitutional right.

It is, moreover, their humble opinion, which they express with the greatest deference to the wisdom of the Parliament, that the Acts made there, imposing Duties on the people of this province, with the sole and express purpose of raising revenue, are infringements of their natural and constitutional rights; because, as they are not represented in the British Parliament, his Majesty's Commons in Britain, by those Acts, grant their property without their consent.

This House further are of opinion, that their constituents, considering their local circumstances, cannot by any possibility be represented in the Parliament; and that it will forever be impracticable, that they should be equally be represented there; and consequently not at all; being separated by an ocean of a thousand leagues: That his Majesty's royal predecessors, for this reason, were graciously pleased to form a subordinate legislative here, that their subjects might enjoy the unalienable right of a representation; Also, that considering the utter impracticability of their ever being fully and equally represented in Parliament, and the great expence that must unavoidably attend even a partial representation there, this House think that a taxation of their constituents, even without their consent, grievous as it is, would be preferable to any representation that could be admitted for them there.

Upon these principles, and also considering, that were the right in the Parliament ever so clear, yet, for obvious reasons, it would be beyond the rules of equity, that their constituents should be taxed, on the manufactures of Great-Britain here, in addition to the duties they pay for them in England, and other advantages arising to Great-Britain from the acts of trade, this House have preferred a humble, dutiful and loyal petition to our most gracious Sovereign, and made such representations to his Majesty's Ministers, as they apprehended would tend to obtain redress.

They have also submitted to consideration, whether any people can be said to enjoy any degree of freedom, if the Crown, in addition to its undoubted authority of constituting a Governor, should appoint him such a stipend as it shall judge proper, without the consent of the people, and at their expence: And whether, while the Judges of the land and other civil officers hold not their commissions during good behavior, their salaries appointed for them by the Crown, independent of the people, hath not a tendency to subvert the principles of equity, and endanger the happiness and security of the people.

In addition to these measures, the House have wrote a letter to their agent, Mr. Deberdt,[3] the sentiments of which he is directed to lay before the Ministry; wherein they take notice of the hardship of the Act for preventing mutiny and desertion; which requires the Governor and Council to provide enumerated articles for the King's marching troops, and the people to pay the expence: and also the commission of the Gentlemen appointed Commissioners of the Customs to reside in America, which authorizes them to make as many appointments as they think fit, and to pay the appointees what sums they please, for whose mal-conduct they are not accountable: from whence it may happen, that officers of the Crown may be multiplied to such a degree, as to become dangerous to the Liberty of the people, by virtue of a commission which doth not appear to this House to derive any such advantages to trade as many have been led to expect.

These are the sentiments and proceedings of this House: And as they have too much reason to believe that the enemies of the Colonies have represented them to his Majesty's Ministers and the parliament as factious, disloyal, and having a disposition to make themselves independent of the Mother Country, they have taken occasion, in the most humble terms, to assure his Majesty and his Ministers, that with regard to the people of this Province, and, as they doubt not, of all the Colonies, that the charge is unjust.

The House is fully satisfied, that your Assembly is too generous and enlarged in sentiment to believe that this letter proceeds from an ambition of taking the lead, or dictating to the other Assemblies: They freely submit their opinion to the judgment of others; and shall take it kind in your House, to point out to them any thing further that may be thought necessary.

This House cannot conclude, without expressing their firm confidence in the King, our common head and father, that the united and dutiful supplications of his distressed American subjects will meet with his royal and favorable acceptance.

Signed by the Speaker
[Thomas Cushing]

LONDON'S RESPONSE[4]

There are still those who view American Revolutionary history as a morality play, pitting good Americans against bad Britons. Topping the list of bad Britons is King George III; men who advised him like Lord North and George Grenville are not far behind. But as scholars have long contended, George III was no tyrant and he let Parliament take the lead in devising American policy. They have also shown that North, Grenville, and most of those who supported them in Parliament were not anti-American; rather, they were pro-empire and the label of "hardliner" that has been affixed to North and Grenville ought to peeled away. True, they believed that Britain was sovereign and Parliament supreme in their expanding empire. They nevertheless took a more flexible, pragmatic approach to policy-making than their critics have appreciated. Even so, they could not tolerate any questioning of Parliament's ultimate authority and Hillsborough's very first letter to colonial governors expressed concern that they were not keeping London well enough informed of colonial oppositionism. His adverse reaction to the Massachusetts circular letter indicates just how deeply he dreaded what it portended.[5]

Wills Hill has yet to escape the stereotyping that once dogged the king and his chief ministers. The first Earl of Hillsborough, Hill was also first to serve as secretary of state for American affairs. He did not take office with a clearly defined plan to make the colonists toe the behavioral line. Even so, the new post was created, with Hillsborough appointed to it, in part because of political infighting where supporters of both the man and the post hoped that a firmer policy would emerge. This latest action by Whitehall and Westminster served only to deepen the resentment among colonists already provoked by Townshend's Revenue Act and the creation of an American Board of Customs.

Rightly or wrongly, Hillsborough bore the brunt of the criticism. Even some contemporaries in Britain singled him out as the proponent of bad policies, one commentator later observing as the War of Independence wound down that "his adversaries have constantly charged him with laying the foundation of the war during the four years he had the administration of the colonies in his hands, by the circular letters he wrote to the governors, enforcing compulsory measures—such as dissolving their assemblies, if they did not comply with the requisitions of government."[6] The most controversial of those circular letters is the one printed below, which Hillsborough wrote in response to the assertions made by the Massachusetts House (Document 1). He did so with the king's explicit endorsement and the tacit approval of many leaders in Parliament.

The post of American secretary of state, which Hillsborough filled in January 1768, came late for a variety of reasons—because overseas empire and American holdings within it became important only over time, and even because of political rivalries in Parliament and the administrative jealousy of the other two secretaries of state.[7] But by 1767 there were enough parliamentary leaders who shared a gloomy view that the post could no longer be avoided, because, as the Earl of Chesterfield put it, "if we have no Secretary of State with full and undisputed powers for America, in a few years we may as well have no America."[8]

Hillsborough was typical of the leading British politicians in his age. As a wealthy Anglo-Irishman he would eventually have estates, with titles to match, on both sides of the Irish Sea. More importantly, he began public life early, with a seat in the House of Commons by the age of twenty-one before he was advanced to the peerage. Like Grenville, North, and so many others, he served on the king's Privy Council and held a number of minor governmental positions at the same time, before he received a cabinet-level appointment. He spent a fair amount of time jockeying for power behind the scenes as ministries rose and fell, but that is the nature of the beast and far too much has been made of the coalition governments and political rivalries of the era as an underlying cause of revolution. Such developments did shape public policy— and still do in Britain and elsewhere, for that matter. But as Hillsborough and his colleagues discovered—too late, it could be argued—they needed to develop new attitudes to keep pace with an ever-changing imperial reality. Their imaginations may have failed them but their failure was not the result of simple pigheadedness.

* * *

Sir,

I have his Majesty's Commands to transmit to you the inclosed copy of a letter from the Speaker of the House of Representatives of the Colony of Massachusets Bay, addressed by order of that House to the Speaker of the Assembly of each Colony upon the Continent of North America.

As his Majesty considers this Measure to be of a most dangerous & factious tendency calculated to inflame the minds of his good Subjects in the Colonies, to promote an unwarrantable combination and to excite and encourage an open opposition to and denial of the Authority of Parliament, & to subvert the true principles of the constitution; It is his Majesty's pleasure that you should immediately upon the Receipt hereof exert your utmost influence to defeat this flagatious attempt to disturb the Public Peace by prevailing upon the Assembly in your Province to take no notice of it, which will be treating it with the contempt it deserves.

The repeated proofs which have been given by the Assembly [space left blank for the name of each respective colony] of their Reverence and respect for the laws, and of their faithful Attachment to the Constitution, leave little Room in his Majesty's Breast to doubt of their showing a proper Resentment of this unjustifiable Attempt to revive those distractions which have operated so fatally to the prejudice of this Kingdom and the Colonies; and accordingly his Majesty has the fullest confidence in their affections. But if notwithstanding these expectations and your most earnest endeavours, there should appear in the Assembly in your Province a disposition to receive or any Countenance to this Seditious Paper, it will be your duty to prevent any proceeding upon it, by an immediate Prorogation of Dissolution.

I am &ca.
Hillsborough

A Governor's Lament[9]

As unpopular, even reviled, as Francis Bernard was in most Boston circles before he returned to England in 1769, few could have predicted such an outcome upon his arrival nine years before. Bernard had first gone to the colonies as governor of New Jersey, an appointment secured through family connections—a fairly typical way to advance one's career in Georgian England. His family had been on the fringe of the Berkshire squirearchy, with barely the means to send him to Westminster School and from there to Christ Church, Oxford. He enrolled at the Middle Temple to train as a barrister without taking an Oxford degree, but whatever plans that he had for improving his social station took years to bear fruit.

Failure to secure a lucrative position in England eventually drove him to seek his fortune in the colonies through a government appointment—a more common decision than is often appreciated. Bernard seemed always to be on the hunt for a better-paying, less demanding post, and his quest became urgent in 1765, by which time it was obvious that whatever power base he had in Massachusetts had eroded in the backwash of the Stamp Act crisis.

During his first few years as governor he tried to placate potential political opponents in Massachusetts as well as impress his superiors in London. The General Court bestowed Mount Desert Island on him as a gift, as much to head off a break as to solidify any sort of political partnership. But as historian William Pencak put it, in "his efforts to please everybody, he pleased nobody."[10] He had not supported Grenville's program, but then he was in no position to oppose it either and he was increasingly associated in dissident minds with London's bad policies. It did not help that he lacked political skill and too often alienated those he needed to please. There began the long process of *"demonizing" him, as his biographer put it,[11] and he is hardly remembered now, except as one of the legion of bureaucrats who helped precipitate an imperial crisis.*

Bernard fancied himself an imperial reformer and he had begun to consider various changes to improve Britain's colonial administration, to some extent along the lines of his friend, Thomas Pownall, before he arrived in Massachusetts. Although he did not make his reformist views public until a 1774 pamphlet,[12] he had made reform a topic of private conversation and correspondence for fully a decade before then. Distressed by the Stamp Act riots that rocked Boston and the larger problems that then loomed, he sighed, "the question will not be whether there shall be a Stamp Act or not; but whether America shall be Subject to the Legislature of Great Britain."[13]

Bernard felt that the colonists enjoyed too much autonomy. He was also convinced that poor direction from London explained the breakdown in social control. Hence the tone of the letter printed below. For some historians this letter is significant, not just for what it says about his impotence as governor, but for its impact on Hillsborough, who put great stock in what Bernard relayed to him by mail. Even if this letter did not alone cause Hillsborough to decide that troops needed to be sent to Boston, it reinforced impressions already formed. The portrait Bernard paints is of a town—and potentially a province—in danger of devolving into anarchy, the people being duped by demagogues and the king's representatives being prevented through inti-midation from performing their rightful duties. What he did not include was an admission that he had kept his distance from the customs commissioners as a function of political survival, a reminder to us that imperial authorities themselves did not always work in close partnership with one another.

Bernard had wanted troops sent to Boston in the aftermath of riots there in August 1765, but his Council would not support him. Their disagreement widened a political breach that had already opened, so by the time Bernard again sought troops in late 1767 and early 1768, he had little support left. That he went about getting them anyway—making it seem that they were necessary, but without directly requesting their dispatch—added to his opponents' belief that he was devious and disingenuous. Personal foibles aside, Bernard's behavior was also the result of an ill-defined imperial structure. The reforms he had in mind would not have solved the problem. That he and others discussed them is proof that there were men on both sides of the Atlantic who understood that, in some parts of the world, the imperial family had become dysfunctional.

* * *

My Lord[14]   Boston March 19, 1768

I expected that the Appointment of the Commissioners of the Customs in Office would have made it unnecessary for me to have troubled your Lordship with any Representations upon the Subject of the Customs. But I see such an Opposition to the Commissioners and their Officers and such a Defiance of the Authority by which they are appointed continually growing, that I can no longer excuse my informing your Lordship of the Detail of Facts from whence the most dangerous Consequences are to be expected.

It is some time since there have been frequent Reports of Insurrections intended, in which it has been said the Houses of one or more of the Commissioners and their Officers would be pulled down: two were more particularly fixed upon. Upon one of these Nights a Number of Lads, about 100, paraded the Town with a Drum and Horns, passed by the council Chamber whilst I was sitting there in the Council, assembled before Mr Paxton's (a commissioner) House & huzzaed; and to the Number of at least 60 lusty Fellows (as I am assured) invested Mr Burch's (another Commissioner) House for sometime; so that his Lady and Children were obliged to go out of the back Door to avoid the Danger which threatned: This Kind of Disturbance was kept up all the Evening; and after all was treated as the Diversion of a few Boys, a Matter of no Consequence. This was all I think on March 4.

After this it was reported that the Insurrection was postponed till Mar. 18 which was the Anniversary of the Repeal of the Stamp Act; upon which Days Effigies were to be exhibited, and two Persons, Mr Paxton a commissioner and Mr Williams one of the Inspectors were mentioned as devoted to the Resentment of the Mob. I took all the Pains I could to discover the Truth of this Report; but could get no other Answer but Assurance that no such thing would be done or suffered. On the very Day before I spoke with the most knowing Men I could procure; who were very positive that no Effigies would be hung up. And yet late that Evening I had certain Advice the Effigys were prepared: but it was too late to do any thing, & my Information was of that Nature that I could not make use of it in public.

Early the next Morning, the Shireff came to me to inform me that the Effigys of Mr Paxton and Mr Williams were hanging upon Liberty Tree. I had the Day before appointed a Council to meet, & I now sent round to get them together as soon as possible it might be. Before I went to Council I learnt that the Effigys had been taken down by some of the neighbours without any Opposition. At Council I set it forth in Strong Terms the notoriousness of this Insult, the Danger of it being followed by actual Violence and the Necessity there was of providing for the Defence of the Town. But all I could say made no Impression upon the Council: they persevered in treating the Affair as of no Consequence and assuring me that there was no

Danger of any Commotion. After they had given their Opinion as in the inclosed Copy of the Minutes, I received a Letter from the Commissioners setting forth the Insults they had received, the Danger they apprehended, and desiring the Protection of the Government. I communicated this to the Council and proposed that they should reconsider their Business, but finding them not inclined to depart from their Opinion as before given, I adjourned the Reconsideration till the Afternoon. In the afternoon the Question being again put to them, They adhered to their former Opinion.

I should have mentioned before that under all the Assurances I had that there would be no Disturbances, it was never understood, that the Day, the Anniversary of the Repeal of the Stamp Act, should not be celebrated. Accordingly at Break of Day there were beating of Drums and firing of Guns heard, and the whole Town was adorned with Ships Colours: and to add to the Celebration, the Feast of St. Patrick being the Day before was postponed to this Day. However great Pains were taken by the Select Men of the Town & some other Gentlemen that the Festivity should not produce a Riot in the Evening, and so far it succeeded that it produced Terror only and not actual Mischief. There was a Number of Gentlemen dined at the Tavern near the Townhouse, upon the Occasion of the Day. These broke up in good Time, after which many of the same and other Gentlemen kept together at the Coffee House (one of the Taverns) all the Evening. These prevented the lighting a Bonfire in that Street, which was several Times attempted, and would probably have been a Prelude to Action. But the assembling a great Number of People together of all Kinds, Sexes and Ages, many of which shewed a great Disposition to the utmost Disorder, could not be prevented. There were many hundred of them paraded the Streets with Yells and outcries which were quite terrible. I had in my House Mr Burch (one of the Commissioners) and his Lady & Children, who had the Day before moved to our House for Safety. I had also with me the Lieut Governor & the Sheriff of the County. But I had taken no Steps to fortify my House, not being willing to shew an Apprehension of Danger to myself. But at that Time there was so terrible a Yell from the Mob going by, that it was apprehended that they were breaking in: but it was not so. However it caused the same Terror as if it had been so; and the Lady, a stranger to this Country who chose our House for Asylum, has not recovered it as yet.

They went on and invested Mr Williams' House but he showed himself at a Window & told them that he was provided for their Reception, & they went off, and either did not intend or dared not to attack his House. They also at two different Times about Midnight made outcrys about Mr Paxtons House out of mere Wantonness to terrify his Family. The whole made it a very terrible Night to those who thought themselves subjects of the popular Fury: and yet if I should complain of it, I should be told that it was nothing but the common Effect of festivity and rejoicing; and there was no Harm intended.

Your Lordship will perhaps ask what I have been doing all this while, that this Spirit of Disorder is got to such a Pitch: I answer, every Thing in my Power to prevent it. Since first these Tumults were apprehended, the Commissioners, with whom (I mean 4 of the 5[15]) I am upon the most intimate Terms, have often asked me what Support to their Office or Protections for themselves I can afford: I answer none in the World. For tho' I am allowed to proceed in the ordinary Business of the Government without Interruption, in the Business of a popular Opposition to the Laws of Great Britain founded upon Pretensions of Rights & Privileges, I have not the Shadow of Authority or Power. I am just now in the Situation I was in above 2 Years ago, sure to be made obnoxious to the Madness of the People by the Testimony I am obliged to bear against it and yet left exposed to their Resentment without any possible Resort for Protection. I am then asked why I don't apply for Troops as well as to Support the Kings Government as to protect the Persons of his Officers. I answer because I don't think it proper or prudent to make such Application upon my own Opinion. All the Kings Governors are directed to take the Advice of the Council in military movements; And in this Government, where the Governor is in a more peculiar Manner obliged to have the Advice of the Council for almost every Thing he does, it would be dangerous to act in such an Important Business without such Advice. And is in Vain to put such a Question to the Council, for considering the Influence they are under from their being Creatures of the people & the personal Danger they would be subject to in assisting in the restraining them, it is not probable that the utmost Extremity of Mischief & Danger would induce them to advise such Measures. I have once before tried the Experiment when the Danger was more urgent and immediate than it is now; and the Success then fully convinced me that it is to no Purpose ever again to Repeat the Question. His Majesty's Ministers have within these 3 Years been fully acquainted with the defenceless State of this Government, and therefore I trust that I shall be excused leaving it to The Administration to determine upon Measures which they are much more able to judge of & be answerable for than I can be. I shall have trouble and Danger enough when such Orders arrive, tho' I keep ever so clear of advising or promoting them. These my Lord are the Answers I have given to the Commissioners in the Course of Conversation; which I have thought proper to recapitulate in this Place for my own Vindication, if it should be needful.

I should have mentioned before, but for not interrupting the Narrative, that in the Debate at the Council, One Gentleman said that there were associations formed for preserving the Peace of the Town. I said that I had not been made acquainted with them: that if there were any such, they ought to have been formed with my privity and confirmed by my Authority. That if a general Association for supporting the Authority of the Government & preserving the peace of the Town could be brought about, it would be of great Service, & I should be glad to see it set about immediately. Upon this A Councellor got up with Vehemence & said that such a Subscription was illegal and unconstitutional, & he should protest against it as tending to bring an Opprobrium upon the Town. I said that at a Time when a Subscription was handed about the Town in direct Opposition to the Parliament and People of Great Britain and was every Day enforced by Menaces and other unfair Methods, it was very extraordinary at that Board to hear a Subscription for the Support of Government & preservation of the Peace called illegal. That I should not endeavour to press a Measure which would derive its chief Efficacy from being voluntary; but I feared they would see the Expediency of such a Measure when it was too late. From this and the generality of the Assurances that no Mischief would be done, I am to understand that the Preservation of the Peace of this Town is to depend upon those who have the Command of the Mob & can restrain them (& of course let them loose) when they please; and Civil Authority is not to interpose in this Business. And indeed I have with Attention observed, that all the Assurances that no Mischief was intended at present are founded upon the Impropriety of using Violence at a Time when they were applying to the Government and Parliament of Great Britain for redress. But it is inferred & sometimes expressly declared that when they have Advice that the Redress which they expect is denied, they will immediately proceed to do themselves Justice: and it is now become common Talk that they will not submit to Duties imposed by Parliament, not only by the late Acts but all others which raise a Revenue. This is publick Talk: As for the sanguine Expectations which the Faction from whose Cabinet all these Troubles have arose, has formed for controlling and triumphing over Great Britain, I dare not repeat what I have heard till their Purposes become more apparent.

In this Narrative I have taken no Notice of the Town Meetings, meetings of Merchants, Subscriptions for not importing English goods, proposals for Manufactures &c which have been carrying on before and during the whole forementioned Time. I intend to make separate Letter upon these Subjects, which possibly may accompany this, as I am not at present apprised of a Conveyance safe enough to trust this by.

I am &c

A BOSTONIAN'S PROTEST[16]

"Vindex"—Latin for "Champion" or "Avenger"—wrote pieces for the Boston Gazette, *protesting the soldiers' arrival in 1768 and their actions culminating in the massacre two years later. Tradition as well as some evidence have assigned the pieces to Samuel Adams. The first in the series is transcribed below. Writing essays pseudonymously was no mere literary affectation. Authors in Britain as well as the colonies who penned pieces critical of government policy used assumed names as a protection against prosecution for seditious libel. If convicted they faced fines and possible jail time, but they were fortunate that seditious libel was no longer considered a capital offense.*

Adams has long been considered the American Revolutionary par excellence, a personification of the American spirit of independence. In reality he was, like most of his colleagues who defended colonial rights, a reluctant revolutionary. He predicted an outbreak of hostilities as early as 1768 with the sending of troops to Boston but he did not openly advocate American independence as the only solution to the imperial problem until 1775, well after the fighting at Lexington and Concord. When he first talked of an American union, it was within the context of a better, more balanced imperial community, where the colonies would enjoy greater political autonomy—even though, like many of his contemporaries, he looked to a time when mother country and colonies would part. So, contrary to stereotype, Adams worked as hard to stave off the inevitable as he did to hasten it.[17]

Adams came from a relatively prosperous background. He earned two Harvard degrees and was no mobocrat, no demagogue, though political opponents accused him of being both. He did not instigate the massacre, he did not singlehandedly orchestrate the Tea Party, he did not manipulate people

Figure 10 John Singleton Copley's justly famous portrait of Samuel Adams, one of Copley's finest, completed in 1772 or thereabout. Boston-born and self-taught, Copley had impressed London artists with his skill in samples they had seen of his work long before he crossed the Atlantic. Diffident about moving to London to hone his skills and make his fortune, he was equally diffident in his politics. That he, a "tory" painter, should have done such a stirring representation of Adams, a leading Boston "whig," is not that surprising. He had already painted flattering portraits of his Beacon Hill neighbor John Hancock and Judge Richard Dana. Hancock commissioned the Adams portrait, which showed Adams as he appeared before Thomas Hutchinson the morning after the massacre to demand that the troops be withdrawn from the town. Photograph © 2010 Museum of Fine Arts, Boston.

and events to produce the "shot heard round the world." He lived frugally, by choice and necessity, after he had whittled away the modest fortune left by his father, and he preferred debate to confrontation. Perhaps his most important writing came with the instructions that he helped draft for Boston's representatives to the Massachusetts House when they prepared for new legislative sessions. He was in his forties before he rose to any notable prominence in the town meeting, but when he teamed with men like Thomas Cushing and Joseph Warren he proved that the pen could be as mighty as the sword. And when the sword was unsheathed without cause he could be adamant in his demands for justice, as Hutchinson learned the day after the massacre, when Adams and other town leaders insisted that the troops be removed from Boston altogether.

Adams's "Vindex" essays in 1768 show his sense of history and his efforts to shape and mobilize an informed opinion, not just provoke mindless resentment, as the basis for political action. Although many of his readers did not have his grounding in the classics, the allusions that he made to seventeenth-century English history may have resonated with many Bostonians who gathered at coffee houses to discuss the issues of the day, even those who had the pieces read to them because they could not read themselves. As "Vindex," Adams reflected the tendency of protesting colonial Americans to emphasize their Englishness, with rights rooted in a shared tradition. He knew that calls for protest could lead to resistance, but—in this early stage, at least—he did not anticipate how protest could trigger a revolt that would eventually lead to revolution.

* * *

I can very easily believe that the officers of the regiments posted in this town, have been inform'd by our *good friends*, that the inhabitants are such a rude unpolish'd kind of folks, as that they are in danger, at least of being affronted during their residence here; and therefore their placing centinels at their respective dwellings seems to be a natural precaution, and under that apprehension may be a necessary step to guard their persons from injury. Or if it be only a piece of respect or homage every where shown to the superior officers of the army, it is a matter which concerns no other persons that I know of, I am sure it is no concern of mine: In this view it is a military custom, in no way interfering with, obstructing or infringing the common rights of the community.—But when these gentlemens attendants take upon them to call upon every one, who passes by, to know *Who comes there* as the phrase is, I take it to be in the highest degree impertinent, unless they can shew a legal authority for so doing.—There is something in it, which looks as if the town was altogether under the government &

controul of the military power: And as long as the inhabitants are fully perswaded that this is not the case at present, and moreover hope and believe that it never will be, it has a natural tendency to irritate the minds of all those who have a just sense of honour, and think they have the privilege of walking the streets without being controul'd.

I have heard that some of these attendants, when question'd by gentlemen who have tho't themselves affronted in this manner, have pleaded orders from their officer: This I am not apt to believe; but should I be under a mistake, the question still occurs, What right have their officers to give them such orders in this town? It is a question which appears to me to be of *present* importance, and ought to be decided: For if the gentlemen of the army should differ in their sentiments respecting this matter, from the inhabitants and freemen of the town, the posting a *standing army* among us, especially if it is *without* and *against our consent*, instead of preventing tumults, which it is said was the profess'd design of the troops being *sent for*, and ordered here, it is to be feared, will have a tendency quite the reverse—I am informed that not less than nine gentlemen of character, some of them of the first families in this province, were stop'd and put under guard the other evening, for refusing to submit to this *military novelty*: And still more alarming, that even one of his Majesty's Council was stop'd, in his chariot in the day time, when going out of town, under a flimsy pretence that possibly he might have conceal'd a deserter in his chariot and was treated with insolence. The hon. Gentleman I dare say felt his resentment kindle; and every one who hears of so high handed an insult must feel anger glowing in his breast.—I forbear to mention the constant practice of challenging, as it is called, the country people when passing and repassing, upon their lawful business, thro' the gates of the city, where a guard house is erected, upon land belonging to the publick, and it is commonly said, without the leave, or even asking the leave of the publick!

Are we a garrison'd town or are we not? If we are, let us know by whose authority and by whose *influence* we are made so: If not, and I take it for granted we are not, let us then assert & maintain the honor—the dignity of free citizens and place the military, where all other men are, and where they always ought & always *will* be plac'd in every free country, *at the foot of the common law of the land.*—To submit to the civil magistrate in the *legal* exercise of power is for ever the part of a good subject: and to *answer* the watchmen of the town in the night, may be the part of a good citizen, as well as to afford them all necessary countenance and support: But, to be called to account by a common soldier, or any soldiers, is a badge of slavery which none but a *slave* will wear.

It was an article of complaint in the memorable petition of right in the reign of King Charles the first, that certain persons exercis'd a "power to proceed *within the land* according to the justice of *martial law*," even against soldiers, "by such *summary* course and order as it is agreeable to *martial* law, and as is used in armies *in the time of war.*" And by the bill of rights it is declared that "the raising and keeping a *standing army* within the kingdom in a time of peace is *against law.*" It seems that in the reign of K. Charles the first, it was look'd upon to be "against the form of the great charter and law of the land" that any man *within the land*, tho' a *soldier* or *mariner*, should be judg'd and executed by martial law; "lest by color thereof, any of his Majesty's subjects be destroy'd or put to death contrary to the law or franchise of the land": and therefore the lords and commons, the guardians of the people, *demanded* of the King as *their right*, and according to the laws and statutes of the realm, the revoking and annulling for such purpose, and even that Prince revok'd and annull'd them.

Is there any one who dares to say that Americans have not the rights of subjects? Is Boston disfranchised? When, and for what crime was it done? If not, Is it not enough for us to have seen *soldiers* and *mariners* forejudg'd of life and executed *within the body of the county by martial law?* Are *citizens* to be called upon, threatnd, ill used at the will of the soldiery, and put under arrest, by the pretext of the law military, in breach of the fundamental right of subjects, and contrary to the law and franchise of the land? And are the inhabitants of this town still to be affronted in the night as well as the day by soldiers arm'd with muskets and fix'd bayonets? Are these the blessings of government? Is this the method to reconcile the people to the temper of the *present* administration of government in this province? Will the spirits of people, as yet unsubdued by tyranny, unaw'd by the menaces of arbitrary power, submit to be *govern'd* by military force? No, let us rouze our attention to the common law, which is our birthright—our great security against all kinds of insult & oppression—The law, which when rightly used, is the *curb* and the *terror* of the haughtiest tyrant—Let our magistrates execute the good and whole some laws of the land with reso- lution and an intrepid firmness—aided by the posse comitatus, the body of the country, which is their only natural and legal strength. They will see their authority rever'd: The boldest transgressors will then tremble before them, and the *orderly* and *peaceable* inhabitants will be restored to the rights, privileges and immunities of *free subjects*.

VINDEX

PARLIAMENT'S FRUSTRATIONS WITH MASSACHUSETTS[18]

Parliamentary inconsistency and instability have often been pointed to as causes of the subsequent revolution. To say that Parliament was inconsistent because it changed policies—passing the Stamp Act, then repealing it; implementing the Townshend duties, then dropping all of them except the duty on tea—is a half truth. That inconsistency masked a deeper consistency in Parliament's desire somehow to remind Americans of their proper place in the empire and have them bear a greater share of the burden in financing it. But then defining that "proper" place and determining a "fair" share proved impossibly difficult, and not just because of colonial resistance to changed policies in London.

In one sense, Parliament could be considered unified in that virtually all of its members, in the Lords as well as the Commons, accepted the Glorious Revolution as a defining moment in settling the relationship with the crown. All were "whigs" rather than "tories," despite lingering use of the old language, because they rejected the pretensions of royal prerogative that had been associated with Stuart kings. Even so, the lack of clear whig and tory allegiances, or older "court" and "country" divisions, did not mean that Parliament was a placid place. There were groupings around powerful families in both the Lords and the Commons; there were still those who allied themselves with Whitehall rather than with colleagues at Westminster. In the Commons, representatives for county constituencies were often considered more independent than those who sat for boroughs, where only a dozen or so electors might hold the franchise.

A handful of men in Parliament—most notably, perhaps, William Pitt—did not think that Parliament, though supreme over the empire, had the constitutional authority to tax the colonists.[19] Taxation, as a "gift of the people," required representation, and the Americans were not—and could not effectively be—represented at Westminster, Pitt contended. Leading colonial protesters argued likewise; thus they considered Pitt their friend. Still, it needs to be remembered that the Townshend Program came into being during Pitt's ministry. Pitt protested the dispatch of troops to Boston in 1768; he would do so again in 1774, in the aftermath of the Tea Party. But he did not rule out the use of coercive policies if Americans strayed too far out of line. That their behavior did not warrant it, in his eyes, in those moments, does not mean it never could.

The vast majority in Parliament operated on the belief that parliamentary supremacy meant that there could be no limit to Parliament's authority over the colonies: the authority to legislate ipso facto included the authority to tax. Where they differed was how to go about doing it. The Rockingham ministry had pushed for repeal of the Stamp Act because it had been the wrong tax; Rockingham differed from Grenville and North on timing and tactics, not on the issue of overall authority. Edmund Burke, who was a member of Rockingham's camp, fell into the same category. True, he argued famously for reconciliation in both 1774 and 1775. And in May 1770, when Parliament received word of the massacre, he introduced a motion in the Commons sharply critical of British policy toward the colonies, criticism aimed especially at Hillsborough and Bernard, though he did not identify them by name.[20] His motion failed, as he had probably guessed it would; he had basically made it for the record.

By contrast, the resolutions printed below passed both houses of Parliament handily. They made it through the Commons in December 1768 and, with some slight revisions, through the Lords the following February. They took their final form on February 9. One condemned the Massachusetts House for its incorrect views as well as its unjustifiable actions. Another blamed the people of Boston for the dispatch of troops—their lawlessness had left London no choice. In what proved to be an especially galling recommendation, the closing resolution urged the king to revive an old statute that would make it possible for those accused of treason in the colonies to be tried in Britain. He did not; no treason prosecutions would ever follow. That they had been suggested at all, and that the colonists reacted so viscerally, is a reminder, again, that political adversaries on both sides of the Atlantic responded to wrongs anticipated as often as to wrongs actually experienced.

* * *

Resolved,

By the Lords Spiritual and Temporal, and Commons, in Parliament assembled, That the Votes, Resolutions, and Proceedings of the House of Representatives of *Massachuset's Bay*, in the Months of *January* and *February*, One thousand Seven hundred and Sixty-eight, respecting several late Acts of Parliament, so far as the said Votes, Resolutions, and Proceedings, do import a Denial of, or do draw into Question, the Power and Authority of His Majesty, by and with the Advice and Consent of the Lords Spiritual and Temporal, and Commons, in Parliament assembled, to make Laws and Statutes of sufficient Force and Validity to bind the Colonies and People of *America*, Subjects to the Crown of *Great Britain*, in all Cases whatsoever, are illegal, unconstitutional, and derogatory of the Rights of the Crown and Parliament of *Great Britain*.

That the Resolution of the said House of Representatives of the Province of *Massachuset's Bay*, to write Letters to the several Houses of Representatives of the *British* Colonies, on the Continent, desiring them to join the said House of Representatives of the Province of *Massachuset's Bay*, in Petitions which do deny, or draw into Question, the Right of Parliament to impose Duties and Taxes, are stated to be Infringements of the Rights of His Majesty's Subjects of the said Province; are Proceedings of a most unwarrantable and dangerous Nature, calculated to inflame the Minds of His Majesty's Subjects in the other Colonies, tending to create unlawful Combinations, repugnant to the Laws of *Great Britain*, and subversive of the Constitution.

That it appears, that the Town of *Boston*, in the Province of *Massachuset's Bay*, has for some Time in the past been in a State of great Disorder and Confusion, and that the Peace of the said Town has at several Times been disturbed by Riots and Tumults of a dangerous Nature, in which the Officers of His majesty's Revenue there have been obstructed, by Acts of Violence, in the Execution of the Laws, and their Lives endangered.

That it appears, that neither the Council of the said province of *Massachuset's Bay*, nor the ordinary Civil Magistrates, did exert their Authority, for suppressing the said Riots and Tumults.

That in these Circumstances of the Province of the *Massachuset's Bay*, and of the Town of *Boston*, the Preservation of the Public Peace, and the due Execution of the Laws has become impracticable without the Aid of a Military Force to support and protect the Civil Magistrate and the Officers of His Majesty's Revenue.

That the Declarations, Resolutions, and Proceedings in the Town Meeting at *Boston*, on the 14th of *June*, and 12th *September*, were illegal and unconstitutional, and calculated to excite Sedition and Insurrections in His Majesty's Province of *Massachuset's Bay*.

That the Appointment at the Town Meeting, on the 12th *September*, of a Convention to be held in the Town of *Boston*, on the 22nd of that Month, to consist of Deputies from the several Towns and Districts in the Province of the *Massachuset's Bay*, and writing a Letter by the Select Men of the Town of *Boston*, to each of the said Towns and Districts, for the Election of such Deputies, were Proceedings subversive of His Majesty's Government, and evidently manifesting a Design in the Inhabitants of the said Town of *Boston*, to set up a new and unconstitutional Authority, independent of the Crown of *Great Britain*.

That the Elections by several Towns and Districts in the Province of *Massachuset's Bay* of Deputies to sit in the said Convention, and the Meeting of such Convention in consequence thereof, were daring Insults offered to His Majesty's Authority, and audacious Usurpations of the Powers of Government.

We beg leave to express to Your Majesty our sincere Satisfaction, in the Measures which Your Majesty has pursued for supporting the Constitution, and for inducing a due Obedience to the Authority of the Legislature; and to give Your Majesty the strongest Assurances, that we will effectually stand by and support Your Majesty, in such further Measures as may be found necessary to maintain the Civil Magistrates in a due Execution of the Laws within Your Majesty's Province of *Massachuset's Bay*: and as we conceive that nothing can be more immediately necessary, either for the Maintenance of Your Majesty's Subjects therein, from being further deluded by the Arts of wicked and designing Men, than to proceed, in the most speedy and effectual Manner, for bringing to condign Punishment the chief Authors and Instigators of the late Disorders, we most humbly beseech Your Majesty, that You will be graciously pleased to direct Your Majesty's Governor of *Massachuset's Bay* to take the most effectual Methods for procuring the fullest Information that can be obtained, touching all treasons, or Misprisions of Treason committed with his Government, since the Thirtieth Day of *December* One thousand Seven hundred and Sixty-seven, and to transmit the same, together with the Names of the Persons who were most active in the Commission of such Offences, to One of Your Majesty's Principal Secretaries of State, in order that Your Majesty may issue a Special Commission, for inquiring of, hearing, and determining the said Offences within this Realm, pursuant to the Provisions of the Statute, of the Thirty-fifth Year of the Reign of King *Henry* the Eight, in case Your Majesty shall, upon receiving the said Information, see sufficient Ground for such a Proceeding.

UNINTIMIDATED MASSACHUSETTS LEGISLATORS[21]

Parliament's resolutions prompted the response transcribed here. The battle of the resolutions underscores how political disputes only deepened differences in constitutional perspective. Superficially, the inevitable battles that pitted governors against legislators revolved around the control of finances—the governor's salary, other uses of public monies, the executive prerogative—but beyond such matters lay differences over ultimate sovereignty. If the people were in some sense sovereign, if government existed first and foremost to serve them, then how could the executive—a governor or a king—be superior to an elected representative? As the 1760s gave way to the 1770s, colonial politicians found it more difficult to avoid asking such questions, as provincial and imperial controversies increasingly overlapped.

The Massachusetts General Court had begun as the governing body for the Massachusetts Bay Colony, when Charles I granted the founding company its charter in 1629. Company shareholders, called "freemen," were all members of the General Court; they appointed a governor and assistants to serve as the chief executive officer and his advisors. The colony quickly swallowed the corporation, which fell by the wayside. Within less than a generation governmental forms had been adapted to local circumstances and remained relatively unchanged until Massachusetts lost its charter and was subsumed within the Dominion of New England, London's one grand attempt at imperial restructuring. With the Dominion's fall, Massachusetts received a new charter and the colony would be governed under it for over eighty years, until London all but set the charter aside in one of the bitterly resented Coercive Acts of 1774.[22] Alterations made in the original charter by the 1691 version—such as making the governor a royal appointee instead of being elected by the freemen of the colony—had irritated many in an earlier generation; still, those complaints paled in comparison with the uproar caused in 1774. By that point, some were as attached to the 1691 charter as others two generations before had been to the 1629 original.

The political point to all of this, which too few in London ever appreciated, was that the "people" of Massachusetts were both proud of and insecure about their provincial government. Change, as they had embraced it, had given them a sense of accomplishment and even, oddly enough, permanence; change imposed by London had done just the opposite. With nearly a century and a half of political experience behind them, many Bay Colonists had come to see the House as the primary protector of their rights. The men who sat there did not always distinguish between themselves as representatives of the people and the people at large—those with the franchise, and those without. In that they were very much like their counterparts in other colonial assemblies. Consequently, disputes over the range of and limits to the authority of the Massachusetts House—as with the lower houses of the assembly in other colonies—raised fundamental questions about rights and privileges, and about liberty and authority, that no one on either side of the Atlantic could answer satisfactorily. As the resolutions printed below demonstrate, many Massachusetts legislators linked the quartering of troops to the issue of parliamentary taxation, which showed that repeal of the Stamp Act had not resolved much at all. Moreover, the language and form of protest used in the resolutions anticipated what would be drafted into the Declaration of Independence seven years later for more avowedly revolutionary purposes.

* * *

THE General Assembly of this his Majesty's Colony of the *Massachusetts-Bay*. Convened by his Majesty's Authority, and by Virtue of his Writ issued by his Excellency the Governor, under the great Seal of the Province; and this House, thinking it their Duty at all Times to testify their Loyalty to his Majesty, as well as their inviolable Regard to their own and their Constituents Rights, Liberties and Privileges, do pass the following Resolutions to be entered on their Journal.

Resolved, That this House do, and ever will bear the firmest Allegiance to our Rightful Sovereign King GEORGE the Third; and are ever ready with their Lives and Fortunes to defend his Majesty's Person, Family, Crown and Dignity.

Resolved, as the Opinion of this House, "That the sole Right of imposing Taxes on the Inhabitants of this his Majesty's Colony of the Massachusetts-Bay, is now, and ever hath been legally and constitutionally vested in the House of Representatives, lawfully convened according to the antient and established practice, with the Consent of the Council, and of his Majesty, the King of Great-Britain, or his Governor for the Time being.

Resolved, as the Opinion of this House, That it is the indubitable Right of the Subject in general, and consequently of the colonists, jointly or severally to petition the King for Redress of Grievances; and that it is lawful, whenever they think it expedient to confer with each other, in Order to procure a joint Concurrence, in dutiful Address for Relief from common Burthens.

Resolved, That Governor Bernard by a wanton and precipitate Dissolution of the last Year's Assembly, and refusing to call another, tho' repeatedly requested by the People, acted against the Spirit of a free Constitution; and if such Procedure be lawful, it may be in his Power whenever he pleases to render himself absolute.

Resolved, That a general discontent, on Account of the Revenue Acts, an Expectation of the sudden Arrival of a Military Power to enforce the Execution of those Acts, an Apprehension of the Troops being quartered upon the Inhabitants, when our Petitions were not permitted to reach the Royal Ear, the General Court at such a Juncture dissolved, the Governor refusing to call a new one, and the people reduced almost to a State of Despair, rendered it highly expedient and necessary for the People to convene by their Committees, associate, consult and advise the best Means to promote Peace and good Order; to present their united Complaints to the Throne, and jointly to pray for the Royal Interposition in Favour of their violated Rights. Nor can this Procedure possibly be illegal, as they expressly disclaimed all Governmental Acts.

Resolved, That Governor Bernard in the Letters before mentioned, by falsely representing that it was become "necessary the King should have the Council Chamber in his own Hands, and should be enabled by Parliament, to supercede by Order in his Privy Council Commissions granted in the name and under his Seal throughout the Colonies," has discovered his Enmity to the true Spirit of the British Constitution, to the Liberties of the Colonies; and has struck at the Root of some of the most invaluable Constitutional and Charter Rights of this Province: The Perfidy of which, at the very Time he profess'd himself a warm Friend to the Charter is altogether unparalleled by any in his Station, and ought never to be forgotten.

Resolved, That the Establishment of a Standing Army, in this Colony in a Time of Peace, without the Consent of the General Assembly of the same, is an Invasion of the natural Rights of the People, as well as of those which they claim as freeborn Englishmen, confirmed by Magna Charta, the Bill of Rights as settled at the Revolution, and by the Charter of this Province.

Resolved, That a Standing Army is not known as a Part of the British Constitution in any of the King's Dominions; and every attempt to establish it has been esteemed a dangerous Innovation, manifestly tending to enslave the People.

Resolved, That the sending an armed Force into this Colony, under a Pretence of aiding and assisting the Civil Authority, is an Attempt to establish a Standing Army here without our Consent; is highly dangerous to this People;—is unprecedented, and unconstitutional.

Resolved, That whoever has represented to his Majesty's Ministers, that the People of this Colony in general, or the Town of Boston in particular, were in such a State of disobedience and Disorder, as to require a Fleet and Army to be sent here, to aid the Civil Magistrate, is an avowed Enemy to this Colony, and to the Nation in general; and has by such Misrepresentation endeavoured to destroy the Liberty of the Subject here, and that mutual Union and Harmony between Great-Britain and the Colonies, so necessary for the Welfare of both.

Resolved, as the Opinion of this House, That the Misrepresentations of the State of this Colony, transmitted by Governor Bernard, to his Majesty's Ministers, have been the Means of procuring the Military Force now quartered in the Town of Boston.

Resolved, That whoever *gave Order* for Quartering even common Soldiers and Camp Women in the Court-House in Boston, and in the Representatives Chamber, where some of the principal Archives of the Government had been usually deposited; making a Barrack of the same, placing a Main Guard with Cannon pointed near the said House, and Centinels at the Door, *designed* a high Insult, and a triumphant Indication that the Military Power was Master of the whole Legislative.

WHEREAS his Excellency General Gage in his Letter to Lord Hillsborough, dated October 31st, among other exceptionable Things expressed himself in the following Words; "From what has been said, your Lordship will conclude, That there is no Government in Boston; in Truth there is very little at present, and the Constitution of this Province leans so much to the Side of Democracy, That the Governor has not the Power to remedy the Disorders that happen in it."

Resolved, as the Opinion of this House, That his Excellency General Gage, in this and other Assertions, has rashly and impertinently intermedled in the Civil Affairs of this Province, which are altogether out of his Department; and of the internal Police of which, by his Letter, if not altogether his own, he has yet betrayed a degree of Ignorance equal to the Malice of the Author.

With Respect to the Nature of our Government, this House is of Opinion, that the Wisdom of that great Prince William the Third who gave the Charter, aided by an able Ministry, and Men thoro'ly versed in the English Constitution and Law; and the happy Effects derived from it to the Nation, as well as this Colony, should have placed it above the Reprehension of the

General, and led him to enquire, whether the Disorders complained of, have not arisen from an arbitrary Disposition of the Government than from too great a Spirit of Democracy in the Constitution. And this House cannot but express their deep Concern, that too many in Power at Home and Abroad, so clearly avow not only in private Conversation, but in their public Conduct, the most rancorous Enmity toward the *free Part* of the British Constitution, and are indefatigable in their Endeavours to render the Monarchy absolute, and the Administration arbitrary, in every Part of the British Empire.

Resolved, That this House after the most careful Inquiry, have not found an Instance of the Course of Justice being interrupted by Violence. Except by a Rescue committed by Samuel Fellows, an Officer in the Navy, and by the Appointment of the Commissioners an Officer also in the Customs; nor of a Magistrate's refusing to enquire into, or redress any Injury complained of: While it is notorious to all the World, that even such Acts of Parliament as by the whole Continent are deemed highly oppressive, have never been opposed with Violence, and the Duties imposed and rigorously enacted, have been punctually paid.

Resolved, That the frequent entries of *Nolle Prosequi*[23] by the Attorney and Advocate General, in Cases favorable to the Liberty of the Subject; and rigorous Prosecutions by Information and otherwise in those in Favour of Power, are daring Breaches of Trust, and insupportable Grievances on the People.

Resolved, as the Opinion of this House, That the late Extension of the Power of the Courts of Admiralty in America, is highly dangerous and alarming; especially as the Judges of the courts of Common Law, the alone Check upon their inordinate Power, do not hold their Places during good Behaviour: And those who have falsely represented to his Majesty's Ministers, that no Dependence could be had on Juries in America, and that there was a Necessity of extending the Power of the Courts of Admiralty there, so far, as to deprive the Subjects of the inestimable Privilege of a Trial by a Jury, and to render the said Courts of Admiralty uncontrouable by the ancient Common Law of the Land, are avowed Enemies to the Constitution; and manifestly intended to introduce and establish a System of insupportable Tyranny in America.

Resolved, as the Opinion of this House, That the constituting a Board of Commissioners of Customs in America, is an unnecessary Burthen upon the Trade of these Colonies, and that the unlimited Power the said Commissioners are invested with of making Appointments, and paying the Appointees what Sums they please, unavoidably tends so enormously to increase the Number of Placemen and Pensioners, as to become justly alarming, and formidable to the Liberties of the People.

Resolved, That it is the Opinion of this House, "That all Trials for Treason, Misprision of Treason, or for any Felony or Crime whatsoever, committed or done in this his Majesty's Colony, by any Person or Persons residing therein, ought of Right to be had and conducted in and before his Majesty's Courts held within the said Colony, according to the fixed and known Course of Proceedings; and that the seizing any Person or Persons residing in this Colony, suspected of any Crime whatsoever, committed therein, and sending such Person or Persons to Places beyond the Sea, to be tried, is highly derogatory of the Rights of British Subjects; as thereby the inestimable Privilege of being tried by a Jury from the Vicinage, as well as the Liberty of summoning and producing Witnesses on such Trial, will be taken away from the Party accused."

A BRITISH SOLDIER'S COMPLAINT[24]

British soldiers living in Boston fretted at being subject to local law, which they felt was used as a political bludgeon. Army lieutenant Alexander Ross related his sad experience with being on the wrong side of the law in the deposition transcribed below. Although he gave the deposition in August 1770, he referred to a series of events that began over a year earlier. The events that he described had taken on a significance in the aftermath of the massacre that they lacked before. Supporters of empire cast about to find instances of local law's perversion in the days and months leading up to the massacre, just as those on the other side of the political contest searched for proof of their allegations about the oppressive nature of imperial policies.

The initial episode in court that Ross described took place before Justice Edmund Quincy. Because of the incident that occurred there, Ross would later be examined by three Suffolk County justices of the peace, one of whom was Richard Dana. Not charged there, he would later be indicted and tried in the Superior Court. Convicted of committing "riot and rescue," he appealed, eventually had his appeal denied, and was ordered to pay a hefty £20 fine. Note Ross's prosecution for being involved in a "rescue"—that is, interfering with a legal procedure by helping someone about to be arrested escape. The more common "rescue," however, occurred when local residents interfered with customs officials going about their duties. Lawbreakers in either instance, whether soldiers refusing to comply with local authorities or local residents whisking away goods about to be confiscated, they would justify their actions by contending that the law obstructed justice.

One can sense that it was especially galling for Ross to have to appear before Richard Dana, who made no bones about his opposition to the presence of soldiers among civilians—even saying so from the bench, when ruling on cases only tangentially connected to that issue. Dana was nearly seventy at the time of Ross's day in court before him, in what amounted to a preliminary hearing. Cambridge native and Harvard graduate, Dana had been a justice of the peace in Boston for well over a decade and kept at his private legal practice over part of the period, too. Most famous for administering an oath to Andrew Oliver requiring Oliver to resign his commission as a stamp distributor in 1765, Dana had long been a leader in the town meeting and shared the political views of those most critical of imperial policy—as Alexander Ross learned, to his chagrin. A member of the Sons of Liberty, Dana detested Thomas Hutchinson and took depositions that ended up in A Short Narrative. *Shrill as Dana appeared to Ross, Dana and Edmund Trowbridge, whose politics were much more conservative and whose instructions to jurors in the soldiers' trial follows (Document 25), remained close friends. Dana was married to Trowbridge's sister.*

*   *   *

I Alexr. Ross, Lieut. in his Majesty's 14th Regiment of Foot, Being duly Sworn & Depose that in the Month of July 1769, I was desired by Capt. Fordyce of the same Regt. to use my endeavours, with Justice Quincey, being known to him, in order to Compound an affair of John Riley's, a Soldier in his Company, who had been brought before the said Justice for striking a Butcher.—

Accordingly the Day following I went at which time the said Riley was before the Justice. Upon entering his house I found the Justice makeing out a Mittimus[25] for Rileys Committment for the Non-payment of a fine, which with Fees &c. amounted to Thirteen Shillings and four pence Lawfull Money, he pleading at the same time his incapacity to pay such a Sum. After useing some endeavours, to the purport of my Comeing, but finding them of no Effect, and a Mob Collecting, seemingly very insulting and abusive, I immediately proposed going away, when Riley says he would follow me. On hearing which I told him in a very peremptory manner by no means to do so, but wait the Determination of the Justice.

However without regarding me he made towards the Door, on which he was instantly Seized by a Constable, and some others, but he Quickly disengaged himself from their hold, and made his Escape, notwithstanding my calling to him several times and as long as I could be heard for the Crowd not to do so. I afterwards went through the Mob that were Collected at the Door; and as there was likely to be some disturbance between them and several Soldiers I immediately order'd the Latter home, to their Barracks, which they Obey'd.

About a Week after I was greatly Surpriz'd to find my Name Mention'd, with Serjeant Phillips, Corporal Findley, Corpl. Dundass, Corpl. Thornley, Corpl. Arnold, John Lane, and Francis Jackson, Soldiers in the same Regt., in order to be Summon'd before a Bench of Justices for a Riot, and the Rescue of the said Jon. Riley; on hearing which I, together with the Men above-Mentioned, went before the Three Justices Denna [Dana], Hill and Ruddock, who had met on purpose for our Examination.

Every matter that could be Alledged against us was Attentively listened to, and even Exaggerated by the Justices. Mr. Denna in particular demanded of us in a threatening manner "what brought you here? Meaning to this Province, by whose Authority came you amongst us?" &c. And when Capt. Fordyce (who was present) attempted to speak for any of the Deffendants, he was Immediately Silenced by the Bench, nor suffered to say a Single word in favour of them. After all the Witnesses were heard (which were only those who could Advance any thing against us) The said Justice Denna made a Speech fill'd with much Invective, and Abuse, against the Military in General, and those before him in Particular. Towards the Close of which, he gave those present, and all the Troops in Boston this Precaution, to behave with Circumspection, nor Offer the least insult to any of the Inhabitants in Town, for that to his knowledge, many carry'd conceal'd weapons about them, and that they would one Day give the Troops a Crush, when they were not expecting it, they being but a handfull when compared with the Inhabitants. He was still going on in this same Manner when one of his Brother Justices, thinking, I suppose, he had rather said too much, gave him a Jog which prevented his going any farther.

Serjeant Phillips and I were then Acquitted no Evidence Appearing against us, the other Six above Mentioned, were Bound Over in the Sum of Forty pounds Lawfull Money Each, for their Appearance at the next Superiour Court, there to stand their Tryals. Gentlemen of Credit were Deny'd being admitted for their Bail, and much hesitation was used with those who at last were Accepted of, tho' of Character, and known Property.

I then thought myself secure from all further Trouble on Account of the above Affair, but at the Meeting of the next Superiour Court, which was held the September following, The Grand Jury found a Bill against me with Four of the Deffendants Guilty of a Riot and a Rescue. The four Men were each fin'd Seven Pounds Lawfull Money and Costs of Suit, and Bound over for some Months to their Good behaviour in the Sum of Five Pounds more. My Lawyer Pleaded an Arrest of Judgment, and was in hopes of bringing on a Fresh Tryal. The former was granted, but I was Bound over for my Appearance in one Hundred pounds Lawfull, at the next Superiour Court, or be Committed to Gaol. However I procured Bail, and when the

Judges met, (which was some time in March 1770) I was Sentenced a fine of Twenty Pounds Lawfull and Costs of Suit. No fresh Tryal being Obtain'd.

Suffolk Is. Castle William Alexdr. Ross

August 25th, 1770

Sworn before me

Ja[mes] Murray [justice of the peace]

DOCUMENT **8**

A MARTYR IS MADE[26]

We can only wonder what Christopher Seider would have thought of his posthumous fame. The Boston Gazette *account of his death on February 22, 1770 turned him into a martyr. He appears to have been the eleven- or twelve-year-old son of working-class German immigrants in Boston. He may have been among the fifty or sixty boys who had originally gathered outside Theophilus Lillie's house. They taunted Lillie, a merchant, with chants and placards for refusing to support a non-importation agreement prompted by the Townshend duties. Ebenezer Richardson impetuously—and dangerously—drew attention to himself by trying to disrupt the proceedings; the crowd of mostly boys followed him to his house. Some among them broke his windows with rocks. He fired his bird-shot-filled musket at the crowd. Seider was hit and died; at least one other boy was wounded at the same moment.*

Dragged out of his house by angry adults who had joined with the boys in the crowd, Richardson was lucky that he and George Wilmot, who had taken shelter with him, were not lynched. Seider's funeral became a public occasion, anticipating the even more dramatic display less than two weeks later with the massacre funeral. Richardson and Wilmot went to trial in April and pleaded self-defense. The judges—the same four who would preside in Preston's and the soldiers' trials—encouraged jurors to acquit them on the basis of a justifiable homicide. The jury returned with a guilty verdict for Richardson, showing a very different response in this case than the jurors would to Trowbridge's instructions in the soldiers' trial (see Document 25). Wilmot was found not guilty and walked away. Richardson, meanwhile, remained in jail for nearly two years. The judges never did pronounce sentence; Richardson received a royal pardon and fled town before any action could be taken against him. By

Figure 11 The Monument to the Fallen, in the Granary Burying Ground. It is located close to the wrought-iron fence facing the sidewalk that runs along Tremont Street. Seider is here Snider. A rougher stone just off to the right marks Samuel Adams's grave. Monuments to Paul Revere and John Hancock are elsewhere in the cemetery. The Old Granary is a featured stopping point along the Freedom Trail. Photo by the author.

going to the king (through Hillsborough) and not pressuring the judges to rule, Hutchinson made even better use of the passage of time than he did in the aftermath of the massacre.[27]

Seider's death and Richardson's drawn-out legal fate played a significant part in the political unrest that troubled Boston. As John Bell has noted, Seider and the other "saucy" boys, as John Adams would label them in the soldiers' trial, helped shape the course of events.[28] *In part they mimicked the actions of adults, singling out for harassment men who had already been ostracized by the adult community. And yet, just as it will not do to reduce crowds to mobs that did Samuel Adams's bidding, so it should be accepted that adults did not simply call forth youth to do their political dirty work. Moreover, some of the "saucy boys" were in fact more men than boys, apprentices in their late teens, streetwise and street tough, who may have been a match for soldiers and adult civilians in a brawl.*

* * *

On Thursday last in the Forenoon a barbarous Murder attended with *many* aggravating Circumstances, was committed on the Body of a young lad of about eleven Years of Age, Son to Mr. — Snider of this Town. A Number of Boys had been diverting themselves with the Exhibition of a Piece of Pageantry near the house of *Theophilus Lillie*, who perhaps at this Juncture of Affairs may with the most Propriety be describ'd by the Name of an IMPORTER. This Exhibition naturally occasion'd Numbers to assemble, and in a very little Time there was a great Concourse of persons, especially the *younger Sett.*—One *Ebenezer Richardson*, who has been many Years employ'd as an under Officer of the Customs, long known by the Name of an INFORMER, and consequently a Person of a most abandon'd Character, it seems, took Umbrage at the suppos'd Indignity offer'd to *the Importers*, and soon became a Party in the Affair—He first attempted to demolish the Pageantry; and failing in the Attempt he retired to his House which was but a few Rods from the Exhibition. Several Persons passing by the House, Richardson who seem'd to be determin'd to take the Occasion to make a Disturbance, without the least Provocation, gave them the most opprobrious Language, charging them with Perjury, &c. which rais'd a dispute between them—This, it is suppos'd, occasion'd the Boys to gather near Richardson's House; and he thinking he had *now* a good Colouring to perpetrate the Villainy, threatned to fire upon them, and swore by GOD that he would make the Place too hot for some of them before Night, and that he would make a Lane through them if they did not go away. Soon after a Number of Brickbats or Stones were thrown among the People from Richardson's House; but the Witnesses, who were sworn before the

Magistrates, declared that it did not appear to them, that till then any Sort of Attack was made by the People on the House. This however brought on a Skirmish, and Richardson discharg'd his Piece loaden with Swan Short at the Multitude, by which the unhappy young Person above-mentioned was mortally wounded, having since died of his Wounds—A Youth, Son to Capt. John Gore, was also wounded in one of his Hands and in both his Thighs, by which his Life was endanger'd; but he is likely soon to recover of his Wounds—during this tragical scene, one *George Wilmot*, who was a Seaman or an Officer on Board the Liberty Sloop lately in the Service of the Commissioners, was present in the House, and an Abettor to Richardson, and appears by the Evidence to have been very active in the Affair—As soon as they could be taken, for they made all possible Resistance, being armed with Musquets and Cutlasses, they were carried to Faneuil-Hall; and upon Examination before four of his Majesty's Justices of the Peace, a Cloud of Witnesses appearing before them, they were committed to the County Gaol under close Confinement, for a legal Trial before the Superiour Court of the Province to be held here next Month.

The worthy Mr. McDougal of New-York will be justly celebrated by Posterity as the first who has suffer'd *actual Imprisonment* for asserting the Cause of American Liberty. A very distinguish'd Patriot in this Town was *long before* made the Object of the Fury of the cursed Cabal; and by the good Providence of GOD escap'd an Assassination evidently intended in September last, tho' not without the Loss of Blood: And the barbarous Treatment of this Gentleman then met with, tho' not yet revenged, is not forgot—Others have suffer'd in their Reputation—Others in their Estates; having endur'd the fiery Trial of modern Courts of Admiralty, where they have been harras'd and distress'd for no other apparent Reason but their being steady & able Advocates for the Cause.—This innocent Lad is the first, whose LIFE has been a Victim to the Cruelty and Rage of *Oppressors*! Young as he was, he died in his Country's Cause, by the Hand of an execrable Villain, directed by others, who could not bear to see the Enemies of America made the *Ridicule of Boys*. The untimely Death of this amiable Youth will be a standing Monument to Futurity, that the Time has been when *Innocence itself was not safe!* The Blood of *young Allen* may be cover'd in Britain:[29] But a thorough Inquisition will be made in *America* for that of *young Snider*, which crieth for Vengeance, like the Blood of righteous *Abel*. And surely, if Justice has not been *driven from its Seat*, speedy Vengeance awaits his Murderers and their *Accomplices*, however secure *they* may think themselves *at present*; For who so sheddeth, or *procureth the shedding* of Man's Blood, BY MAN SHALL HIS BLOOD BE SHED.

DOCUMENT 9

A MOST SHOCKING SCENE[30]

Copied below is the most famous contemporaneous newspaper report of the massacre. It ran in the Boston Gazette *exactly a week later, covering one full page and part of another.[31] Reprints appeared in other colonial papers and even across the Atlantic. Business partners for over fifteen years, Benjamin Edes and John Gill, the men behind the paper, printed pamphlets as well, including* A Short Narrative; *they also sold books. For years their shop stood on Queen Street, situated on the opposite side of the town house from King Street. Edes and Gill held close ties with town leaders; their* Boston Gazette *account was easily the longest and most inflammatory of Boston's four weekly newspapers in reporting the events of March 5.*

By contrast, the Boston Chronicle *ran but a brief notice just three days after the affair and anticipated* A Fair Account *by referring to the "unfortunate affair" in a barebones summary. "We decline at present, giving a more particular account of the unhappy affair," commented the printer John Fleeming, "as we hear the trial of the unfortunate prisoners is to come next week."[32] But no trial followed for months and the* Chronicle *had almost nothing more to say on the matter—an unpleasant subject, best forgotten, the printer seemed to imply by his silence.*

Richard Draper's Massachusetts Gazette, *published that same day, devoted more space to the affair than did Fleeming. Although Draper's paper, like Fleeming's, had closer ties to Hutchinson than to town leaders—being even in some sense the administration paper—Draper was more critical of the soldiers than the civilians for their general conduct. He nevertheless stopped short of condemning anyone for what happened on King Street.*

Brothers Thomas and John Fleet, whose Boston Evening-Post *ran on Mondays, just like Edes and Gill's paper, offered a report very close to it, with portions being virtually identical. They were not as caustic as Edes and Gill's but they did not hide their anger. They too reported soldiers harassing civilians, Preston ordering his men to fire, and those men attempting to bayonet people who were simply trying to aid the wounded. Aiming their words at imperial authorities on both sides of the Atlantic, they asked "How the authors" of this near "subversion of BRITISH FAITH, BRITISH LIBERTY,* Justice, HUMANITY, *and* mutual Affection *of ALL TO ALL, can bear to read this tale, let others imagine!"*[33]

With time, the position taken by the Boston Gazette *would appear to have better reflected the prevailing view in the town and around the province than that of the* Chronicle *or the* Massachusetts Gazette. *Edes and Gill connected the stationing of troops with foolish, unconstitutional policies designed to raise revenue in the empire. Attempting a transatlantic connection, they also underscored that what happened in Boston was far more serious than what had transpired on St. George's Field in London—a warning "for both Countries."*[34] *It was a message that apparently resonated with many readers. Indeed, the* Chronicle *went out of business by the summer of 1770 and the* Massachusetts Gazette *survived only by altering its content and tone. The* Boston Gazette *and the* Evening-Post *both closed down in Boston in the aftermath of Lexington and Concord and the beginning of a siege: the latter to cease publishing altogether, the former to take up the patriot cause at a press in Watertown.*

That the Boston Gazette *and the* Evening-Post *could be said to have won the press war for hearts and minds between 1765 and 1775 is an important commentary on the larger political battle being waged in the town. But exactly in what sense remains an unanswered, even unanswerable, question. All four papers had struggled to shape public opinion. The degree to which they succeeded can only be inferred. Influence is what many intellectual historians would most like to establish and yet, except in rare instances, they cannot prove it. Nor can they say, with Boston's newspapers in the Revolutionary Era as a case in point, how much print culture shapes, or is shaped by, the reading public. What the papers printed mattered; exactly how it mattered is more difficult to determine.*

* * *

The Town of Boston affords a recent and melancholy Demonstration of the destructive Consequences of quartering Troops among Citizens in a Time of Peace, under a Pretence of supporting the laws and aiding Civil Authority; every considerate and unprejudic'd Person among us was deeply imprest with the Apprehension of these Consequences when it was known that a

Number of Regiments were ordered to this Town under a Pretext, but in reality to enforce oppressive Measures; to awe & controul the legislative as well as executive Power of the Province, and to quell a Spirit of Liberty, which however it may have been basely oppos'd and even ridicul'd by some would do Honor to any Age or Country. A few Persons among us had determin'd to use all their Influence to procure so destructive a Measure with a View to their securing the Profits of an American Revenue, and unhappily for both Britain and this Country, they found the Means to effect it.

It is to Governor Bernard, the Commissioners, their Confidents and Coadjutors, that we are indebted as the procuring Cause of a military Power in this Capital—The Boston Journal of Occurrences, as printed in Mr Holt's New York Gazette, from Time to Time, afforded many striking Instances of the Distresses brought upon the Inhabitants by this measure, and since those journals have been discontinued, our Troubles from that Quarter have been growing upon us: We have known a Party of Soldiers in the face of Day fire off a loaden Musket upon the Inhabitants, others have been pricked with Bayonets, and even our Magistrates assaulted and put in Danger of their Lives, when Offenders brought before them have been rescued; and why those and other bold and base Criminals have as yet escaped the Punishment due to their Crimes, may soon be a Matter of Enquiry by the representative Body of this People—It is natural to suppose that when the Inhabitants of this Town saw those Laws which had been enacted for their Security, and which they were ambitious of holding up to the Soldiery, eluded, they should more commonly resent for themselves—and accordingly it has happened; many have been their Squabbles between them and the Soldiery; but it seems their being often worsted by our Youth in those Recounters, has only served to irritate the former—What passed at Mr. Gray's Rope-walk, has already been given the Public, & may be said to have led the way to the late Catastrophe—That the Rope-walk Lads when attacked by superior Numbers should defend themselves with so much Spirit and Success in the Club-way, was too mortifying, and perhaps it may hereafter appear, that even some of the Officers were *unhappily* affected with the Circumstance: Divers Stories were propagated among the Soldiery, that serv'd to agitate their Spirits; particularly on the Sabbath, that one Chambers, a Sergeant, represented as a sober Man, has been missing the previous Day, and must have therefore been murdered by the Townsmen; an Officer of Distinction so far credited this Report, that he enter'd Mr. Gray's Rope-walk that Sabbath, and when required by that Gentleman, the Occasion of his so doing, the Officer reply'd, that it was to look if the Serjeant said to be murdered had not been there; this sober Serjeant was found on Monday unhurt, in a house of pleasure—The Evidence already collected shew, that many Threatnings had been thrown out by the Soldiery, but we do not pretend to say that there was any preconcerted Plan, when the Evidences are published, the World will judge—We may however venture to declare, that it appears too probable from their conduct, that some of the Soldiery aimed to draw and provoke the Townsmen into Squabble, and that they intended to make Use of other Weapons than Canes, Clubs or Bludgeons.

Our Readers will doubtless expect a circumstantial account of the tragical Affair on Monday Night last; but we hope they will excuse our being so particular as we should have been, had we not seen that the Town was intending an Enquiry & full Representation thereof.

On the Evening of Monday, being the 5th Current, several Soldiers of the 29th Regiment were seen parading the Streets with their drawn Cutlasses and Bayonets, abusing and wounding Numbers of the Inhabitants.

A few minutes after nine-o'clock, four youths, named Edward Archbald, William Merchant, Francis Archbald, and John Leech, jun. came down Cornhill together, and seperating at Doctor Loring's corner, the two former were passing the narrow alley leading to Murray's barrack, in which was a soldier brandishing a broad sword of an uncommon size against the walls, out of which he struck fire plentifully. A person of mean countenance armed with a large cudgel bore him company. Edward Archbald admonished Mr. Merchant to take care of the sword, on which the soldier turned round and struck Archbald on the arm, then pushed Merchant and pierced thro' his cloaths inside the arm close to the arm-pit and grazed the skin. Merchant then struck the soldier with a short stick he had, & the other Person ran to the barrack & bro't with him two soldiers, one armed with a pair of tongs[,] the other with a shovel: he with the tongs pursued Archbald back thro' the alley, collar'd and laid him over the head with the tongs. The noise bro't people together, and John Hicks, a young lad, coming up, knock'd the soldier down, but let him get up again; and more lads gathering, drove them back to the barrack, where the boys stood some-time as it were to keep them in. In less than a minute 10 or 12 of them came out with drawn cutlasses, clubs and bayonets, and set upon the unarmed boys and young folks, who stood them a little while, but finding the inequality of their equipment dispersed.—On hearing the noise, one Samuel Atwood, came up to see what was the matter, and entering the alley from dock square, heard the latter part of the combat, and when the boys had dispersed he met the 10 or 12 soldiers aforesaid rushing down the alley towards the square, and asked them if they intended to murder people? They answered, Yes, by G-d, root and branch! With that one of them struck Mr. Atwood with a club, which was repeated by another, and being unarmed he turned to go off, and received a wound on the left shoulder which reached the bone and gave him much pain. Retreating a few steps, Mr. Atwood met two officers and said, Gentlemen, what is the matter? They answered, you'll see by and by. Immediately after, those heroes appeared in the square, asking where were the boogers? Where were the cowards? But notwithstanding their fierceness to naked men, one of them advanced towards a youth who had a spit of raw stave in his hand, and said damn them here is one of them; but the young man seeing a person near him with a drawn sword and a good cane ready to support him, he held his stave in defiance, and they quietly passed by him up the little alley by Mr. Silsby's to Kingstreet, where they attacked single and unarmed persons till they raised much clamor, and then turned down Cornhill street, insulting all they met in like manner and pursuing some to their very doors. Thirty or forty persons, mostly lads, being by this means gathered in Kingstreet, Capt. Preston, with a party of men with charged bayonets, came from the main guard to the Commissioners house, the soldiers pushing their bayonets, crying, Make way! They took place by the custom house, and continuing to push to drive people off, pricked some in several places; on which they were clamorous, and, it is said, threw snow balls. On this, the Captain commanded them to fire, and more snow balls coming, he said, Damn you, Fire, let the consequence be what it will! One soldier then fired, and a townsman with a cudgel struck him over the hands with such force that he dropt his firelock; and rushing forward aimed a blow at the Captain's head, which grazed him and fell pretty heavy upon his arm; However, the soldiers continued to fire, successively, till 7 or 8, or as some say, 11 guns were discharged.

By this fatal maneuvre, three men were laid dead on the spot, and two more were struggling for life; but what shewed a degree of cruelty unknown to British troops, at least since the house of Hanover has directed their operation, was an attempt to fire upon or push with their bayonets the persons who undertook to remove the dead and wounded!

Mr. Benjamin Leigh, now undertaker in the Delph Manufactory, came up, and after some conversation with Capt. Preston, relative to his conduct in this affair, advised him to draw off his men, with which he complied.

The dead are Mr. Samuel Gray, killed on the spot, the ball entering his head and bearing off a large portion of his skull.

A mulatto man, named Crispus Attucks, who was born in Framingham, but lately belonged to New Providence and was here in order to go to North Carolina, also killed instantly, two balls entering his breast, one of them in special goring the right lobe of the lungs, and a great part of the liver most horribly.

Mr. James Caldwell, mate of Capt. Morton's vessel, in like manner killed by two balls entering his back.

Mr. Samuel Maverick, a promising youth of 17 years of age, son of the widow Maverick, and an apprentice to Mr. Greenwood, Ivory-Turner, mortally wounded, a ball went through his belly & was cut out his back: He died the next morning.

A lad named Christopher Monk, about 17 years of age, an apprentice to Mr. Walker, Shipwright; wounded, a ball entered his back about 4 inches above the left kidney, near the spine; and was cut out of the breast on the same side; apprehended he will die.

A lad named John Clark, about 17 years of age, whose parents live at Medford, and an apprentice to Cpt. Samuel Howard of this town; wounded, a ball entered just above his groin and came out at his hip, on the opposite side; apprehended he will die.

Mr. Edward Payne, of this town, Merchant, standing at his entry-door, received a ball in his arm, which shattered some of the bones.

Mr. John Green, Taylor, coming up Leverett's Lane, received a ball just under his hip, and lodged in the under part of his thigh, which was extracted.

Mr. Robert Patterson, a seafaring man, who was the person that had his trowsers shot through in Richardson's affair, wounded; a ball went through his right arm, and he suffered great loss of blood.

Mr. Patrick Carr, about 30 years of age, who work'd with Mr. Field, Leather Breeches-maker in Queen-street, wounded, a ball enter'd near his hip and went out his side.

A lad name David Parker, an apprentice to Mr. Eddy the Wheelwright, wounded, a ball entered his thigh.

The People were immediately alarmed with the Report of this horrid Massacre. The Bells were set ringing, and great numbers soon assembled at the Place where the tragical Scene had been acted; their Feelings may be better conceived than express'd; and while some were taking Care of the Dead and Wounded, the Rest were in Consultation about what to do in these dreadful Circumstances.—But so little intimidated were they, notwithstanding their being within a few Yards of the Main-Guard, and seeing the 29th Regiment under Arms, and drawn up in King-Street; that they kept their Station and appear'd as an Officer of Rank express'd it, ready to run upon the very Muzzles of their Muskets—The Lieut. Governor soon came into the Town-House, and there met some of his Majesty's Council, and a Number of Civil Magistrates; a considerable Body of the People immediately entered the Council chamber, and expressed themselves to his Honor with a Freedom and Warmth becoming the occasion. He used his utmost Endeavours to pacify them, requesting that they would let the Matter subside for the Night, and promising to do all in his Power that Justice should be done, and the Law have its Course; Men of Influence and Weight with the People were not wanting on their part to procure their Compliance with his Honor's Request, by representing the horrible Consequences of a promiscuous and rash Engagement in the Night, and assuring them that such Measures should be entered upon in the Morning, as would be agreeable to their Dignity, and a more likely way of obtaining the best Satisfaction for the Blood of their fellow Townsmen. —The Inhabitants attended their Suggestions, and the Regiment under Arms being ordered to their Barracks, which was insisted upon by the people, they then separated & returned to their Dwellings by One o'Clock. At 3 o'Clock Capt. Preston was committed, as were the Soldiers who fir'd, a few Hours after him.

Tuesday Morning presented a most shocking Scene, the Blood of our fellow Citizens running like Water thro' King-street, and the Merchants Exchange[,] the Principal Spot of the Military Parade for about 18 Months past. Our Blood might also be track'd up to the head of Long-Lane, and through divers other Streets and Passages.

REVERE'S RENDERING

If not for the antiquarian interests of Mellen Chamberlain we would probably know even less about the massacre than we do now. Chamberlain served as librarian of the Boston Public Library from 1878 to 1890 and added significantly to the library's Revolutionary Era collections. A good part of what he acquired—or donated from his own documentary trove—was connected to the massacre. Having once sat on the bench of Boston's municipal court, Judge Chamberlain, as he was widely known, well understood that the remembered past slips ever further away with the passage of time; memory survives only through conscious efforts to form and preserve it.

One of the items that Chamberlain donated is this diagram of King Street, showing the position of the soldiers and the killed and wounded in the moments immediately following the massacre. Chamberlain was convinced that Paul Revere drew it because the handwriting matched known examples left by the silversmith; Esther Forbes, in her Pulitzer Prize-winning biography of Revere, concurred.[35] Even so, whether it was used during the trial by any of the parties involved remains an unanswered question.

The circles to the right in front of the custom house obviously represent the soldiers. There are three darker circles there as well. Do they signify where Preston stood at various points in the incident or does the bottommost of them, which seems to have an extension to it indicating a musket, like those of the soldiers in line, represent an eighth enlisted man? Recall that Revere showed seven men firing in his engraving. Was this eighth not shown because Revere hid him from view? Again, with the conflicting testimony coming from the depositions that ended up in A Short Narrative *and* A Fair Account, *Revere may have decided that the sentry, Hugh White, or one of those who marched down the street to relieve him, had not been in the firing line.*

Is it wrong, then, to say that Revere erred in showing only seven men shooting at the civilians? This issue is unresolved and Revere's drawing only adds more mystery to it. What do the circles, numbers, and letters placed on the street, beyond Preston and the soldiers, represent? Local historian Charles Bahne has studied the drawing and mulled over the meaning of Revere's symbols.[36] The prostrate figures closest to the soldiers, marked A1 and G2, no doubt represent Attucks and Gray, he concludes, as have many others. Likewise, the circle with P8, across the street and down, unquestionably marks the spot where Edward Payne was wounded. Does C3, in the middle of the street, mark where James Caldwell fell, and, to the left, does 4G in Quaker Lane represent Patrick Carr? With good reason, Bahne says "yes," though he admits that marking Carr's spot with a G rather than a C is perplexing. Since Samuel Maverick fled the scene before collapsing and being taken to his mother's house, where he died the next morning, Revere may have decided not to mark the spot where he had been hit. But then Carr did not die on the street either and lived much longer than did Maverick.

There are six more circles, four in a rough line down the right side of King Street, one closer to the Exchange Tavern, and then, of course, the one marking Payne's house at the lower left. One of those circles has a letter (M) with no number by it; one has a number (5) but no letter. As Bahne suggests, the circle by P6, below Attucks and Gray, and the circle by P7, nearer the town house, could stand for Robert Patterson and David Parker. Which is which, however, is difficult to say, based on the depositions taken to that point. Did the circle with M9 stand for Christopher Monk, another of the wounded, or is it the circle above, with M to its left, or the one with 5 under it but no letter, to the right and below? Attempting any more matches beyond that takes us to even broader conjectures, since there is no letter to match the names of the remaining wounded (John Clark and John Green).

Perhaps some day the key to the drawing will turn up and the questions about letters and numbers will then be answered. Naturally, if still more evidence turns up, then still more questions will be answered. And yet, even with more evidence, the most important questions will never be answered—indeed, those questions may never have had answers. For soldiers, if asked precisely when and why they fired, and for members of the crowd, if asked why they were in King Street at all, the answers given may or may not have matched real actions and real motives. The stories that we tell ourselves about ourselves, after all, may or may not be true; and we, like others, may not even know the difference.

* * *

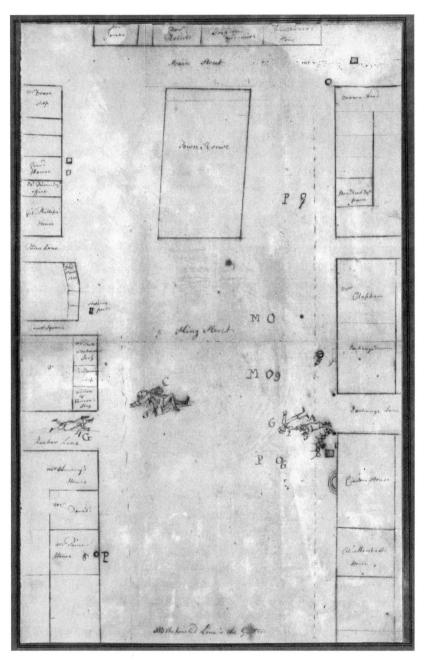

Document 10 Paul Revere's drawing of the massacre scene. Courtesy of the Trustees of the Boston Public Library/Rare Books.

DOCUMENT **11**

HUTCHINSON UNDER PRESSURE[37]

Thomas Hutchinson served as acting governor for nearly two years before becoming governor in his own right. He was still in that interim position at the time of the massacre. It is as much a commentary on historical memory as on Hutchinson that he is normally thought of only in connection with executive power, because he began his political career in the Massachusetts House. But that was in the 1730s, when he was a young man. He was nearing sixty at the time of the massacre and had become a lightning rod for controversy, like Bernard before him. If that hardly seems fair for a native son of Massachusetts who always considered himself as loyal to the colony as he was to the empire, he knowingly chose the wrong side in the imperial dispute: knowingly, in that he could see that he was out of step with political leaders in both town and province; wrong, in that his view could be sustained only by a London unwilling, perhaps even incapable, of doing what needed to be done for him to prevail.[38]

Hutchinson had once favored imperial reform, even along the lines suggested by Franklin's 1754 Albany Plan. He did not back every policy that came out of London enthusiastically, as can be seen with his adverse reaction to the Stamp Act. Still, he disliked politics that became too contentious and politicians who raised constitutional questions that he felt were best left unasked. And yet, once an issue was raised he found it difficult not to engage his opponents, sometimes writing anonymous pieces for the Boston press and most famously —infamously, for his local reputation—in early 1773 when he debated his Council and the House on the nature of colonial rights. In a technical sense his argument was as sound as theirs.[39] But they played out their constitutional dispute in a political context and it was there that Hutchinson's skills fell short.

Figure 12 Edward Truman's portrait of Thomas Hutchinson, painted in 1741, nearly thirty years before the massacre. Though hardly a tragic figure in the traditional sense of being brought down by his own hubris, Hutchinson nonetheless stands for many as the man sadly out of step with his times, the Boston native made homeless by political and social change that he could neither prevent nor embrace. He was no mindless law- and-order man and proved during the massacre crisis that he could use time to his advantage. Though hardly inept—if Hutchinson had been as politically unskilled as his critics charge, he never would have risen as far as he did—his notion of the empire, and of Massachusetts's proper place within it, eventually became impossible to sustain. He died in London in 1780 after six years of exile, in some sense a man without a country. Courtesy of the Massachusetts Historical Society.

In arguing for Parliament's complete supremacy and the need for the colonists to accept something less than the full rights of Englishmen he said nothing that he had not said before. His timing, however, could not have been worse.

By the time that he decided he needed to take a leave and defend his behavior before officials in London, he had been effectively stripped of his power even though he still had nominal authority. He had cut a truly pathetic figure nine years before in the aftermath of the Stamp Act riots, appearing in court the day after his house had been utterly ransacked, his personal property had been destroyed, and he had had to flee for his life. And yet there he sat on the bench, determined to preside in court. Even his political opponents could not but be impressed by his courage, then and later. Some have contended that he was too legalistic in his thinking, too dogmatic in his belief in the need for deference to rightful authority. Perhaps he was. He definitely had no place in the new social and political order that was emerging in Massachusetts by the late 1760s. Accused by critics of committing treason against the colony as he prepared to leave in 1774, he unrealistically believed that he might return as governor once order had been restored. He would die in exile, no longer a man of Massachusetts and never really an Englishman.

Hutchinson's report to Thomas Gage the day after the massacre is printed below. Hutchinson says little about the incident itself; rather, he emphasizes his role in keeping the lid from blowing off and the whole town going up in smoke. If read too quickly, it could give the impression that Hutchinson wrote as if he were firmly in charge, that he singlehandedly separated the contesting parties and restored order. Read more closely, it is clear—now, if not in Hutchinson's own mind then—that the only way he could preserve the peace was to give the town leaders what they wanted: a soldier-free Boston.

* * *

Sir   Boston 6th March 1770

I beg leave to refer you to Col. Dalrymple for the particulars of a most unfortunate affair which hapned the last Evening so far as they relate to the Troops under his Command. So far as they respect the Inhabitants and my own conduct I must acquaint you that just before ten O'Clock the Bells of the Town were rung as usual in case of fire, but I soon found there was another cause and one upon another came running to my House to inform that unless I went out immediately the whole Town would be in arms and the most bloody scene would follow that had ever been known in America. I went immediately abroad and met a vast crowd of people running for their arms and prevailed on them to turn back and follow me to Kingstreet, promising them justice should be done. I found two persons killed, a third mortally wounded and a fifth[,] Mr. Payne[,] a merchant of the Town[,] shot in his arm and the Bone splintered, as he stood at his door. The people were enraged to a very great degree and could not be pacified until I assured them immediate enquiries should be made by Civil Magistrates which was done and the body of them retired, about 100 only remaining until the examination was over which lasted till 3 or 4 O'Clock in the morning. I ordered a Council to be summoned to meet to day at 11 O'Clock, when I came to them and found the Selectmen and the Justices waiting for me to present that the Inhabitants had insisted upon a Town Meeting, and that it would not be in their power to keep them under restraint if the Troops were not removed to the Barracks at the Castle. I told them this was not in my power. In a short time I received a message from the Town Meeting which I shall enclose. The Committee consisted of the principal Inhabitants, several of them in plain terms declared they knew the people not only in the Town but all the neighbouring Towns were determined to unite and force the Troops out of the Town. I told them that an attack upon the Kings Troops would be high Treason and every man concerned would forfeit his life and Estate, but what I said had no effect. Upon consulting the Council, Colo. Dalrymple and Col. Carr being present they expressed unanimously their desire that the Regiments might be sent to the Castle. As the principal if not all the Quarrels of the Inhabitants had been with the 29th, Colo. Dalrymple so far yielded to their desire as to consent that the 29th should be quartered at the Castle and promised further that the 14th should be kept in the Barracks at Wheelwrights wharfe and all occasion of difference with the Inhabitants prevented. This the Committee of the Town were informed of and reported to the Meeting, but it proved not satisfactory and in the Afternoon a second Committee came to me in Council, Colonels Dalrymple and Carr and also Capt. Caldwell of the Rose being then present and laid before me another vote of the Town declaring they were not satisfied &c which vote I could not avoid asking the opinion of my Council upon. They not only unanimously declared their opinion that it was absolutely necessary that the Troops should be in the barracks at the Castle but most of them declared they had the greatest certainty that the Inhabitants of the Town and the Towns of Charlestown and Cambridge, Dedham, Roxbury[,] Dorchester &c. would infallibly unite and at all events drive the Troops from the Town and that it would admit of no delay, they were sure the night which was coming on would be the most terrible that had ever been seen in America. Two of the Council from Charlestown and Dedham confirmed what had been said of the disposition of the people of those Towns and everyone in the most earnest manner pressed me to communicate their opinion and advice in a formal way to Colo. Dalrymple and to pray him to cause both Regiments to remove to the Barracks at the Castle. I did not see how I could avoid complying with this unanimous Advice of the Council under the circumstances of the Town and Province, especially as I had opportunity of consulting so many Servants of the Crown together with the Secretary who is not of the Council and who saw all the matter in the same light as I did—and I am very certain Colo. Dalrymple was influenced to a compliance with any measure from the representation made in Council of the desperate state of the people and the desire they so strongly expressed which he thought necessary to justify him in his compliance.

I shall immediately represent the fate of this affair to the Secretary of State.[40] A vessel I am informed will sail for London in eight days.

I have the Honor to be very respectively Sir your most humble and most obedt. Servt.

Tho. Huchinson

March 7th. I am now informed that four persons are dead and a 5th lyes very dangerous and that several more were slightly wounded.

GAGE REPORTS TO HILLSBOROUGH[41]

If any British official could have been expected to understand the colonists, it was General Thomas Gage. A seasoned army officer, he fought at Culloden and on the Continent before arriving in the colonies, where he survived Braddock's disastrous 1755 campaign and went on to distinguish himself later in the French and Indian War. He married a young woman from a prominent New Jersey family and in 1763 succeeded Jeffrey Amherst as commander-in-chief of the British armed forces in North America, a post he held for twelve years.

He could be at once astute and inept. Years before the colonists rose in revolt he predicted that they would escalate their protests, starting with denying Parliament's authority to tax them, then they would question Parliament's authority over them altogether, and eventually deny even the authority of the king.[42] Yet, as astute as he could be in predicting American behavior, he seemed utterly incapable of preventing that behavior from developing or from bringing on the very crises that he had foreseen. Just the opposite; he may have hastened them—not simply as a result of his own poor judgment, but because he was called on to implement poorly defined policies.

When Bernard began hinting that he needed troops to bolster his authority, Gage expressed sympathy but made no promises. He told the customs commissioners, whose pleas for intervention were far more direct, the same thing. Gage would not have balked at moving troops to Boston years before, during the Stamp Act crisis, either, were he given orders from London to act. But being commander-in-chief over the armed forces did not give him seniority over governors; indeed, their ambiguous relationship was one of the failures of colonial administration addressed by imperial reformers like Thomas Pownall.

When Hillsborough finally ordered troops to Boston, Gage pledged a decisive response should there be resistance. If civil authority could be maintained simply by the troops' presence, fine; "but if open and declared Rebellion make its Appearance, I mean to use all the Powers lodged in my Hands, to make Head against it."[43] Contrast Gage's tough talk in this letter, as he prepared to send the troops into Boston, with the letter written after the massacre that is printed below, where Gage writes like a mere observer of, rather than a participant in, events. He placed the blame squarely on the civilians rather than the soldiers; he believed local authorities had been agitating the people to get the troops removed altogether; he doubted that a fair trial was possible for Preston or his men. And yet he wrote as if he described circumstances beyond his control— that he acted completely in response to the actions of colonial protesters. The initiative—and the advantage—lay with them.

*   *   *

My Lord,   New York April 10th 1770

Your Lordship will have received by the way of Boston, much earlier Intelligence than it has been in my Power to transmit, of an unhappy Quarrell between the People of that Town and the Soldiers; in which several of the former were killed and wounded. But I take the first opportunity to send your Lordship the best account I have been able to procure of this unfortunate Accident, as well as to represent the critical Situation of the Troops, and the hatred of the People towards them.

The Occasion which brought the Regiments to Boston rendered them obnoxious to the People, and they may have increased the odium them-selves, as —— the Disorders of that Place have mostly sprang from Disputes with Great Britain. The Officers and Soldiers are Britons, and the People found no advocates amongst them. It was natural for them, without exam-ining into the merits of a political Dispute, to take the part of their Country, which probably they have often done with more zeal than Discretion, considering the Circumstances of the Place they were in, for in matters of Dispute with the Mother Country, or relative thereto, Government is at an End in Boston; and in the hands of the People, who have only to assemble to execute any Designs. No Person dares to oppose them or call them to Account; the whole Authority of Government, the Governor excepted, and Magistracy supporting them. The People prejudiced against the Troops lead every Snare to entrap and destroy them, and frequent Complaints have been made, that the Soldiers were daily in publick, and the People encouraged to insult them even by magistrates, that no satisfaction could be obtained, but the Soldiers if found in fault punished with the Rigour of the Law: Such Proceedings could not fail to irritate, but the Troops were restrained by their Discipline; and the Accidental Quarrells happened, mostly were prevented going to Extremitys.

In My Letter to your Lordship no. 40 I mentioned a misunderstanding between the Inhabitants and Soldiers in this Town; soon after which Advice was transmitted from Boston, that the People there had quarrelled with the Troops, and lay in wait for them in the Streets to knock them down; in so much that it was unsafe for Officers or Soldiers to appear in the Streets after dark. A particular Quarrell happened at a Rope-Walk with a few Soldiers of the 29th Regiment; the Provocation was given by the Rope-Makers, tho' it may be imagined in the Course of it, that there were Faults on both sides. The Quarrell it is supposed excited the People to concert a general Rising on the night of the 5th of March. They began by falling upon a few Soldiers in a Lane, contiguous to a Barrack of the 29th Regiment, which brought some Officers of the said Regiment out of their Quarters, who found some of their Men greatly hurt, but carried all the Soldiers to their Barrack. The mob followed, menacing and brandishing their Clubs over the Officers Heads to the Barrack Door, the Officers endeavouring to pacify them and desiring them to retire. Part of the mob broke into a Meeting House and rang the Fire-Bell, which appears to have been the Alarm concerted, for numerous Bodys immediately assembled in the Streets, armed, some with Musquets, but most with Clubs, Bludgeons and such like weapons.

Many People came out of their Houses supposing a Fire in the Town and several Officers on the same Supposition were repairing to their Posts, but meeting with mobs were reviled [and] attacked and those who could not escape knocked down and treated with great Inhumanity. Different mobs paraded through the Streets, passing the several Barracks and provoking the Soldiers to come out. One Body went to the Main Guard, where every Provocation was given without effect for the guard remained quiet. From there the mob proceeded to a Centinel posted upon the Custom House, at a small Distance from the Guard, and attacked him. He defended himself as well as he could, calling out for help; and People ran to the Guard to give Information of his Danger. Captain Preston of the 29th Regiment, being Captain of the Day, his Duty upon the Alarm carried him to the Main Guard, and hearing the Centinel was in Danger of being murdered, he detached a Serjt and twelve Men to relieve him, and soon after followed himself to prevent any rash Act on the part of the troops. This Party as well as the Centinel was immediately attacked, some throwing Bricks, Stones, Pieces of Ice and Snow Balls at them, whilst others advanced up to their Bayonets, and endeavoured to close with them, to use their Bludgeons and Clubs, Calling out to them to fire if they dared, and provoking them to it by the most opprobrious Language. Captain Preston stood between the Soldiers and the Mob, parlying with the latter and using every conciliating method to persuade them to retire peaceably. Some amongst them asked him if he intended to order the Men to fire, he replyed by no means, and observed he stood between the Troops and them. All he could say had no effect, and one of the Soldiers receiving a violent Blow, instantly fired. Captain Preston turned round to see who fired, and received a Blow upon his Arm, which was aimed at his Head, and the mob at first seeing no Execution done and imagining the Soldiers had only fired Powder to frighten, grew more bold and attacked with greater violence, continually striking at the Soldiers and pelting them, and calling out to them to fire. The Soldiers at length perceiving their Lives in Danger, and hearing the word Fire all round them, three or four of them fired one after another; and again three more in the same hurry and Confusion. Four or five Persons were unfortunately killed, and more wounded. Captain Preston and the Party were soon afterwards delivered into the hands of the magistrates who committed them to Prison.

The misunderstanding between the People and the Troops in this Place,[44] was contrived by one Party, not only to wound their Adversarys, who had voted to supply the Troops according to Act of Parliament, through the sides of the Soldiers, by making them and their Measures odious to the People, but also to have a Pretence to desire the Removal of the Troops, which I am assured was mentioned, if not moved at the time of the Council. This Plan of getting the Troops removed by quarrelling with them was soon transmitted to Boston, where they immediately put it in Execution, by Endeavours to bring on a general Quarrell between them and the Towns People. We fortunately found not only magistrates but many People of Consequence in this Place, who discovered the Designs of the adverse Party, and exerted themselves in keeping the People quiet and preventing mischief without whose Assistance, I am confident something very disagreeable must have happened here, notwithstanding the uncommon Pains taken with the Soldiers. And had the magistrates and those who have Influence over the Populace in Boston, taken as much trouble to appease and restrain, as they have on too many occasions, to inflame and excite the People to tumults and Mischief, I am as confident that no Blood would have been shed in that Place. But it appears unfortunately that their schemes were not to be brought about through Peace and Tranquility, but by promoting Disorders.

Some have swore that Captain Preston gave Orders to fire, others who were near that the Soldiers fired without Orders upon the Provocation they received. None can deny the attack made upon the Troops, but differ in the Degree of violence in the Attack.

I hope and believe, that I have given your Lordship in general a true Relation of this unhappy Affair, and sorry I am to say, there is too much Reason to apprehend neither Captain Preston or the Soldiers can have a fair and impartial Tryal for their Lives. The utmost malice and malevolence has been shewn already, in Endeavours to bring on the Tryals whilst the People are heated by Resentment, and the Thirst of Revenge. And Attempts have been made to overawe the Judges. The Inveteracy of the People against the Commissioners has also appeared in this Affair, for there is Information, that the Grand Jury took Pains to bring them in as conspiracy with the Army to Massacre, as they term it, the Inhabitants. And an officer of the customs belonging to Gaspee with a Gentleman of his Acquaintance, and two Servants of the Board have been committed to Prison, where they have been some Days as Accessories, for firing out of the Custom House upon the Evidence of a French Serving Boy of 14 Years of Age, notwithstanding the Officer by name Manwaring, was apprehended by a warrant from a popular Justice, and dismissed upon the Detection of the Villany of the Boy.

Lieutenant Governor Hutchinson, and Lieutenant Colonel Dalrymple, having acquainted His Majesty's Ministers with the reasons for removing the Troops from Boston to the Island of Castle William, it is needless for me to trouble your Lordship with a Repetition of them. His Majesty alone can judge whether the Lieutenant Colonel, who acted contrary to his own opinion, should have refused to comply with the Desires of every part of the Civil Government in that Respect, as well as most of the Officers of the Crown; in order to avoid greater Evils than they should suffer, from the Absence of the Troops.

Conceiving the Troops to be of no use at the Island, I proposed to the Lieutenant Governor to remove them out of the Province; and one of them immediately. The last measure I shall be obliged to take shortly or run the Risk of some contagious Disorders getting amongst the Men, from their being so much crowded in small Rooms. Not finding the Proposal agreeable, I have consented to let both Regiments remain till the Arrival of the February mail from England, tho' I can't perceive any service is hoped for from them, unless it is to serve in the last Extremity as an Azylum, to which the Officers of the crown might fly, for the security of their Persons. But if there are any Reasons to apprehend Dangers of the kind, I am ignorant of them. It has indeed been proved, that they were of no other use in the Town of Boston, for the People were as Lawless and Licentious after the Troops arrived, as they were before. The Troops could not act by Military Authority, and no Person in Civil Authority would ask their Aid. They were there contrary to the wishes of the Council, Assembly, Magistrates and People and seemed only offered to Abuse and Ruin. And the Soldiers were either to suffer ill usage and even Assaults upon their Persons till their Lives were in

Danger, or by resisting and defending themselves, to run almost a Certainty of suffering by the Law.

I have the honour to be with the greatest Regard, Respect, and Esteem,

My Lord,
Your Lordships's
Most obedient,
And most humble Servant,
Thos. Gage

PRESTON PLEADS HIS CASE TO PITT[45]

Jailed in Boston, facing prosecution in a Massachusetts court before a Suffolk County jury, Thomas Preston feared that he would be convicted and hanged. Desperate, perhaps, to soften local opinion, he made a statement to the Boston Gazette, *which appeared in the same issue as its infuriated report of the massacre. Preston thanked "the Inhabitants in general of this Town—who throwing aside all Party and Prejudice, have with the utmost Humanity and Freedom stept forth Advocates for Truth, in Defence of my injured Innocence." Thus, "I shall ever have the highest Sense of the Justice they have done me, which will ever be gratefully remembered." Whether he hid his true feelings at that moment or changed his mind once he began to ponder his plight as a prisoner, he spoke very differently in the statement transcribed below. Not only did he send it to Gage; he forwarded a copy to William Pitt, now Earl of Chatham in the House of Lords but still venerated by many as "The Great Commoner." Exactly what he thought Pitt could do is unclear, except to hope that he would work behind the scenes to calm the atmosphere at Westminster. Note his attempt to make a family connection in the cover letter introducing his statement about events on the evening of March 5. Note too that he said he sent out a party of thirteen men—six more than would eventually be charged and tried (not counting White, the sentry on duty outside the custom house). Did he misremember or did some unnamed soldiers escape trial? We do not, and probably will never, know.*

* * *

Sir

A very extraordinary Affair has happened here, which as a principal Officer of the Crown, it may be necessary for you to know, and I as a person unluckily concern'd inclose you an Account of. Upon the most perjur'd evidence, and virulent prosecution, I am thrown into a Gaol, strongly secur'd, and charged with a barbarous, cruel, & premeditated murder; my judges intimidated, my Evidence browbeat, & threatned, and to finish the scene, my life left to the mercy of a partial Jury, whose prejudice is kept up by a set of designing Villains, that only draw their subsistence from the disturbances they cause.

I have nothing to support me under these difficulties, but the testimony of a clear conscience, and such Evidence as would easily acquit me in any other place but this, where they are looking for everything that will be a palliative & excuse for their rebellion, and rebellion it certainly is if the Council, & Handcocks words may be taken, for they declared: that 4 or 5000 men were ready arm'd to attack the troops, and drive them out of the Town, if they had not consented to go out themselves, besides they have kept a regular guard ever since.

Copies of my case are sent home to Lord Hillsborough, Lord Barrington, and Genl. Harvey, as also to Col. Evelyn, with copies of all the affidavits that we could get, tho' these were got with the greatest stealth, & several refus'd to swear unless in Court. I must rest there having no hopes but from his Majesty's pardon and God knows if it will come time enough to save me from a shameful end.

If I may judge of your goodness of heart by several circumstances that have come to my knowledge, I shall find very little difficulty in prevailing on you to back the memorial of my friends by your interest, to save the life of an innocent person, who only went to the fatal place to prevent the unfortunate accident that happened.

With the best wishes for Mrs. J. Master Hood, and the rest of your family, I remain with great Respect

Sir, your most obedient and much distress'd humble Servant

Thos. Preston

THE CASE OF CAPTAIN THOS. PRESTON

It is now a matter of too great notoriety to need any Proofs, that the arrival of his majesty's Troops in Boston was extreamly obnoxious to its inhabitants. They have ever since used all means in their power to weaken the Regiments, and to bring them into contempt; by promoting & aiding desertions, and with impunity, even when there has been the clearest Evidence of the fact, and by grosly & falsly propagating untruths concerning them.

On the arrival of the 64th and 65th their ardour seemingly began to abate[,] it being too expensive to buy off so many, and attempts of that kind rendered too dangerous from the Numbers, but the same spirit revived immediately on its being known that those Regiments were ordered for Halifax, and hath ever since their departure been breaking out with much greater violence. After their Embarkation one of their Justices, most thoroughly acquainted with the People & their Intentions, on the Tryal of a man of the 14th Regiment openly & Publickly, in the hearing of great numbers of the People, & from the seat of Justice, declared "that the Soldiers must now take care of themselves, nor trust too much to their Arms, for they were but a handful, that the Inhabitants carried weapons concealed under their cloths, and would destroy them in a moment if they pleased."[46]

This[,] considering the malicious temper of the people, was an alarming circumstance to the Soldiery—Since which, several disputes have happen'd between the Townspeople & the Soldiers of both Regiments, the former being encourag'd thereto by the protections of all the party against Government, in general such disputes have been kept too secret from the Officers.

On the 2d Instant two of the 29th going through one Gray's Ropewalk the Ropemakers insultingly asked them if they would empty a Vault. This unfortunately had the desired effect, by provoking the Soldiers and from words they went to blows. Both parties suffered in this affray, and finally the Soldiers retired to their quarters. The officers on the first knowledge of this Transaction took every precaution in their power to prevent any ill consequences, notwithstanding which, single quarrels could not be prevented, the Inhabitants constantly provoking & abusing the Soldiery. The insolence, as well as utter hatred of the Inhabitants to the Troops encreased daily; in so much, that Monday & Tuesday, the 5th and 6th Instant, was privately agreed for a general attack.—In consequence of which, several of the Militia came from the Country Armed to join their Friends, meaning to destroy any who should oppose them. This plan has been discovered.

On Monday night about 8 o'clock two Soldiers were attacked and beat but the party of the Townspeople, in order to carry matters to the utmost length, broke into two meeting Houses and rang the Alarm Bells, which I supposed was for fire as usual, but was soon undeceived. About 9 some of the Guard came to and informed me, the Town inhabitants were Assembling to attack the Troops, and that the Bells were ringing as the Signal for that purpose, and not for Fire, and the beacon intended to be fired to bring in the distant people of the Country.

This, as I was Captain of the day, occasioned my repairing immediately to the main Guard. On my way there, I saw the people in great commotions and heard them use the most cruel and horrid threats against the Troops.

In a few minutes after I reached the Guard about 100 people past it, and went towards the Customhouse where the Kings money is lodged. They immediately surrounded the Sentry posted there and with Clubs & other weapons threatned to execute their vengeance on him. I was soon informed by a Townsman, their intentions was to carry off the Soldier from his post, and probably murder him. This I feared might be a prelude to their plundering the Kings Chest. I immediately sent a Non Commissioned officer and 12 men to protect both the Sentery and the Kings money and very soon followed myself to prevent, if possible, all disorder; fearing least the officers and Soldiers by the Insults and provocations of the Rioters should be thrown off their Guard, and commit some rash act. They soon rushed through the people and by charging their Bayonets in a half circle kept them at a little Distance.

Nay so far was I from intending the Death of any person that I suffered the troops to go the spot where the unhappy affair took place without any loading in their pieces, nor did I ever give orders for loading them. This remiss conduct in me perhaps merits censure yet it is evidence resulting from the nature of things, which is the best & surest that can be offered that my intentions was not to act offensively, but the contrary part, and that not without compulsion.

The Mob still encreased & were more outragious, striking their Clubs or Bludgeons one against another and calling out, come on you rascals, you bloody backs, you Lobster scoundrels, fire if you dare, G-d damn you, fire & be damn'd. We know you dare not. And much more such Language was used.

At this time I was between the Soldiers and the Mob, parlying with and endeavouring all in my power to persuade them to retire peaceably, but to no purpose. They advanced to the point of the Bayonets[,] struck some of them, and even the Muzzels of the pieces and seemed to be endeavouring to close with the Soldiers. On which some wellbehaved persons asked me, if the Guns were charged. I replied Yes. They then asked me if I intended to order the men to fire. I answered NO, by no means—for please to observe, that I was advanced before the Muzzels of the mens pieces, and must fall a sacrifice if they fired. That the Soldiers were upon the half-lock & Charged Bayonets, and my giving the word fire under those Circumstances would prove me to be no officer.

While I was thus speaking one of the Soldiers[,] having received a severe blow with a stick, step'd a little on one side and instantly fired, on which turning to and asking him why he fired without orders I was struck with a Club on my Arm which for some time deprived me of the use of it, which blow had it been placed on my Head, most probably would have destroy'd me. On this a general attack was made on the men by a great number of heavy Clubs, & snow Balls being thrown at them, by which all our lives were in eminent danger, some persons at the same time, from behind call'd out damn your bloods why don't you fire—instantly three or four of the Soldiers fired one after another, and directly after three more in the same confusion and hurry.

The Mob then ran away, except the unhappy men, who instantly expired, in which number was Mr. Gray at whose Ropewalk the prior quarrel took place, one more is since Dead, and three others are dangerously wounded and four slightly wounded.

The whole of this melancholy affair was transacted in about 20 minutes. On my asking the Soldiers why they fired without orders, they said they heard the word fire, and supposed it came from me. This might be the case, as many of the Mob called out fire, fire, but I assured the Men that I gave no such order, that my words were, don't fire, stop your firing, in short it was scarcely possible for the Soldiers to know who said fire, or don't fire or stop your firing. On the peoples assembling again to take away the dead bodies, the soldiers supposing them coming to attack them, were making ready to fire again, which I prevented by striking up their firelocks with my hands.

Immediately after this a Townsman came & told me that 4 or 5000 people were Assembled in the next street, and had sworn to take my Life with every mans with me. On which I judged it unsafe to remain there any longer, and therefore sent the party and Sentry to the Main Guard, where the street is narrow & short, there telling them off into street firings[,] divided and planted them at each end of the street to secure their Rear. Momently expecting an attack, as there was a constant cry by the Inhabitants to Arms to Arms, turn out with your Guns & the Town drums beating to Arms, I order'd my Drum to beat to Arms & being soon after joined by the different Companies of the 29th Regimt. I formed them as the Guard into street firings. The 14th Regiment also got under Arms, but remained at their bar-racks. I immediately sent a Serjeant with a party to Colo. Dalrymple the Commanding Officer, to acquaint him with every particular. Several officers going to join their Regiments were knock'd down by the Mob, one very much wounded and his Sword taken from him.

The Lieutenant Governor & Colo. Carr soon after met at the head of the 29th Regiment and agreed that the Regiment should retire to their Barracks & the people to their Houses, but I kept the Picket to strengthen the Guard. It was with great difficulty that the Lieut. Governor prevailed on the people to be quiet and retire. At last they all went off, excepting about a hundred.

A Council was immediately call'd on the breaking up of which three justices met and issued a warrant to apprehend me and eight Soldiers. On hearing this procedure I instantly went to the Shireff & surrender'd myself, tho' for the space of four hours I had it in my power to have made my escape, which I most undoubtedly should have attempted & could easily executed had I been the least conscious of any Guilt.

On the examination before the justices, two witnesses swore that I gave the men orders to fire, the one testified he was within two feet of me, the other that I swore at the men for not firing at the first word. Others swore they heard me use the word fire but whether do or not fire, they could not say. Others that they heard the word fire, but could not say if it came from me. The next day they got five or six more to swear I gave the word to fire. So bitter & inveterate are many of the malcontents here, that they are industriously using every method to fish out evidence to prove it was a concerted scheme to murder the Inhabitants. Others are infusing the utmost malice and revenge into the minds of the people who are to be my jurors by false publications, votes of Towns & all other artifices, that so from a settled rancour against the Officers & Troops in general, the suddenness of my Trial after the affair, while the peoples minds are all greatly inflamed I am, tho' perfectly innocent, under most unhappy circumstances, having in reason to expect, but the loss of Life, in a very ignominious manner, without the interposition of his Majesty's royal goodness.

And this must be the fate of all the unhappy Soldiers confined with me. In short, with such jurors and witnesses we have nothing better to expect than be sacrificed as a terror to all others who should oppose the people however wrong. If I am view'd even as a man attacked & insulted, can I be blamed for defending myself, even supposing all they swear against me to be true? If as an Officer at the head of a party, I think it impossible that I should be tax'd as being either passionate or rash, the Commanding Officer with the Officers of both the two Corps and every other dispassionate man here have approved of my conduct and hope it will also deserve the attention of His Majesty.

Boston March 14th 1770
Thos. Preston Capt. in the 29th Regiment of Foot

BOSTON COUNTERS PRESTON[47]

Town leaders learned soon enough that Preston had written to Pitt. He was, after all, being held in their jail. They countered with a letter to Pitt of their own. The three men who signed the letter—James Bowdoin, Samuel Pemberton, and Joseph Warren—were all prominent in their time, but Warren is the only one of the three to survive in popular memory, and that primarily because of his death in the June 1775 fighting at Breed's Hill, not his role in town and provincial politics. Bowdoin in particular was a driving force in the town meeting but later generations were destined not to know just how powerful he was. Son of a wealthy Boston merchant, with both a bachelor's and master's from Harvard, he served in the Massachusetts House before being chosen by his colleagues there to sit on the governor's Council. Bernard and Hutchinson could have tried to prevent his being seated but they probably foresaw the potential political backlash, so he joined the Council. There he acted as a thorn in the side of both governors, causing them every bit as much difficulty as Samuel Adams and John Hancock in promoting the "patriot" cause. They are remembered; he is not. Such are the vagaries of the reconstructed past.

* * *

Figure 13 (opposite) Robert Feke's 1748 portrait of James Bowdoin II, painted, presumably, to mark Bowdoin's marriage to Elizabeth Erving. He had inherited a portion of his father's estate the year before. He was ensconced in town politics and would sit in the Massachusetts House and on the governor's Council, opposing both

Francis Bernard and Thomas Hutchinson on one issue or another. He continued his political involvement through the Revolutionary Era and was twice elected Massachusetts governor after the war. Interested in science as well as politics, his biographer, Gordon Kershaw, called him "the American personification of the eighteenth-century Man of the Enlightenment."[48] In 1767 Bowdoin's daughter Elizabeth married John Temple, a member of the customs commission. Bowdoin's political opponents were convinced that the father-in-law corrupted his son-in-law's thinking, winning him over to the side of Boston's demagogues. Courtesy of Bowdoin College Museum of Art, Brunswick, Maine, Bequest of Mrs. Sarah Bowdoin Dearborn.

It is in Consequence of an Appointment of the Town of Boston, that we have the Honor of writing to your Lordship, and of communicating the enclosed Narrative, relative to the massacre in this Town on the 5th Instant.

After that execrable Deed, perpetrated by Soldiers of the 29th Regiment, the Town thought it highly expedient that a full and just Representation of it should be made to Persons of Character as soon as may be, in Order to frustrate the Designs of certain men who say they have heretofore been plotting the Ruin of our Constitution and Liberties, by their Letters, Memorials and Representations, are now said to have procured Depositions in a private manner, relative to the said Massacre, to bring an Odium upon the Town as the Aggressors in that Affair. But we humbly apprehend your Lordship, after examining the said narrative and the Depositions annexed to it, will be fully satisfied of the Falshood of such a Suggestion, and we take upon ourselves to declare upon our Honor and Consciences, that having examined critically into the matter, there does not appear the least Ground for it.

The Depositions referred to (if any such there be) were taken without notifying the Selectmen of the Town, or any other Person whatever, to be present at the Caption in behalf of the Town: which, as it has been a Thing justly complained of in some other Cases so the Town now renew their Complaints on the same Head and humbly presume such Depositions will have no Weight till the Town has been served with Copies of them, and an Opportunity given them to be heard in their Defence in the matter, and in any other, wherein their Character is drawn into Question, with a View to passing a Censure upon it.

A different Conduct was observed on the Part of the Town. The Justices with a Committee to assist them, made their Examinations publickly: most of them at Faneuil Hall, and the rest where any Persons might attend. Notifications were sent to the Custom House, where the Commissioners of the Customs sit, that they or any Persons in their behalf might be present at the Captions: and accordingly Mr. Sheaffe, the Deputy Collector, and Mr. Green, Tenant of the Custom House under the Commissioners and employed, [were] present at many of them.

One of the said Commissioners, Mr. Robinson, in a secret manner has embarked on board Capt. Robsin, and sailed for London the 16th Instant: which, with three of the other Commissioners retiring from the Town, and not having held a Board for some time since the 5th Instant, gives Reason to apprehend they have planned, and are executing a Libel of misrepresentation to induce Administration to think, that their Persons are not in Safety in this Town in the Absence of Troops. But, my Lord, their safety is no way dependent on Troops: for your Lordship must be sensible, that if any Evil has ever been intended them, Troops would not have prevented it.

It was so apparently incompatible with the safety of the Town, for the Troops to continue any longer in it that His Majesty's Council were unanimous in their Advice to the Lieutenant Governor, that they should be removed to Barracks at Castle Island. And it is the humble and fervent Prayer of the Town and the Province in General, that His Majesty will graciously be pleased, in his great Wisdom and Goodness, to order the said Troops out of the Province; and that his dutiful and loyal Subjects of this Town and Province—dutiful and loyal notwithstanding any Representation to the Contrary—may not again be distressed and destroyed by Troops, for preventing which, We beg Leave in behalf of the Town, to request most earnestly the Favor of your Lordship's Interposition and Influence.

We have the honor to be with the most perfect Regard,

My Lord
Your Lordship's most obedient
And very humble Servants
James Bowdoin
Saml. Pemberton
Joseph Warren

GAGE'S HANDS TIED[49]

In October 1768 Gage had sailed to Boston from New York, not knowing what to expect, given the grim reports he had received from there and rumors that any troops that attempted to land would be resisted. He arrived two weeks after the 14th and 29th regiments came ashore from Halifax and was pleasantly surprised to see that, after some initial friction, they had been bivouacked around the town. He thought about staying until the 64th and 65th regiments arrived from Ireland, but decided to return to New York. He did not anticipate any problem with their finding quarters and more pressing business awaited him back at headquarters.

And indeed, the 64th and 65th arrived in November only to turn around and leave the following July, so peaceful had Boston become—peaceful, that is to say, except for the continued protests against their presence featured in "A Journal of the Times" that circulated in the press,[50] and the occasional confrontation between individual soldiers and civilians. Had Bernard not objected, Gage would have removed the 14th and 29th regiments as well, given the little they had to do. Their continued presence, he realized, meant that there could be an incident. Bernard knew that too, but he feared even worse should they leave. Bernard, Gage, and the customs commissioners did not always agree on the need for or use of military force. Servants of empire all, they nonetheless had different perspectives about how best to impose imperial authority.

Lieut. Col. Dalrymple, who had arrived with the 14th Regiment in October 1768, ended up in overall command soon after the departure of a colonel and then a general before him—neither officer wanting to be posted in a town so potentially hostile, over troops with duties so poorly defined. Dalrymple asked Gage what to do to prevent a possible confrontation between the locals and his *troops; Gage could not tell him anything specific, since Dalrymple's men were not on true military duty. In the event of war with a foreign enemy, orders could be clear; even in the event of a massive riot, where the king's property was in danger, precise orders could be given, but Gage had little to say about the niggling, if constant, problems besetting the soldiers—a verbal exchange here, a shoving match there.*

Gage's orders to Dalrymple on removing the 29th Regiment from Castle William and getting it to New Jersey after the massacre follow below. Like his comments on Preston's actions on March 5, they leave the impression that the soldiers stationed in Boston had been all but orphaned, their continued confused status proof of a policy adrift in the tide. Dalrymple's own regiment, the 14th, would remain at Castle William until relieved in 1772. It was a singularly unappealing posting.

*   *   *

Sir,   New York April 28th 1770

You will receive Orders concerning the March of the 29th Regiment. Major Shirreff goes to Rhode Island to take up Vessels to transport them from Providence to Amboy and Elizabeth Town, from whom you will have due Notice when the Transports are prepared and ready to receive the Regiment; and you will give Orders for their March accordingly.

I write to the Lieut. Governor Hutchinson to give him Notice of the March of this Regiment, and to desire his Directions to the Justices of Peace or other Magistrates, to provide them with Quarters and Carriages, through his Government. And shall write likewise on the same Subject to the Governor of Rhode Island. It will not be possible to provide the Men with regular Quarters in the Straggling Places they March through, but they can Shift for a Night in Barns and Outhouses.

No Determinations, Resolves, or Orders, have appeared in the January and February Mails, to require my keeping the two Regiments any longer at Castle William. With respect to the 14th Regiment, that Corps will be Sufficient for present purposes. If anything is to be done, Measures more forceable must be taken, if not, I hope the Answers to my Dispatches by the Packet just Sailing, will allow me to bring that Regiment away likewise. Troops can be of no use to Government as they are Situated, and serve more to embroil and create Disturbances, than to strengthen the hands of Government and preserve Tranquility.

You will of Course detain all Officers or Men who may be wanted as Evidences at the ensuing Tryals of Captain Preston and the Soldiers. I have transmitted home the best Account I could of that Affair, collected from

Passages of Letters, and such other Materials that I could procure. Shewing withal the little Chance the Prisoners had to escape, whether culpable or not, unless Government interfered and delayed Executions, till a thorough Information was obtained of the true Conduct of the Captain and Soldiers, to enable them to Judge, how far they are Objects of the Royal Mercy. I have done all I could, but unfortunately my Letters go home very late, And I must repeat my Sollicitations to postpone the Tryals as long as possible; to effect which I am assured the Lieutenant Governor will do all that lyes in his Power.

I understand from your first Letters on this Unhappy Subject, that you had transmitted home a Narrative thereof, as well as an Account of all that followed, which occasioned the Removal of the Troops, to the Barracks at Castle William. You don't say to whom you transmitted those Accounts, but I am to hope they are to some Public Office, and that some Measures will be resolved on before my Letters get home.

Captain Preston's own Account I rather wish kept here than sent home. He had no Business to defend the Custom House, unless legaly called upon. I suppose his Motives for sending the Party was, to relieve the Centry who was attacked, and bring him back to the Guard to prevent Mischief. Other Motives were no doubt good, honest and Military, but they may not be good in Law, where a Military Man Acts by his own Authority Solely.

I am with great Regard.

Sir,
&ca

AN EYEWITNESS ACCOUNT[51]

Robert Goddard, whose brief statement appears below, was just one of the townsmen who offered testimony to coroner Thomas Davies the day after the massacre. Only a handful of the depositions offered at the four coroners' inquests survive from the dozens that were taken, and those that do anticipate the general tone that would be taken in A Short Narrative.

Goddard stated that he went to King Street after he heard an alarm bell and stood by the sentry box outside the custom house. He saw Preston and a party of soldiers come to relieve the sentry there, and heard Preston order the men to fire. Indeed, when they hesitated, he repeated the order. Goddard helped carry an already dead Attucks from King Street as Preston, sword drawn, marched his men away. Goddard went to the jail and identified Preston as the officer in command, after Preston had surrendered himself to the town authorities. Goddard also testified for the prosecution in Preston's trial, where he seems to have elaborated on his statement at the inquest, most notably in stating that Preston "stood behind" the enlisted men "all the time."[52]

* * *

I Robert Goddard of lawful age testify and declare that on the Evening of the 5th Instant between the hours of nine & ten, I heard a Bell ring, upon which I ran towards the Town house; I heard a Cry for help, in King Street. I went & stood near the Centry Box by the Custom house; I saw an Officer come towards the Box, with a party of Men, having a drawn Sword in his hand I heard him frequently repeat "Clear the way." The Party then drew up near where the Centinel stood, and order'd his men to stand with their

Bayonets charg'd. He then said "Boys stand off or we shall wound some of you; You had better stand off." And a sailor then struck the Officer, upon which he said "damn you I will not be us'd in such a manner" immediately he said Fire, upon which the Soldiers stood for a short space. The Officer then said "Damn your Blood Fire." I immediately heard & saw One Musquet discharg'd which was directly follow'd by several others & saw four men laying[53] on the ground one of which was the deceas'd Crispus Attucks.[54] The Officer order'd his men to stand with their Bayonets charg'd, after which I helped carry away the deceas'd into Mr. Stones and the Officer march'd off with his party with his drawn Sword in his hand.

Boston 6th March 1770 [signed] Robert Goddard

NB[55] Mr. Goddard was desired to go up to the Gaol in order to see if he knew the man and he was satisfyed that it was the same person, or Officer that Commanded the Detachment.

Lieutenant Jame Bassett Commanded the Main Guard after Capt Preston march'd off with the Detachment. And said before the Jury of Inquest that Corporal Wems, went off with the said Detachment.

The above taken by Thomas Davies Coroner. Inquisition on S. Gray

DOCUMENT **17**

CORONER'S INQUEST FOR CRISPUS ATTUCKS[56]

All but forgotten by his own generation, Crispus Attucks would be rediscovered a century later and in that rediscovery move from member of a mob to martyr for a cause. Attucks's rediscovery demonstrates very nicely the sometimes blurry line separating the folkloric from the historical.

We do not know much more about the historical Attucks than what John Fiske alluded to in his 1888 tribute to the massacre's martyrs (see Document 30). He appears to have been of Natick and African-American ancestry, born in Massachusetts in 1723, raised in the Framingham area, possibly a slave at some point and a sailor later, only temporarily in Boston in March 1770. The first to be slain, there were those who testified that he had been a ringleader who made threatening gestures toward the soldiers and may even have grabbed at their muskets, while others described him as more placid, leaning on, but not wielding, a large stick when the soldiers fired.[57]

Despite what little is known about Attucks, a veritable cottage industry has grown up around him as a Revolutionary Era hero. He has come to symbolize for many, especially African-Americans, resistance to tyranny and a defense of rights, a brave man who died in a just cause. He is the subject of various children's books, with a full past invented for him. He has been celebrated and commemorated on stamps and coins; a philanthropic group took on his name and there is a website devoted to him. Perhaps most famously there is Crispus Attucks High School in Indianapolis, which produced the first all-black championship basketball team in American history and included future NBA hall-of-fame member Oscar Robertson among it stars.

Attucks's rediscovery and reinvention as an American hero is of a piece with the search for heroes and villains throughout our history, not just in the

Revolutionary Era. Trying to sift through the folkloric to find the historical in Attucks's life, as with other leading figures from the past, might strike some as un-American. In that sense, a man associated with the fight to be free has ironically been confined within the limits of a patriotic past.

Reproduced below is the standard printed form for a coroner's inquest that was used for Attucks, with details of the event written by hand and signed by all fourteen members of the coroner's jury for Suffolk County. Their finding was that the deceased "was wilfully and feloniously murdered" between nine and ten o'clock the night before "by the discharge of a Musket or Muskets loaded with Bulletts[,] two of which were shot thro' his body by a party of Soldiers to us unknown[,] then and there headed by Captain Thomas Preston of his Majesty's 29th Regiment of foot against the peace of our Sovereign Lord the King[,] his Crown & dignity and so by that means he came by his death as appears by evidence."

Michael Johnson, not Crispus Attucks, is the name on the form below. Robert Goddard had also referred to the individual in question as Michael Johnson in his deposition (see Document 16), but someone crossed out Johnson and wrote Crispus Attucks above it. By the time of the indictment, Attucks had replaced Johnson altogether. The name change only adds to the mystery surrounding the massacre. There are those who contend that Attucks used the other name as an alias because he was—or had been—an escaped slave. But then again, it could have been a case of mistaken identity, corrected within a matter of days.[58]

* * *

Document 17 The fourteen members of the jury convened for coroner Robert Peirpont on March 6, 1770 are listed at the top and each one signed below. Attucks was identified here as Michael Johnson. He would be correctly identified as Attucks in the subsequent grand jury indictment. Why he was first listed as Johnson remains a mystery, despite various attempts to explain the discrepancy. Courtesy of the Bostonian Society/Old State House Museum.

GRAND JURY INDICTMENT[59]

For an Englishman, a "trial by jury," proclaimed Blackstone in his Commentaries *just a year before the massacre, "is the grand bulwark of his liberties."[60] Trial by jury was a vote of confidence in the ability of untrained men to weigh evidence, understand the concept of reasonable doubt, distinguish the probable from the improbable, and know when circumstantial evidence might be sufficient to warrant a conviction. There might be no reliable eyewitnesses for jurors to rely on; irrefutable evidence was a rarity. And yet these "good and lawful" men, even if they did not themselves pronounce sentence, were expected to decide questions of life and death.*

Nothing better captures the English essence of colonial Massachusetts law than the impaneling of a grand jury, the handing down of an indictment, and a trial before yet another jury, all of the jurors drawn from freemen residing in the same venue where the alleged crime occurred. Going to trial on the basis of an "information"—the attorney general proceeding without a grand jury indictment—was legally correct but politically dangerous, in England as well as Massachusetts.

The Suffolk County grand jurors' indictment identified Preston, the eight accused soldiers, and four civilians by name. It singled out from among them William Warren as the primary perpetrator in the death of Crispus Attucks, with the others acting as accessories to the crime. Ultimately Warren would be acquitted; only Hugh Montgomery would be found guilty of shooting Attucks. Because the case dealt with a capital offense it was argued in the Supreme Court of Judicature, the highest court in the colony. In theory any jury verdict tendered there or decision reached by the court could be appealed to the king in council. But since that appeal could raise questions about provincial judicial autonomy, in practice the Court's decision would most likely stand. Similarly, in theory the Court could get around a jury verdict without formally vacating it, but Massachusetts judges did so reluctantly—again, like their counterparts in England.

Jurors hearing a murder case in both England and Massachusetts were expected to consider questions of law as well as fact. In the case of the accused in the massacre, they would decide on who shot whom (the "fact" in contention) and whether the shooting was, or was not, in self-defense (the question of law).[61] The massacre trials may have come at a "nadir of law, authority, and justice"[62] in Revolutionary Era Massachusetts, as Hiller Zobel put it, but the outcome was sound enough by the standards of the day. Rumors that Whitehall and Westminster intended to move future trials of imperial officials accused of capital offenses in the colonies to England only added to the growing list of American resentments and fears.

* * *

At his Majesty's Superiour Court of Judicature Court of Assize and General Gaol delivery, begun and held at Boston within and for the County of Suffolk, on the second Tuesday of March in the Tenth year of the Reign of George the third by the Grace of God of Great-Britain, France and Ireland, King, defender of the Faith &c.

The Jurors for the said Lord the King upon their oath present that Thomas Preston Esq., William Wemms Labourer, James Hartegan Labourer, William McCauley Labourer, Hugh White Labourer, Mathew Kilroy Labourer, William Warren Labourer, John Carroll Labourer & Hugh Montgomery Labourer, all now residents in Boston, in the County of Suffolk, Hammond Green Boat-Builder, Thomas Greenwood Labourer, Edward Manwaring Esquire[63] & John Munroe Gentleman, all of Boston aforesaid, not having the Fear of God before their eyes, but being moved and seduced by the Instigation of the devil and their own wicked hearts, did on the fifth day of this instant March at Boston, aforesaid within the County aforesaid, with force of arms feloniously, wilfully and of their malice aforethought assault one Crispus Attucks, then and there being in the peace of God, and of the said Lord the King, and the said William Warren, a certain hand gun of the value of twenty shillings, which the said William Warren then and there held in both his hands charged with Gun-powder and two leaden Bullets then and there feloniously, wilfully & of his malice aforethought, did shoot of and discharge at and against the said Crispus Attucks, and that the said William Warren, with the leaden Bullets as aforesaid out of the said hand gun then and there by force of the said Gun-powder so shot of and discharged as aforesaid, did then & there feloniously, wilfully and of his malice aforethought, strike, penetrate and wound the said Crispus Attucks in and upon the right Breast a little below the right pap of him the said Crispus, & in and upon the left Breast, a little below the left pap of him the said Crispus, thereby giving to him the said Crispus, with one of the bullets, aforesaid, so shot of and discharged as aforesaid, in and upon the right Breast a little below the right pap of him the said Crispus, one mortal wound of the depth of six inches & of the width of one inch, and also thereby giving to him the said Crispus, with the other Bullet aforesaid so shot of and discharged, by the said William Warren as aforesaid, in and upon the left Breast a little below the left pap of him the aforesaid Crispus one other mortal wound of the depth of six inches & of the width of one inch, of which said mortal wound the said Crispus Attucks then and there instantly died; and that the aforesaid Thomas Preston, Williams Wemms, Jame Hartegan, William McCauley, Hugh White, Mathew Kilroy, John Carroll, Hugh Montgomery, Hammond Green, Thomas Greenwood, Edward Manwaring & John Munroe, then & there feloniously, wilfully, and of their malice aforethought, were present, aiding, helping, abetting, comforting, assisting, and maintaining the said William Warren to do and contrive the Felony of murder aforesaid. And so the Jurors aforesaid upon their said oath do say that the said Thomas Preston, William Wemms, James Hartegan, William McCauley, Hugh White, Mathew Kilroy, William Warren, John Carroll, Hugh Montgomery, Hammond Green, Thomas Greenwood, Edward Manwaring, & John Munroe, then and there in manner and form aforesaid, feloniously, wilfully, and of their malice aforethought did kill and murder the said Crispus Attucks, against the peace of the said Lord the King, his Crown & Dignity.

> Jon[athan] Sewall Atty. Pro De Rege [attorney for the king]
> This is a true Bill
> W[illia]m Taylor Foreman
> August term 1770

And now the same Thomas Preston, Hammond Green, Thomas Greenwood, Edward Manwaring and John Munroe are brought and set to the Bar and arraigned, and upon their arraignment severally plead not guilty, and for Trial put themselves upon God and the Country.

> Att[ested to] Sam[ue]l Winthrop Clerk

To this Indictment the said William Wemms, James Hartegan, William McCauley, Hugh White, Mathew Kilroy, William Warren, John Carroll, Hugh Montgomery, being also brought and set to the Bar and arraigned, severally plead not guilty—and for trial put themselves upon GOD and country.

> Att[ested to] Sam[ue]l. Winthrop Clerk

A SHORT NARRATIVE [64]

On Tuesday, March 13, the Boston town meeting chose James Bowdoin, Joseph Warren, and Samuel Pemberton to "find out who those Persons are that were the Perpetrators of the horred Murders and Massacres done and committed in King Street." Charged with taking "such Examinations and Depositions as they can procure," they in turn entrusted that task to justices of the peace, who apparently had already begun taking statements.[65] Usually working in twos, those justices of the peace gathered depositions through March 24, ninety-six in all. They and the men who appointed them acted in response to a clamor that erupted during the town meeting the morning after the massacre, when those who claimed to have seen the incident demanded to have their accounts recorded.

The town meeting acted on its own, not waiting for approval from Hutchinson or the General Court. Town leaders believed that time was of the essence—that they had to act quickly to win the battle for public opinion well in advance of anything that might be determined in court. Consequently, they took the depositions that they thought might eventually be used at trial and immediately printed them as A Short Narrative. They cobbled the depositions into a rough story line. The first entries discussed events leading to the massacre, with those devoted to the massacre itself following. Then came depositions dealing with the aftermath.

By the time the justices of the peace began their work the 14th Regiment had left to join the 29th Regiment at Castle William. John Ruddock, a selectman and one of the justices of the peace who would take depositions, had been one of those who waited on Hutchinson in his role as a militia officer to inform the lieutenant governor that the town had formed an armed watch. He had also been a member of the even larger committee that waited on Hutchinson the day after the massacre to demand that the troops be removed from town. He would be involved in recording over forty depositions. Fellow justice of the peace Richard Dana, whose dislike for the presence of soldiers in Boston was well known, would take down even more.

Only a handful of those who gave depositions printed in the Short Narrative testified in the subsequent trials. For example, Samuel Drowne, whose deposition the town committeemen drew attention to in their introduction, was not called on to testify by either prosecution or defense in any of the trials. Henry Knox was one of the notable exceptions among Short Narrative deponents, testifying for the prosecution in Preston's trial and for the defense in the soldiers'. He was decidedly more sympathetic to the soldiers in court than he had been in his original statement, though in neither instance did he justify Preston's actions.

Depositions would be gathered to influence public opinion once again five years later, in the aftermath of the fighting at Lexington and Concord. In that instance the provincial convention, which had become, for all intents and purposes, the new government in the Bay Colony, printed the depositions of militiamen involved in the fighting to prove that British soldiers had attacked innocent Massachusetts civilians.[66] One could be forgiven for having a sense of déjà vu, both with the issues involved and the press tactics used to try to win over public opinion.

The committeemen who wrote the introduction to the 1770 Short Narrative, printed below, organized the depositions taken by the justices of the peace carefully. They did not let the depositions speak for themselves; instead, they laid out the details as they wanted readers to see them, starting with underlying causes. They presented an informal indictment of imperial policy, beginning with policies dating from 1763 and culminating in the slaughter on King Street seven years later. Governor Bernard and the customs commissioners come off as cowardly and conniving, misrepresenting Bostonians as incorrigibly lawless and calling for troops that were not needed.

The committeemen held the soldiers accountable as well, emphasizing that they had conspired against civilians, with the events beginning at Gray's ropewalk on March 2 as proof. "It appears very clearly," the committeemen claimed, that "there was a general combination among the soldiers of the 29th regiment at least, to commit some extraordinary act of violence upon the town." Preston, they noted, "is said to have ordered them to fire, and to have repeated that order"—their Short Narrative thereby underscoring what had already been written in the Boston Gazette account and pictured in Revere's engraving. That the committeemen could not tie the roving gangs of soldiers to events on King Street does not appear to have bothered them much. They asserted that the seemingly unconnected was in fact connected—that the sentry on duty at the custom house, the soldiers who came to relieve him, and others who *accosted civilians elsewhere in town wanted to shed Bostonian blood. The committeemen assigned very specific roles in this drama: townsmen as victims, soldiers as victimizers.*

* * *

It may be a proper introduction to this narrative, briefly to represent the state of things for some time previous to the said Massacre: And this seems necessary in order to the forming of a just idea of the causes of it.

At the end of the late war, in which this Province bore so distinguished a part, a happy union subsisted between Great-Britain and the Colonies. This was unfortunately interrupted by the Stamp-Act; but it was in some measure restored by the Repeal of it. It was again interrupted by other acts of parliament for taxing America; and by the appointment of a Board of Commissioners, in pursuance of an act, which by the face of it was made for the relief and encouragement of commerce, but which in its operation, it was apprehended, would have, and it has in fact had, a contrary effect. By the said act the said Commissioners were "to be resident in some convenient part of his Majesty's dominions in America."—This must be understood to be in some part convenient for the whole.—But it does not appear that, in fixing the place of their residence, the convenience of the whole was at all consulted, for Boston being very far from the centre of the colonies, could not be the place most convenient for the whole.—Judging by the act, it may seem this town was intended to be favored, by the Commissioners being appointed to reside here; and that the consequence of that residence would be the relief and encouragement of commerce: but the reverse has been the constant and uniform effect of it: So that the commerce of the town, from the embarrassments in which it has been lately involved, is greatly reduced. For the particulars on this head, see the state of the trade not long since drawn up and transmitted to England by the merchants of Boston.[67]

The residence of the Commissioners here, has been detrimental not only to the commerce, but to the political interests of the town and province; and not only so, but we can trace from it the causes of the late horrid massacre. Soon after their arrival here in November 1767, instead of confining themselves to the proper business of their office, they became partizans of Governor Bernard in his political schemes; and had the weakness and temerity to infringe upon one of the most essential rights of the house of commons of this province—that of giving their votes with freedom, not being accountable therefor but to their constituents. One of the members of that house, Capt. Timothy Folgier, having voted in some affair contrary to the mind of the said Commissioners, was for so doing dismissed from the office he held under them.

These proceedings of theirs, the difficulty of access to them on office-business, and a supercilious behavior, rendered them disgustful to people in general, who in consequence thereof treated them with neglect. This probably stimulated them to resent it; and to make their resentment felt, they and their coadjutor, Governor Bernard, made such representations to his Majesty's ministers as they thought best calculated to bring the displeasure of the nation upon the town and province: and in order that those representations might have the more weight, they are said to have contrived and executed plans for exciting disturbances and tumults, which otherwise would probably never have existed; and when excited, to have transmitted to the ministry the most exaggerated accounts of them.

These particulars of their conduct in his Majesty's Council of this province have fully laid open in their proceeding in council, and in their address to General Gage, in July and October 1768; and in their letter to Lord Hillsborough of the 15th of April, 1769.—Unfortunately for us, they have been too successful in their said representations, which in conjunction with Governor Bernard's, have occasioned his Majesty's faithful subjects of this town and province to be treated as enemies and rebels, by an invasion of the town by sea and land: to which the approaches were made with all the circumspection usual where a vigorous opposition is expected. While the town was surrounded by a considerable number of his Majesty's ships of war, two regiments landed and took possession of it; and to support these, two other regiments arrived some time after from Ireland: one of which landed at Castle Island, and the other in the town.

Thus were we, in aggravation of our other embarrassments, embarrassed with troops, forced upon us contrary to our inclination—contrary to the spirit of Magna Charta—contrary to the very letter of the Bill of Rights, in which it is declared, that the raising or keeping a standing army within the kingdom in time of peace, unless it be with the consent of parliament, is against the law—and without the desire of the civil magistrates, to aid whom was the pretence for sending the troops hither: who were quartered in the town in direct violation of an act of parliament for quartering troops in America: and all this in consequence of the representations of the said Commissioners and the said Governor, as appears by their memorials and letters lately published.

As they were the procuring cause of troops being sent hither, they must therefore be the remote and a blameable cause of all the disturbances and bloodshed that have taken place in consequence of that Measure.

But we shall leave them to their own reflections, after observing, that as they had some months before the arrival of the troops, under pretence of safety to their persons, retired from town to the Castle, so after the arrival of the troops, and their being quartered in the town, they thought proper to return: having answered, as they doubtless thought, the purpose of their voluntary flight.

We shall next attend the conduct of the troops, and to some circumstances relative to them.—Governor Bernard without consulting the Council, having given up the State-house to the troops at their landing, they took possession of the chambers, where the representatives of the province and the courts of law held their meetings; and (except the council-chamber) of all other parts of that house: in which they continued a considerable time, to the great annoyance of those courts while they sat, and of the merchants and gentlemen of the town, who had always made the lower floor of it their exchange. They had a right to do so, as the property of it was in the town: but they were deprived of that right by mere power.—The said Governor soon after, by every stratagem and by every method but a forcibly entry, endeavored to get possession of the manufactory-house, to make a barrack of it, for the troops: and for that purpose caused it to be besieged by the troops, and the people in it to be used very cruelly; which extraordinary proceedings created universal uneasiness, arising from the apprehension; that the troops under the influence of such a man would be employed to effect the most dangerous purposes: but failing of that, other houses were procured, in which, contrary to act of parliament, he caused the troops to be quartered. After their quarters were settled, the main guard was posted at one of the said houses, directly opposite to, and not twelve yards from, the State-house, (where the General Court, and all the Law Courts for the County were held), with two field pieces pointed to the State-house. This situation of the main guard and field pieces seemed to indicate an attack upon the constitution, and a defiance of law; and to be intended to affront the legislative and executive authority of the province.

The General Court, at the first session after the arrival of the troops, viewed it in this light, and applied to Governor Bernard to cause such a nusance to be removed; but to no purpose. Disgusted at such an indignity, and at the appearance of being under duresse, they refused to do business in such circumstances; and in consequence thereof were adjourned to Cambridge, to the great inconvenience of the members.

Besides this, the challenging the inhabitants by centinels posted in all parts of the town before the lodgings of officers, which (for about six months, while it lasted), occasioned many quarrels and great uneasiness—

Capt. Wilson's, of the 59th, exciting the negroes of the town to take away their masters' lives and property, and repair to the army for protection, which was fully proved against him.—The attack of a party of soldiers on some of the magistrates of the town—the repeated rescues of soldiers from peace officers—the firing of a loaded musket in a public street, to the endangering of a great number of peaceable inhabitants—the frequent wounding of persons by their bayonets and cutlasses, and the numerous instances of bad behavior in the soldiery, made us early sensible, that the troops were not sent here for any benefit to the town or province, and that we had no good to expect from such conservators of the peace.

It was not expected however, that such an outrage and massacre, as happened here on the evening of the fifth instant, would have been perpetrated. There were then killed and wounded, by a discharge of musketry, eleven of his Majesty's subjects, viz.:

Mr. Samuel Gray, killed on the spot by a ball entering his head.

Crispus Attucks, a molatto, killed on the spot, two balls entering his breast.

Mr. James Caldwell, killed on the spot, by two balls entering his back.

Mr. Samuel Maverick, a youth of seventeen years of age, mortally wounded: he died the next morning.

Mr. Patrick Carr mortally wounded: he died the 14th instant.

Christopher Monk and John Clark, youths about seventeen years of age, dangerously wounded. It is apprehended they will die.

Mr. Edward Payne, merchant, standing at his door: wounded.

Messrs. John Green, Robert Patterson, and David Parker: all dangerously wounded.

The actors in this dreadful tragedy were a party of soldiers commanded by Capt. Preston of the 29th regiment. This party, including the Captain, consisted of eight, who are all committed to jail.

There are depositions in this affair which mention, that several guns were fired at the same time from the Custom-House; before which this shocking scene was exhibited. Into this matter inquisition is now making.—In the mean time it may be proper to insert here the substance of some of those depositions.

Benjamin Frizell, on the evening of the 5th of March, having taken his station near the west corner of the Custom-House in Kingstreet, before and at the time of the soldiers firing their guns, declares (among other things) that the first discharge was only of one gun, the next of two guns, upon which he the deponent thinks he saw a man stumble: the third discharge was of three guns, upon which he thinks he saw two men fall, and immediately after were discharged five guns, two of which were by soldiers on his right hand; *the other three, as appeared to the deponent, were discharged from the balcony, or the chamber window of the* CUSTOM-HOUSE, *the flashes appearing on the left hand, and higher than the right hand flashes appeared to be, and of which the deponent was very sensible,* although his eyes were much turned to the soldiers, who were all on his right hand.

Gillam Bass, being in King-street at the same time, declares that they (the party of soldiers from the main guard) posted themselves between the custom-house door and the west corner of it; and in a few minutes began to fire upon the people: *Two or three of the flashes so high above the rest, that he the deponent verily believes they must have come from the* CUSTOM-HOUSE *windows.*

Jeremiah Allen declares, that in the evening of the 5th day of March current, being at about nine o'clock in the front chamber of the house occupied by Col. Ingersoll in King-street, he heard some guns fired, which occasioned his going into the balcony of the said house.—That when he was in the said balcony in company with Mr. William Molineux jun'r. and John Simpson, he heard the discharge of four or five guns, the flashes of which appeared to be to the westward of the centry box, and immediately after, he the deponent *heard two or three more guns and saw the flashes thereof from out of the house, now called the* CUSTOM-HOUSE, *as they evidently appeared to him*, and which he said the deponent at the same time declared to the aforesaid Molineux and Simpson, being then near him, *saying to them*, (at the same time pointing his hand toward the custom-house), *there they are out of the custom-house.*

George Coster, being in King-street at the time above-mentioned, declares that in five or six minutes after he stopped, he heard the word of command given to the soldiers *fire*; upon which one gun was fired, which did no execution, as the deponent observed; about half a minute after two guns, one of which killed Samuel Gray, a ropemaker, the other a molatto man, between which two men the deponent stood, after this the deponent heard the discharge of four or five guns more, by the soldiers; immediately after which the *deponent heard the discharge of two guns or pistols, from an open window of the middle story of the* CUSTOM-HOUSE, near to the place where the centry box is placed, and being but a small distance from the window, he heard the people from within speak and laugh, and soon after saw the casement lowered down; and after which the deponent assisted others in carrying off one of the corpses.

Cato, a negro man, servant to Tuthill Hubbart, Esq., declares that on Monday evening the 5th of March current, on hearing the cry of fire, he ran into Kingstreet, where he saw a number of people assembled before the Custom-House; that he stood near the centry-box and saw the soldiers fire on the people, who stood in the middle of said street; directly after which *he saw two flashes of guns, one quick upon the other, from the chamber window of the* CUSTOM-HOUSE; and that after the firing was all over, while the people were carrying away the dead and wounded, *he saw the Custom-House door opened, and several soldiers (one of whom had a cutlass), go into the Custom-House* and shut the door after them.

Benjamin Andrews declares, that being desired by the committee of enquiry to take the ranges of the holes made by the musket balls, in two houses nearly opposite the Custom-House, he finds the bullet hole in the entry-door post of Mr. Payne's house (and which grazed the edge of the door, before it enter'd the post, where it lodged, two and a half inches deep), *ranges just under the stool of the westernmost lower chamber window of the* CUSTOM-HOUSE.

Samuel Drowne, towards the end of his deposition (which contains a pretty full account of the proceedings of the soldiers on the evening of the 5th instant) declares, that *he saw the flashes of two guns fired from the* CUSTOM-HOUSE, *one of which was out of a window of the chamber westward of the balcony, and the other from the balcony; the gun (which he clearly discerned) being pointed through the ballisters, and the person who held the gun, in a stooping posture withdrew himself into the house, having a handkerchief or some kind of cloth over his face.*

These depositions show clearly that a number of guns were fired from the Custom-House.—As this affair is now enquiring into, all the notice we shall take of it is, that it distinguishes the actors in it into Street-Actors and House-Actors; which is necessary to be observed.

What gave occasion to the melancholy event of that evening seems to have been this. A difference having happened near Mr. Gray's ropewalk, between a soldier and a man belonging to it, the soldier challenged the ropemakers to a boxing match. The challenge was accepted by one of them, and the soldier worsted. He ran to the barrack in the neighbourhood, and returned with several of his companions. The fray was renewed, and the soldiers were driven off. They soon returned, with recruits and were again worsted. This happened several times, till at length a considerable body of soldiers was collected, and they also were driven off, the ropemakers having been joined by their brethren of the contiguous ropewalks. By this time Mr. Gray being alarmed interposed, and with the assistance of some gentlemen prevented any further disturbance. To satisfy the soldiers and punish the man who had been the occasion of the first difference, and as an example to the rest, he turned him out of his services; and waited on Col. Dalrymple, the commanding officer of the troops, and with him concerted measures for preventing further mischief. Though this affair ended thus, it made a strong impression on the minds of the soldiers in general, who thought the honor of the regiment concerned to revenge those repeated repulses. For this purpose they seem to have formed a combination to commit some outrage upon the inhabitants of the town indiscriminately; and this was to be done on the evening of the 5th instant or soon after: as appears by the depositions of the following persons, viz.:

William Newhall declares, that on Thursday night the 1st of March instant, he met four soldiers of the 29th regiment, and that he heard them say *there were a great many that would eat their dinners on Monday next, that should not eat any on Tuesday.*

Daniel Calfe declares, that on Sunday evening of the 3d of March, a camp-woman, wife to James McDeed a grenadier of the 29th, came into his father's shop, and the people talking about the affrays at the ropewalks, and blaming the soldiers for the part they had acted in it, the woman said, the soldiers were in the right; adding, *that before Tuesday or Wednesday night they would wet their swords or bayonets in New-England people's blood.*

Mary Brailsford declares, that on Sabbath evening the 4th of March instant, a soldier came to the house of Mr. Amos Thayer, where she then was. He desiring to speak with Mr. Thayer, was told by Mrs. Mary Thayer, that her brother was engaged, and could not be spoke with. He said, your brother as you call him, is a man I have a great regard for, and I came on purpose to tell him to keep in his house, for *before Tuesday night next at Twelve o'clock, there will be a great deal of bloodshed, and a great many lives lost*: and added, that he came out of a particular regard to her brother to advise him to keep in his house for then he would be out of harm's way. He said, your brother knows me very well: my name is Charles Malone. He then went away.—Of the same import, and in confirmation of this declaration, are the depositions of Mary Thayer and Asa Copeland, who both live with Mr. Thayer, and heard what the soldier said as abovementioned. It is also confirmed by the deposition of Nicholas Ferriter.

Jane Usher declares, that about 9 o'clock on monday morning the 5th of March current, from a window she saw two persons in the habit of soldiers, one of whom being on horse back appeared to be an officer's servant. The person on the horse first spoke to the other, but what he said, she is not able to say, though the window was open, and she not more than twenty feet distant: the other replied, *He hoped he should see blood enough spilt before morning.*

Matthew Adams declares, that on Monday evening the 5th of March instant, between the hours of 7 and 8 o'clock, he went to the house of corporal Pershall of the 29th regiment, near Quaker Lane, where he saw the corporal and his wife, with one of the fifers of said regiment. When he had got what he went for, and was coming away, the corporal called him back, and desired him with great earnestness to go home to his master's house as soon as business was over, and not to be abroad on any account that might in particular, for *the soldiers were determined to be revenged on the ropewalk people; and that much mischief would be done.* Upon which the fifer (about eighteen or nineteen years of age) said, *he hoped in God they would burn the town down.* On this he left the house, and the said corporal called after him again, and begged he would mind what he said to him.

Caleb Swan declares, that on monday night, the 5th of March instant, at the time of the bells ringing for fire, he heard a woman's voice, whom he knew to be the supposed wife of one Montgomery, a grenadier of the 29th regiment, standing at her door, *and heard her say, it was not fire; the town was too haughty and too proud; and that many of their arses would be laid low before the morning.*

Margaret Swansborough declares, that a freewoman named Black Peg, who has kept much with the soldiers, on hearing the disturbances on monday evening the 5th instant said, *the soldiers were not to be trod upon by the inhabitants, but would know before morning, whether they or the inhabitants were to be masters.*

Joseph Hooton, junr. declares, that coming from the South-end of Boston on monday evening the 5th of March instant, against Dr. Sewall's meeting he heard a great noise and tumult, with the cry of murder often repeated. Proceeding towards the town-house he was passed by several soldiers running that way, with naked cutlasses and bayonets in their hands. He asked one of them what was the matter, and was answered by him, by God you shall all know what is the matter soon. Between 9 and 10 o'clock he went into King-street, and was present at the tragical scene exhibited near the Custom-house; as particularly set forth in his deposition.

Mrs. Mary Russell declares, that John Brailsford a private soldier of the *fourteenth* regiment, who had frequently been employed by her (when he was ordered with his company to the Castle, in consequence of the murders committed by the soldiers on the evening of the 5th of March), coming to the deponent's house declared, that THEIR *regiment were* ORDERED *to hold themselves in readiness, and accordingly was ready* THAT EVENING, *upon the inhabitants firing on the soldiery, to come to the assistance of the soldiery.* On which she asked him, if he would have fired upon any of the inhabitants of this town. To which he replied, yes, if he had orders; but that if he saw Mr. Russell, he would have fired wide of him. He also said, *it's well there was no gun fired by the Inhabitants, for had there been,* WE *should have come to the soldiers assistance.*

By the foregoing depositions it appears very clearly, there was a general combination among the soldiers of the 29th regiment at least, to commit some extraordinary act of violence upon the town; that if the inhabitants attempted to repel it by firing even one gun upon those soldiers, the 14th regiment were ordered to be in readiness to assist them; and that on the late butchery in King-street they actually were ready for that purpose, had a single gun been fired on the perpetrators of it.

It appears by a variety of depositions, that on the same evening between the hours of six and half after nine (at which time the firing began), many persons, without the least provocation, were in various parts of the town insulted and abused by parties of armed soldiers patrolling the streets; particularly—

Mr. Robert Peirpont declares, that between the hours of 7 and 8 in the same evening, three armed soldiers passing him, one of them who had a bayonet gave him a back-handed stroke with it. On complaint of this treatment, he said the deponent should soon hear more of it, and threatened him very hard.

Mr. Henry Bass declares, that at 9 o'clock, a party of soldiers came out of Draper's alley, leading to and from Murray's barracks, and they being armed with large naked cutlasses, made at every body coming in their way, cutting and slashing, and that he himself very narrowly escaped receiving a cut from the foremost of them, who pursued him.

Samuel Atwood, declares, that 10 or 12 soldiers armed with drawn cutlasses, bolted out of the alley leading from Murray's barracks into dock-square, and met the deponent, who asked them if they intended to murder people? they answered, yes, by God, root and branch; saying, here is one of them; with that one of them struck the deponent with a club, which was repeated by another. The deponent being unarmed turned to go off, and he received a wound on the left shoulder, which reached the bone, disabled him, and gave him much pain. Having gone a few steps the deponent met *two officers*, and asked them, gentlemen, what is the matter? *They answered, you will see by and by*; and as he passed by Col. Jackson's he heard the cry, turn out the guards.

Capt. James Kirkwood, declares, that about 9 o'clock in the evening of the 5th day of March current, he was going by Murray's barracks: hearing a noise he stopt at Mr. Rhoads's door, opposite the said barracks, where said Rhoads was standing, and stood some time, and saw the soldiers coming out of the yard from the barracks, armed with cutlasses and bayonets. And rushing thro' Boylstone's alley into cornhill, two officers, viz. Lieuts. Minchin and Dickson, came out of the mess house, and said to the soldiers, my lads, come into the barracks and don't hurt the inhabitants, and then retir'd into the mess house. Soon after they came to the door again, and found the soldiers in the yard; and directly upon it, *Ensign Mall* came to the gate of the barrack yard and *said to the soldiers, turn out and I will stand by you*; this he repeated frequently, adding, *kill them! stick them! knock them down, run your bayonets thro' them*, with a great deal of language of like import. Upon which a great number of soldiers came out of the barracks, with naked cutlasses, *headed by said Mall*, and went through the aforesaid alley; that some officers came & got the soldiers into their barracks, and that

Mall with his sword or cutlass drawn in his hand, as often had them out again, but were at last drove into their barracks by the aforesaid Minchin and Dickson.

Mr. Henry Rhoads's declaration agrees with Captain Kirkwood's.

Mr. Matthias King, of Halifax, in Nov Scotia, declares, that in the evening of the fifth day of March instant, about nine of the clock, he was at his lodgings at Mrs. Torrey's near the town pump, and heard the bells ring and the cry of fire; upon which he went to the door and saw several soldiers come round the south side of the town house, armed with bayonets, and something which he took to be broad swords; that one of those people came up almost to him and Mr. Bartholomew Kneeland; and that they had but just time to shut the door upon him; otherwise he is well assured they must have fell victims to their boundless cruelty. He afterwards went into the upper chamber of the said house, and was looking out of the window *when the drum and the guard went to the barrack,* and he saw one of the guards kneel and present his piece, with a bayonet fixed, and heard him swear he would fire upon a parcel of boys who were then in the street, but he did not: He further declares, that *when the body of troops was drawn up before the guard house (which was presently after the massacre) he heard an officer say to another, that this was fine work, and just what he wanted;* but in the hurry he could not see him, so as to know him again.

Robert Polley declares, that on monday evening, the 5th instant, as he was going home, he observed about ten persons standing near Mr. Taylor's door, after standing there a small space of time, he went with them towards Boylston's alley, opposite to Murray's barracks; we met in the alley about eight or nine arm'd soldiers, they assaulted us, and gave us a great deal of abusive language, we then drove them back to the barracks with sticks only; we looked for stones or bricks, but could find none, the ground being covered with snow; some of the lads dispersed, and he, the said Polley, with a few others were returning peaceably home, when we met about nine or ten other soldiers armed: one of them said, "Where are the sons of bitches": They struck at several persons in the street, and went towards the head of the alley. Two officers came and endeavored to get them into their barracks; one of the lads proposed to ring the bell; the soldiers went thro' the alley, and the boys huzza'd and said they were gone through royal exchange into Kingstreet.

Samuel Drowne declares that, about nine of the clock of the evening of the fifth of March current, standing at his own door in Cornhill, he saw about 14 or 15 soldiers of the 29th regiment, who came from Murray's barracks, arm'd with naked cutlasses, swords, &c. and came upon the inhabitants of the town, then standing or walking in Cornhill, and abused some, and violently assaulted others as they met them; most of whom were without so much as a stick in their hand to defend themselves, as he very clearly could discern, it being moon light, and himself being one of the assaulted persons. All or most of the said soldiers he saw go into King-street (some of them through Royal Exchange lane), and there followed them, and soon discovered them to be quarrelling and fighting with the people whom they saw there, which he thinks were not more than a dozen, when the soldiers came first, armed as aforesaid. Of those dozen people, the most of them were gentlemen, standing together a little below the Town-House, upon the exchange. At the appearance of those soldiers so arm'd, the most of the twelve persons went off, some of them being first assaulted.

The violent proceedings of this party, and their going into King-street, "quarrelling and fighting with the people whom they saw there" (mentioned in Mr. Drowne's deposition), was immediately introductory to the grand catastrophe.

These assailants, who issued from Murray's barracks (so called), after attacking and wounding divers persons in Cornhill, as above mentioned, being armed, proceeded (most of them) up the Royal Exchange lane into King-street; where making a short stop, and after assaulting and driving away the few they met there, they brandished their arms and cried out, Where are the Boogers! where are the Cowards! At this time there were very few persons in the street beside themselves.—This party in proceeding from the Exchange lane into King-street, must pass the centry posted at the westerly corner of the Custom House, which butts on that lane and fronts on that street. This is needful to be mentioned, as near that spot and in that street the bloody tragedy was acted, and the street actors in it were stationed: Their station being but a few feet from the front side of the said Custom House.—The outrageous behavior and the threats of the said party occasioned the ringing of the meeting house bell near the head of King-street, which bell ringing quick as for fire, it presently brought out a number of the inhabitants, who being soon sensible of the occasion of it, were naturally led to King-street, where the said party had made a stop but a little while before: and where their stopping had drawn together a number of boys, round the centry at the Custom-House. Whether the boys mistook the centry for one of the said party, and thence took occasion to differ with him, or whether he first affronted them, which is affirmed in several depositions,—however that may be, there was much foul language between them: and some of them, in consequence of his pushing at them with his bayonet, threw snowballs at him:[68] which occasioned him to knock hastily at the door of the Custom-House. From hence two persons thereupon proceeded immediately to the main guard, which was posted (opposite the State-house) at a small distance near the head of the said street. The officer on guard was Capt. Preston, who with seven or eight soldiers with fire arms, and charged bayonets, issued from the guard house, and in great haste posted himself and his soldiers in front of the Custom House near the corner aforesaid. In passing to this station the soldiers pushed several persons with their bayonets, driving through the people in so rough a manner that it appeared they intended to create a disturbance. This occasioned some snow-balls to be thrown at them which seems to have been the only provocation that was given. Mr. Knox (between whom and Capt. Preston there was some conversation on the spot) declares, that while he was talking with Capt. Preston, the soldiers of his detachment had attacked the people with their bayonets; and that there was not the least provocation given to Capt. Preston, or his party: the backs of the people being toward them when the people were attacked. He also declares, that Capt. Preston seemed to be in great haste and much agitated; and that, according to his opinion, there were not then present in Kingstreet above seventy or eighty persons at the extent.

The said party was formed into a half circle; and within a short time after they had been posted at the Custom-House, began to fire upon the people.

Captain Preston is said to have ordered them to fire, and to have repeated that order. One gun was fired first: then others in succession, and with deliberation, till ten or a dozen guns were fired; or till that number of discharges were made from the guns that were fired. By which means eleven persons were killed and wounded, as above represented.

These facts with divers circumstances attending them, are supported by the depositions of a considerable number of persons, and among others of the following viz.:—Messir's. Henry Bass[,] Samuel Atwood, Samuel Drowne, James Kirkwood, Robert Polley, Samuel Condon, Daniel Usher, Josiah Simpson, Henry Knox, Gillam Bass, John Hickling, Richard Palmes, Benjamin Frizzel, and others; whose depositions are in the appendix.

Soon after the firing, a party from the main guard went with a drum to Murray's and the other barracks, beating an alarm as they went, which, with the firing, had the effect of a signal for action. Whereupon all the soldiers of the 29th regiment, or the main body of them, appeared in Kingstreet under arms; and seemed bent on a further massacre of the inhabitants, which was with great difficulty prevented. They were drawn up between the State House and main guard: their lines extending across the street and facing down Kingstreet, where the town-people were assembled. The first line kneeled; and the whole of the first platoon presented their guns ready to fire, as soon as the word should be given. They continued in that posture for a considerable time. But by the good Providence of God they were restrained from firing.

That they went into Kingstreet with such a disposition will appear probable by the two following depositions.

Mrs. Mary Gardiner, living in Atkinson street, declares, that on Monday evening the 5th of March current, and before the guns fired in Kingstreet, there were a number of soldiers assembled from Green's barracks towards the street, and opposite to her gate; that they stood very still until the guns were fired in Kingstreet, then they clapped their hands and gave a cheer, saying, *this is all that we want.* They ran to their barrack, and came out again in a few minutes, all with their arms, and ran towards Kingstreet.

William Fallass declares, that (after the murder in Kingstreet) on the evening of the 5th instant, upon his return home he had occasion to stop opposite to the lane leading to Green's barracks, and while he stood there, the soldiers rushed by him with their arms, towards Kingstreet, saying, *this is our time or chance*: and that he never saw men or dogs so greedy for their prey as those soldiers seemed to be, and the sergeants could hardly keep them in their ranks.

These circumstances with those already mentioned, amount to a clear proof of a combination among them to commit some outrage upon the town on that evening; and that after the enormous one committed in Kingstreet, they intended to add to the horror of that night by making a further slaughter.

At the time Capt. Preston's party issued from the main guard, there were in Kingstreet about two hundred persons, and those were collected there by the ringing of the bell in consequence of the violences of another party, that had been there a very little while before. When Captain Preston had got to the Custom-house, so great a part of the people dispersed at sight of the soldiers, that not more than twenty or thirty then remained in Kingstreet, as Mr. Drowne declares, and at the time of the firing not seventy, as Mr. Palmes thinks.

But after the firing, and when the slaughter was known, which occasioned the ringing of all the bells of the town, a large body of the inhabitants soon assembled in Kingstreet, and continued there the whole time the 29th regiment was there under arms, and would not retire till that regiment, and all the soldiers that appeared were ordered, and actually went, to their barracks: after which, having been assured by the Lieutenant-Governor, and a number of the civil magistrates present, that every legal step should be taken to bring the criminals to justice, they gradually dispersed. For some time the appearance of things were dismal. The soldiers outrageous on the one hand, and the inhabitants justly incensed against them on the other: both parties seemed disposed to come to action. In this case the consequences would have been terrible. But by the interposition of his Honor, some of his Majesty's council, a number of civil magistrates, and other gentlemen of weight and influence, who all endeavored to calm and pacify the people, and by the two principal offices interposing their authority with regard to the soldiers, there was happily no further bloodshed ensued; and by two o'clock the town was restored to a tolerable state of quiet. About that time, Capt. Preston, and a few hours after, the party that had fired, were committed to safe custody.

One happy effect has arisen from this melancholy affair, and it is the general voice of the town and province it may be a lasting one—All the troops are removed from the town.—They are quartered for the present in the barracks at Castle-Island; from whence it is hoped they will have a speedy order to remove entirely out of the province, together with those persons who were the occasion of their coming hither.

*A FAIR ACCOUNT*⁶⁹

Despite the criticism, then and since, of Thomas Hutchinson's political skills, the lieutenant governor was astute enough to realize that the court of public opinion could be as powerful as a court of law, and that he could not leave that arena to his opponents. James Murray, a justice of the peace in sympathy with him, began taking depositions on the same day as others acting for the town. Hutchinson hoped those statements, brought together as A Fair Account, *could somehow neutralize the effects of what became* A Short Narrative.*

Interestingly enough, A Fair Account *challenged the validity of* A Short Narrative *and yet it started the numbering of its depositions at ninety-seven in a futile attempt to make it seem that it simply extended the town's record. In it Hutchinson assembled twenty-five depositions from twenty-seven deponents in all—five civilians and twenty-two soldiers. As in the* Short Narrative, *a long introduction designed to shape readers' impressions preceded the depositions in* A Fair Account. *Likewise, deeper causes were located years before, but there the similarity ends. As the* Fair Account *told it, those underlying causes were not traceable to flaws in the navigation system but, instead, to selfish Bostonians who had wrongly denied Parliament's authority to regulate their trade. Petty, meanspirited, even treasonous, Bostonians had harassed the soldiers from the moment they came ashore.*

Whoever wrote the preface to A Fair Account *concurred with the towns-men behind* A Short Narrative *that the March 2 fight at Gray's ropewalk led to the confrontation on King Street the following Monday night. According to this rendition, however, the soldiers had been lured into an ambush of fists and clubs. Gangs of local ruffians disingenuously turned the soldiers' acts of self-defense on March 5 into a pretext to roam the streets, indiscriminately waylaying and accosting any soldiers who crossed their path—officers or enlisted men, members of the 29th or the 14th Regiment; it did not matter to Boston's countless hoodlums.*

The soldiers' depositions in particular corroborated each other in claiming that snarling Bostonians had shouted, "Murder, kill all the dogs" in their desire to drive the "bloody-back rascals" out of town. But not one could speak as a witness to what Preston and the men with him outside the custom house had done. A few testified that they heard "fire and be damned" from a mob that numbered in the hundreds, but none could identify any individual who committed a violent or provocative act. To that extent, A Fair Account *suffered from the same evidentiary failings as* A Short Narrative.

✶ ✶ ✶

WHOEVER has conversed much with those who have been lately at Boston must know that the arrival of the King's troops at that town in 1768 was exceedingly disgustful to all that part of the people who call themselves *the sons of liberty*, and deny the authority of the British parliament to pass the late acts for imposing duties upon certain articles of trade imported into America, and who certainly form a great majority of the people in that town, though perhaps not of the persons of the best fortunes and most respectable characters in the place. Whether they are right in this opinion, I shall not here inquire. But it ought to be clear beyond the possibility of a doubt on the side of the Americans, in order to justify the violent measures that have been taken in Boston to carry it into practice, which have amounted to little less than a forcible opposition to those acts of parliament, or, in the language of the statute of treason, a levying of war against the King.[70]

And in the conduct of this opposition (even if we suppose for a moment that the opposition itself could be justified upon the principles of the law of nature, which in some cases of extreme necessity allows of a resistance against illegal exercises of power), they have not behaved with that openness and candour that would have been suitable to the dignity of their pretensions, but have persecuted both those of their own countrymen who presumed to differ from them in opinion, and the King's troops who were sent thither to preserve the public peace, with the utmost malice and injustice. It has been deemed a crime to affirm that the authority of the British parliament was supreme in all respects throughout all the dominions of the crown of Great Britain, and that a forcible resistance to the acts established by it was unlawful; and those bold and honest men who have ventured to affirm this have been stigmatized by the name of *tories*, as persons insensible of public liberty and devoted to the old exploded doctrines of passive obedience and non-resistance.

And it has been made a crime of a still blacker die to continue a commercial intercourse with the mother-country, or to refuse to enter into their non-importation agreements, or illegal combinations. And those who have presumed to do so, in the pursuit of their usual and lawful callings, and in compliance with what they took to be their duty to the public as obedient subjects of the crown, have been marked out by advertisements in their public news-papers as traitors and enemies to their country and fit victims to the fury of a licentious and deluded populace.

And as to the King's troops, who were sent thither in October 1768, they have been treated by these *sons of liberty* and *well-disposed* persons (as they stile themselves) with a degree of cruelty that could not have been justified, and probably would not have been practised by them, towards prisoners of war of the nation with which we are oftenest at enmity. For they not only, upon the first arrival of these troops at Boston, did every thing in their power to prevent their having quarters assigned them, and to oblige them to continue in camp, though the rigour of the winter-season was beginning to be felt; but they have ever since been traducing them with the most scurrilous and abusive language, and harrassing them with vexatious actions at law for trifling trespasses occasioned by provocations designedly given by themselves in order to draw them into difficulties; and with malicious accusations, oftentimes intirely false and always overcharged; and with every other low and spiteful device that rage and disappointment at the check they received in their design by the arrival of those regiments at Boston, could suggest.

I must add also the perversion of justice in the most flagrant manner in their courts of judicature, so far as the juries were concerned in the administration of it, by finding verdicts upon almost any evidence against a soldier, while, if the soldier was the complaining party, no proof was deemed to be sufficient to produce one *for* him.

These are facts of such notoriety, that it is presumed the sons of liberty themselves will hardly think to deny them; but will rather endeavour to excuse and vindicate their conduct upon the principles of jesuitical morality and the lawfulness of using any means to obtain so glorious an end as the recovery of public liberty. But if they should deny them, I must refer the reader to the testimony of all the Englishmen, of every rank and profession of life, that have been at Boston within the last two years, for the proof of them.

This ill disposition of the inhabitants of Boston towards the King's troops had gone on increasing from the time of their arrival there till the late Unhappy Disturbance by which some of them have lost their lives, and had proceeded to such a length that, as two gentlemen of the 29th regiment, Lieutenant Dickson and Ensign St. Clair, declare in their deposition[71] it was become unsafe for an officer or soldier to walk the streets, and that they had been desired to take care of themselves by an inhabitant of the town, who had heard several of the people say that they would kill all the officers in town, and that after that they should be able to manage the soldiers by giving them land and settling them in the back parts of the province.

Such was the temper of the people with respect to the King's troops for some time before the late accident; and it seems to have occasioned a pretty strong degree of resentment in the latter, and perhaps made them not unwilling to embrace any opportunity that chance might offer, consistently with their duty and the law, to take some revenge on those who had so long ill-treated them. That it should have such an effect, is probable in itself from the natural passions of mankind; and that it did produce this natural resentment, may be collected from some of the depositions in the Boston Narrative, particularly those of Mary Thayer and Bartholomew Broaders, supposing those testimonies, which carry in them strong marks of a party bias,[72] deserve in this particular to be believed: but I do not think it can be inferred from their conduct on the 5th of March, or, as the Boston narrative calls it, the horrid Massacre. The natural desire of defending themselves, and the sense of the duty incumbent upon them in that unhappy moment to repel force by force in order to defend a centinel's post which they were called upon to guard, and which when attacked by at least an hundred people, armed with bludgeons, sticks, and cutlasses, will be sufficient to account for their firing on the assailants on that occasion without any mixture of revenge. The circumstances of this unfortunate affair, and of the previous quarrel with the rope-makers, which gave rise to it, so far as they can be collected from the Boston Narrative (to which I refer the reader for them) and those printed at the end of this tract, seem to have been as follows:

On Friday the 2d of March last, between ten and eleven o'clock in the forenoon, as three soldiers of the 29th regiment of foot were passing by Mr. John Gray's rope-walk in a peaceable and inoffensive manner, one Green a rope-maker, who as at work there, asked one of the soldiers whether he wanted work; to which the soldier answered that he did; "Then," said Green, "you shall go and clean my necessary-house." (See Samuel Bostwick's evidence.[73]) This insult provoked the soldier to use a good deal of ill language in return, and to swear that he would have satisfaction for it. Upon this one of the rope-makers, named Nicholas Ferriter, came up to him and tripped up his heels, and, after he was fallen, another of them, named John Wilson, took his sword from him, (which, Ferriter says, appeared naked under his coat,) and carried it into the rope-walks. The soldier then went to Green's barrack, and in about twenty minutes returned with about eight or nine more soldiers, armed with clubs, who began with three or four men in

Mr. Gray's warehouse by asking them why they had insulted the soldier aforesaid? These men immediately called out for assistance, upon which they were joined by a number of rope-makers, with whose help they beat off the soldiers. The soldiers upon this returned to their barrack, and in a few minutes appeared again in the rope-walk with a stronger party, making now about thirty or forty, armed with clubs and cutlasses, and headed by a tall negroe drummer. This party fell upon the rope-makers coming up to the assistance of their companions, the soldiers were again beat off with considerable bruises, and followed by the rope-makers as far as Green's lane, when a corporal came and ordered the soldiers into their barracks; and Mr. John Hill, an elderly gentleman of the town, who seems to have been a magistrate, persuaded the rope-makers to go back, and they readily obeyed him.

Hitherto we see no footsteps of a massacre, or intended massacre, of the inhabitants. Some soldiers, having been affronted by the rope-makers, go out to take revenge on them without their military weapons, armed only with clubs, in order to give them a beating. The occasion of the quarrel was sudden, and the duration of it short. No officers, not even the serjeants and corporals, appear to have been concerned in it; and a single corporal had influence enough to put an end to it.

On the next day, Saturday the 3d of March, there happened another fray in Mr. Mac Neil's rope-walk between three grenadiers and six or seven rope-makers, in which the rope-makers had again the advantage.

These contentions heightened the animosities of both parties. The soldiers wished for another engagement to revenge themselves on the rope-makers; and the towns-people seem to have resolved to make use of their vast superiority of numbers, which had given them the advantage in the former encounters, either to destroy the soldiers intirely, or to drive both them and the commissioners of the customs out of the town. With this view they seem to have intended to draw the soldiers out of their barracks to a general engagement of the same kind as the former, that is, with sticks and clubs, and to assemble a large mob for that purpose, of which the rope-makers should be the leaders, that it might seem to be only a renewal of the quarrel that had lately happened, and not a general design of the inhabitants to rise upon them. This at least appears to me to have been the plan formed by the towns-people on this occasion, upon a careful perusal of all the evidences relating to this unhappy business, which are submitted to the reader's consideration.

These animosities were considerably heightened by the sudden absence of a serjeant of the 14th regiment on the evening of Saturday the 3d of March, which continued likewise on the following day, Sunday the 4th of March, and gave rise, in that time of jealousy, to a suspicion among the soldiers that he had been murdered by the rope-makers. This suspicion proved to be ill-grounded: but, while it continued, it occasioned Colonel Carr, the Lieutenant Colonel of the 14th regiment, and his officers, to go, on the Sunday, into Mr. Gray's rope-walk, and search for him in every part of it with the greatest anxiety and diligence, to the surprize, and, it seems, not much to the satisfaction, of Mr. Gray. Mr. Gray upon this went directly to Colonel Dalrymple (the Lieutenant Colonel of the 29th regiment, and commanding officer of the troops then in Boston[74]) and related to him what he understood had passed at the rope-walk two days before; to which the Colonel replied that it was much the same as he had heard from his people, and then said that Mr. Gray's man was the aggressor by affronting one of the soldiers by asking him if he wanted work, and then telling him to clean his little-house. Mr. Gray made answer that he would dismiss his journey-man the next morning for that insolent expression, and would further do every thing in his power to prevent from his people giving the soldiers any affront for the future. And Colonel Dalrymple in like manner assured Mr. Gray that he had done, and should do, every thing in his power to keep the soldiers in order and prevent their any more entering Mr. Gray's enclosure. Presently after Colonel Carr came in and asked Colonel Dalrymple what they should do; for that they were daily losing their men; and that three of his grenadiers passing quietly by the rope-walks had been greatly abused, and one of them so much beat that he was likely to die of his bruises. He then said that he had been searching for a serjeant who had been murdered.—Upon which Mr. Gray said, "Yes, colonel; I hear you have been searching for him in my rope-walks;" and asked him whether that serjeant had been in the affray there on the Friday? The Colonel replied, "No; for he was seen on the Saturday." Mr. Gray then asked him how he could think of looking for him in his walks, and said that, if he had applied to him, he would have waited on him and have opened every apartment he had for his satisfaction. This is the substance of John Gray's deposition[75] and shews how greatly the suspicions of the officers and soldiers were alarmed by the sudden and unaccountable absence of the serjeant.

On Monday, the 5th of March, the day of the disturbance that proved fatal to some of the inhabitants, about seven o'clock in the evening, numbers of the towns-people of Boston were seen walking in the streets, in several different parties from about three to six men each, armed with clubs. Mr. John Gillespie, in his deposition,[76] declares that, as he was going to the south end of town, to meet some friends at a public house, he met several people in the streets in parties of this kind, to the number, he thinks, of forty or fifty persons; and that while he was sitting with his friends there, several persons of his acquaintance came in to them at different times, and took notice of the numbers of persons they had seen in the streets armed in the above manner; and that about eight o'clock one Mr. Fleming came in and told them that three hundred people were assembled at Liberty-Tree armed with sticks and clubs to beat the soldiers. Mr. Gillespie goes on and says, that about half an hour after eight the bells rung, which he and his company took to be for fire; but they were told by the landlord of the house that it was to collect the mob. Mr. Gillespie upon this resolved to go home, and in his way met numbers of people who were running past him, of whom many were armed with clubs and sticks, and some with other weapons. At the same time a number of people passed by him with two fire-engines, as if there had been a fire in the town. But they were soon told that was no fire, but that the people were going to fight the soldiers; upon which they immediately quitted their fire-engines, and swore they go to their assistance. All this happened before the soldiers near the custom-house fired their muskets, which was not till half an hour after nine o'clock; and it shews that the inhabitants had formed, and were preparing to execute, a design of attacking the soldiers on that evening. This account is confirmed by the deposition of William Davies, serjeant-major to the 14th regiment, who declares that, on the same evening about eight o'clock, as he was going towards the north end on regimental business, he saw in the streets a large body of the inhabitants, armed some with fire-arms, and others with cutlasses and bludgeons, crying out, that "they would do for those rascals, the officers and soldiers, that night." This was more than an hour before the firing. He says further, that he returned home about nine o'clock, and as he came near the market-place, he saw a greater number of people than before, tearing up the butchers stalls for clubs, and swearing they would murder the first officer or soldier they should meet with. They then gave three huzzas, and cried, "Now for the bloody-back rascals." And some of them said, "Let us attack the main-guard." Others proposed to attack Smith's barracks; and others said, "Away to the rope-walk." And instantly the mob divided into three divisions, of some hundred men in each division: and the bells at the same time were ringing. The serjeant-major then went to a friend's house and changed his dress: and in repairing from thence to his barrack through the several streets that led to it, he saw several armed towns-people crying out, "Murder, kill all the dogs; for we will have no commissioners nor soldiers in Boston. And damn the scoundrel that first ordered them here. We will soon rid the town of them all:" or words to that effect. And all this he saw and heard before the firing in King's-street. Nothing, as I conceive, can prove more clearly the design of the towns-people to make an attack that evening on the soldiers.

The custom-house and the centry posted there to defend it seem to have been a principal object of the people's fury. For they began to assemble about it in great numbers before it was dark, that is, before seven o'clock, or more than two hours before the extremity of violence that obliged the soldiers to fire. Thomas Lochead, in his deposition,[77] declares, that as he was passing through King's-street, a little before dark, he observed a number of towns-people standing almost close to the centry then on duty at the custom-house, and presently after he saw several of them throwing snow-balls and pieces of ice at him, upon which the centry said, *"Gentlemen, I beg you will let me alone and go away from my post; for, if you do not, you must take the consequences."* Upon this a gentleman dressed in a red cloak went to the people and spoke to them, and advised them to let the centry alone. They accordingly went to the other side of the street, and there remained. In about an hour after, that is, about eight o'clock, Thomas Lochead had occasion to pass by the people standing in the same place as before, armed with sticks and large clubs, who threw snowballs at him as he passed by, and called him a bloody-back rascal, notwithstanding he said nothing to provoke them.

About nine o'clock Edward Hills, being among the mob near the town-house at Boston, when the bells were set a ringing to bring the people together, heard some of them say, they would go down to the custom-house, where there was a centry placed, and would take him off his post. Upon this Mr. Hill went immediately to the main-guard to acquaint the soldiers with what he had heard. In the mean time the mob surrounded the centry, and began to attack him by striking at him with clubs, swearing they would be revenged on the soldiers. The centry defended himself, as well as he could, with his bayonet, and desired them to keep off, saying, *"He durst not quit his post; and that, if they did not desist, he must call the guard."* They did not however desist, but pelted him with sticks and large pieces of ice picked up from the streets. This obliged him to retreat to the door at the custom-house, where, getting upon the steps of it, he loaded his musket in the sight of the people, and, after he had loaded it, he struck the butt-end of it against the steps three or four times, hoping, as it should seem, that the sight of the danger they were running, if they pressed upon him any further, would induce the people to keep off. (See Thomas Cain's deposition.[78]) But it had not this effect; for the people assembled in greater numbers, and set him at defiance, crying, *"Fire, fire, and be damned."* And some of them drew quite near to him; Mr. Knox says, within the distance of ten feet: upon which he snapped his piece upon them, but did not fire it, endeavouring again to frighten them from approaching any nearer to him. Mr. Knox upon this went up to him, and told him that, "if he fired, he died;" to which he bravely answered, *"that he did not care, and that, if they touched him, he would fire;"* which it is generally understood to be the duty of every centinel to do that is attacked upon his post. The people however continued to defy him, telling him to fire and be damned: upon which Mr. Knox, who seems to have done every thing in his power to prevent mischief on this occasion, went to the people, and endeavoured to keep them from going up: but without success. (See Mr. Knox's deposition.[79]) The centry, being thus hard pressed, knocked at the custom-house door very hard for assistance: and in a few minutes a party of twelve soldiers, headed by Captain Preston, came to him from the main-guard, with their arms in a horizontal posture, and their bayonets fixed. They drew up immediately before the door of the custom-house with their faces towards the people, and held their guns breast high, in order to defend the centinel; and Captain Preston stood before them near the ends of their guns. Mr. Richard Palmes at this time went up to the captain, and asked him if the soldiers guns were loaded; to which the captain answered that they were loaded with powder and ball. Mr. Palmes then said to him, "*I hope you do not intend they shall fire upon the inhabitants*;" to which he answered, "*by no means*," which indeed might have been concluded from the position he had chosen to stand in, directly before the muzzles of their guns. (See Mr. Palmes's depositions.[80]) But the people continued to insult and defy this party of soldiers in the same manner as they had done the single centinel, pelting them with sticks and balls of ice, and calling out to them "*Damn you, you rascals; fire. You dare not fire. Fire, and be damned.*" These expressions were frequently repeated; during which time Captain Preston spoke often to the mob, desiring them to be quiet and disperse; for that, if they continued their attack upon him and his party, he should be obliged to fire upon them. But his humane endeavours were to no purpose. The people continued their attack upon the soldiers, till they were provoked beyond all patience. A large stick, or, as Mr. Palmes says, a piece of ice, that was thrown at a grenadier on the right of the party, struck him with violence and made him stagger, upon which both he and the soldier next him fired their pieces without any order from Captain Preston for that purpose, (See John Hickling's deposition, and Thomas Greenwood's depositions,[81] and Richard Palmes's depositions) and soon after the rest of the party did the same; by which three men were killed on the spot, and eight wounded, of whom two have since died of their wounds. Presently after the last gun was fired off, Captain Preston sprung before the soldiers, and waiving his sword or stick, said, "*Damn ye, rascals, what did ye fire for?*" and struck up the gun of one of the soldiers who was loading again; whereupon they seemed confounded, and fired no more. (See William Wyat's deposition.[82])

This is the whole of what the Boston Narrative calls *the horrid Massacre*. How far it deserves that appellation, let the unprejudiced reader judge. For my part, I cannot but think it a very gross abuse of language, and highly injurious to the unhappy officer and soldiers who were concerned in this affair, to call it by the same name that has heretofore been used to describe such wanton, unnecessary, and premeditated acts of general destruction as the slaughter of the Protestants of France in the year 1572, and of the Protestants of Ireland in 1641; to which a resistance made by twelve soldiers against more than an hundred people armed with sticks and bludgeons, in defence of a post which it was their duty to defend, seems to me to bear no resemblance.

I shall mention but slightly what happened after the soldiers had fired, as it is not material to the justification of their conduct in the act of firing, which is the ground for charging them with the perpetration of a horrid massacre. As soon as the firing was over, all the bells of the town were set a ringing, (whereas before the firing only one of them had been rung,) and the inhabitants gathered together in vastly greater numbers than before; and on the other hand the soldiers drew out from their barracks in proper order, and stood under arms to defend themselves against any further assaults, which there was then great reason to apprehend. And now indeed dreadful evils might have ensued, and a slaughter, less improperly to be stiled a massacre than the former, might in a few minutes have been committed, if the principal persons of both parties had not immediately interposed their authority and influence to prevent any further mischief. But by the endeavours of the worthy Lieutenant-governor Hutchinson and the council of the province on the one part, and of the commanding officers of the two regiments on the other, the people were persuaded to disperse, and the soldiers to retire to their barracks.

After this account of the foregoing unfortunate transaction, (which, when the reader shall have compared it with the depositions from which it is extracted, I flatter myself, he will judge to be a fair one;) I presume that no impartial person will be inclined to consider either the officer or soldiers who were concerned in it guilty of wilful murder of malice afore-thought. Whether their conduct can be wholly justified in point of law upon the principles of self-defence and the obligations of military duty, I will not take upon me to determine: I leave to others the discussion of those nice points of law. But if they cannot be intirely justified, they ought at least to be considered as persons who have been provoked by repeated insults and attacks to commit a rash and hasty act of violence, and consequently as being intitled, in a legal view, to the benefit of their clergy, and, in a moral view, to the compassion, rather than the indignation, of their countrymen. May the people of Boston, in whose hands they now are, be inclined to think of them in this manner, and regain the good opinion of their fellow subjects of Great Britain by so honourable an instance of their justice and moderation.

In the Boston Narrative of this affair there is an attempt to make it believed that some guns were fired upon the people from the windows of the custom-house. But this is so very improbable in itself, and so ill supported by proof, that I imagine few of the readers of that account will give any credit to it.

However, lest the confidence with which this charge is brought should mislead any person into a belief that it is true, I will venture to subjoin a few observations on the weakness of the evidence by which it is supported.

In the first place, some of the witnesses mentioned in the Boston Narrative say, they saw the flashes of guns at the custom-house.

This deserves little or no regard: for in the hurry and confusion of that time it must have been almost impossible to distinguish with exactness the places and heights from which the flashes came. The soldiers stood just at the custom-house door, and the flashes of their guns might naturally enough seem to a hasty observer to come from the custom-house itself.

In the next place, some stress is laid on the directions of three of the balls, as collected from the holes made by them in the houses into which they entered. Now these directions, as they were taken by Mr. Andrews, (see his deposition[83]) are just such as one would suppose they should be from guns fired by men standing before the custom-house door; and the two latter of them are found to range breast-high, that is, at much the same height as they would have ranged if they had been fired from the ground-floor of the custom-house itself, supposing that floor to be nearly upon the same level with the street. They consequently could not be fired from the windows up one pair of stairs, as they are said to have been in the charge. Further, the second ball is found to range breast-high from the ground, and between two of the windows of the custom-house; consequently it could not have been fired from either of them, but by some person without the custom-house standing between those two windows. And for a like reason the first ball could not be fired from a window in the custom-house, because it ranges below the stool of the westernmost lower chamber window: for if it had been fired from that window, it must have ranged above the stool of it.

The last and strongest evidence that is brought in support of this charge is that of Charlotte Bourgate,[84] Mr. Edward Manwaring indented servant. This indeed would be very material, if he were a person that deserved any credit, and if his testimony was not invalidated by contrary evidence of the strongest kind. For he has positively charged Mr. Manwaring with firing off a gun out of the window. But he has confessed in this very deposition,[85] that he had denied before a justice of the peace every word of its contents after he had first sworn that they were true, though he then (more than a fortnight after the affair, to wit, March 23, when the soldiers were gone out of the town and the people were in possession of every thing) thought fit to swear to them a second time. Such a witness destroys his own credit, if he ever had any; which, it seems, this boy, from the sadness of his character, never had. But, to come to a more particular examination of the contents of his deposition; he says in the first place, that there were four or five men in the custom-house, (whom he does not name, and therefore does not pretend to have known) at the time of the soldiers firing, who went up stairs and pulled and haled him after them—that one of them a tall man, loaded a gun twice, and gave it to him to fire, and forced him by threats of immediate violence to fire it off twice out of the window—that he did not fire it against the people who were assembled near the custom-house, but sideways up the street—and secondly, that Mr. Manwaring and Mr. Munroe were both in the custom-house at the time of this firing, and that Mr. Manwaring fired off a gun himself out of the window.

This is the substance of that boy's evidence. Now, if the first part of it was true, of the tall man's forcing him to fire the gun off twice, it would not be much worth inquiring into, as it would relate only to persons unknown, and, we might well presume, not belonging to the custom-house. For, if they had belonged to it, this boy, who is a servant of Mr. Manwaring, who has an employment in the customs, must in all probability have known them. But it is a strange and incredible story. For if the tall man, as the story supposes, meant to do the people mischief, why did he not fire the gun himself rather than force the boy to do it, especially when he observed that the boy had fired the first time sideways up the street instead of directly forwards upon the people? I know no way of accounting for this, if we admit the fact to be true, but by supposing that some of the inhabitants themselves had thrust themselves into the custom-house, and had forced the boy to fire a gun out of the window for the sake of charging the custom-house officers with having had a hand in the destruction of the inhabitants that evening, but at the same time had taken care that he should fire in such a direction as not to do them any real mischief. But 'tis more probable that the whole fact is false, and therefore needs no explanation; for there were in the house at the same time Mr. Hammond Green, who, as this boy says, let him in, and three women, Elizabeth Avery, Mary Rogers, and Ann Green.

Of these four persons Hammond Green alone has been examined: and he says in his deposition,[86] that he went up stairs into the lower west chamber, and saw the guns fired by the soldiers: but says not a word about the four or five men and the boy, Charlotte Bourgate, whom they forced to fire off a gun twice out of the window, which he could not but have known if it had happened. He says also, that the three women before-mentioned, Elizabeth Avery, Mary Rogers, and Ann Green, were up stairs likewise at the time of the soldiers firing. They therefore must likewise have seen these four or five men and the boy Charlotte Bourgate, and have known of his firing the gun, if it was true that he had done so. But it has not been thought fit to examine them, or at least to publish their depositions.

As to the other part of this boy's charge, to wit, that Mr. Manwaring and Mr. Munroe were both present at the custom-house at the time of the soldiers firing, and that Mr. Manwaring did himself fire a gun out of the window, this is proved to be utterly false, and even impossible, by the deposition of Michael Angelo Warwell[87] who declares, that these gentlemen were at the same time at a distance from the custom-house, to wit, in Mr. Manwaring's lodgings in Back-street, and had been there from seven o'clock in the evening, that is, more than two hours before the soldiers fired, and continued there till half an hour after ten o'clock, when, the tumult occasioned by the firing being subsided, Mr. Munroe ventured to leave Mr. Manwaring's lodging and go home. Mr. Manwaring continued in his own lodgings the whole night.

This charge therefore against the people at the custom house must be looked upon as an idle, ill-grounded accusation, proceeding solely from the prejudices of the inhabitants of Boston against the commissioners of the customs and every body that has any connection with them, which disposes them to imagine and believe every thing that may tend to their disadvantage.

DOCUMENT **21**

ADDITIONAL OBSERVATIONS[88]

So anxious were town leaders that they not lose the battle for public opinion to Hutchinson and his supporters that they rushed Additional Observations *into print before they had even seen* A Fair Account. *The recriminations printed there went well beyond the criticisms expressed in the original* Short Narrative. *The entire pamphlet, with only ancillary material deleted, appears below.*

Town leaders once again blamed the customs commissioners for much of what had befallen Boston. They opened with John Robinson's oceanic dash for London, charging that Robinson left in secret and effectively abandoned his post. The other commissioners too had left their posts while pretending that the people of Boston made it too dangerous for them to perform their duties. This might seem an odd complaint from men who disliked enforcement of the navigation system, unless part of their intended audience is remembered: Britons in general and members of the ministry in particular who could be both embarrassed and upset by such behavior. The townsmen then posed a rhetorical question: "Is it possible they indicate any thing less than a design to take occasion from the outrages and murders committed on the evening of that day by the soldiers (assisted perhaps from the custom-house) to represent the town in a disadvantageous light?" If the depositions—as yet apparently unseen—Hutchinson gathered suggested that the custom house was under attack, they lied; if they stated that the "revenue chest" was in danger of being stolen, that too was a lie; if they claimed that the troops had been forced out of town, again, they lied. Any allegation that government was "at an end" or that the province was "in a state of rebellion" should be dismissed as utter nonsense.

"When a people have lost all confidence in government, it is vain to expect a cordial obedience to it," the men behind these Additional Observations *warned. Had the troops not been removed from town and had they continued their behavior as before the people of Boston would have been within their rights to force them out—by "that law of nature, which superceeds all other laws."*

Having made their threat, town leaders closed with an appeal to the king to see that the people of Massachusetts were his faithful subjects. They distinguished between him and foolish policies passed by Parliament that, implicitly, they were calling upon him to disavow. It was a distinction typical of patriot protest at this point in the imperial controversy. Most aggrieved colonists still sought to build some sort of transatlantic community of protest, condemning parliamentary policies without condemning Parliament altogether, rejecting Parliament's authority to raise revenue through new navigation acts without denying its superintending authority over the empire. And the king still stood rhetorically as the one who united them all, Americans and Britons, into one grand transatlantic family.

*   *   *

THE extraordinary conduct of the Commissioners of the Customs since the 5th of *March*, and their perseverance in it, make it necessary to bestow a few observations upon it; and upon divers matters, with which it seems to be connected.

The said commissioners (excepting Mr *Temple*) have all retired from the town: and we find, on particular enquiry, that they have not held a meeting of their board since the 9th of *March*. How they have disposed of themselves since that time we shall relate here.

Mr *Robinson* is gone to *England*: He sailed the 16th of *March*, and went not only without the leave but, as it is said, contrary to the minds of his superiors, signified to him from home. None but the few, intrusted the secret, knew any thing of his going til after the departure of the vessel in which he went.

Mr *Paxton* retired to *Cambridge*, four Miles from *Boston*, and for the most part has continued there. He has divers times however visited the town since that retiring.

Mr *Hulton* sometime ago purchased a place at *Brooklyn* [Brookline], five Miles from *Boston*, and has ever since resided there.

Mr *Burch*, with his wife, has retired to Mr *Hulton's*, who, together with Mr *Burch* (leaving their wives behind them) are now on a tour to *Portsmouth*, in the province of *New-Hampshire*, where the last Account from thence left them. It is now above six weeks since a board of Commissioners was held: and it is utterly uncertain when there will be another.

From their first establishment here, to the 11th of *June*, 1768, they held their boards regularly four days every week. They then retired on board the *Romney* man of war, and from thence to the castle: for what purpose, their letters and memorials lately published have sufficiently informed the world. From their re-establishment in *Boston* in *November* 1768, to the 5th of *March*, 1770, they held their boards at the same regular manner. Since that time there have been but two board meetings, the last of which was on the 9th of *March*.

Now what do all these manoeuvres since the 5th of *March* indicate? Is it possible to suppose they indicate any thing less than a design to take occasion from the outrages and murders committed on the evening of that day by the soldiers (assisted perhaps from the custom-house) to represent the town in a disadvantageous light? And does not their former conduct render this highly probable?—Besides, it is a fact, that depositions have been taken in a secret manner, relative to that unhappy affair, to the prejudice of the town; and it is no way improbable that Mr *Robinson* is gone home with memorials and letters from the commissioners and others, accompanying such depositions.

By some escapes, as well as by what the circumstances above mentioned make possible, a pretty good judgment may be formed on the substance of those Memorials, Letters, and Depositions, namely, that the Custom-house was attacked—the revenue chest in danger, but saved by the firing on the *mob*—The King's troops compelled to leave the town—the commissioners thence obliged for their safety to quit it also—the consequent impossibility of their holding boards—the detriment thence arising to the revenue and his Majesty's service—all government at an end, and the Province in a state of rebellion.

If these be, either in whole or in part, the subjects of the dispatches sent home, it is very proper a few observations should be made upon them.

The Custom-house attacked—a falshood. The people drawn into *Kingstreet*, were drawn thither by the cry of fire, and the outrages of the Soldiers, which occasioned it. From the first appearance of the people in *Kingstreet*, to the time of the firing upon them, there had not passed fifteen minutes. It might with as much truth be affirmed, that they made an attack upon the Custom-house in *London*, as upon the Custom-house in *Boston*: of which latter there was not even a pane of glass broken.

The Revenue Chest in danger—a falshood. It is not probable the chest is kept at the Custom-house: but if it be, there was, and is, at least as much danger of it from some of the out-door people employed under the Commissioners, as from any body else. It is certain that some of them are of an infamous character.

The troops compelled to quit the town—a falshood. They quitted the town by the orders of their Commanding Officer, in consequence of a *request* from the Lieutenant Governor, who was advised by the council to *pray* the said Officer to remove the troops. This *request* and this *prayer* was obtained by an application from the town to the Lieutenant Governor. Into what times are we fallen, that the government of the province is reduced to the humiliating condition of making *such a prayer*.

But supposing the troops had been compelled *vi & armis*[89] to quit the town. It would have been a measure justifiable in the sight of God and man. When the Soldiers sent hither for the declared purpose of assisting the Civil Magistrate to keep the peace, were themselves in a remarkable manner the breakers of the peace—When, instead of assisting, they insulted him; and rescued offenders of their own camps from justice—when they frequently abused the inhabitants in the night—when they had entered into a combination to commit some extraordinary acts of violence upon the town; and in consequence of it, on the evening of the Massacre, attacked the inhabitants wherever they met them; afterwards firing upon, and killing and wounding a number of them. When all this had been done, and more threatened, it was high time they should be removed from the town. If there had been no other means of getting rid of them, the inhabitants would have had a right by that law of nature, which superceeds all other laws, when they come in competition with it—the law of self-preservation—to have compelled them to quit the town. This law is radical in our nature, indelible from it, and uniformly operating, where it can operate, to the removal or destruction of everything incompatible with it; and is abrogable by no other lawgiver than God himself, the great author of it. Therefore, although the resisting the King's troops in any thing they have a right by law to do, may be adjudged treason, yet when they act contrary to law, especially in so outrageous a manner as in the present case, and retain a disposition to repeat it, whereby the lives of the King's subjects are in danger, they then cease to be the King's troops: that is, they are not the King's troops for any such purpose, but so far become traitors; and on the failure of other means of riddance from them, which the time and circumstances may make eligible and are lawful, they may (by the principles of all law, as well as by the great law above-mentioned, into which those principles are resolvable) be resisted and expelled: and not to do it, where it can be done, is a species of treason against the constitution, and consequently treason in an equal degree against the King, and all his subjects.

The Commissioners obliged for their safety to quit the town—If one falshood can be more so than another, this is the greatest yet mentioned, and is as ridiculous as it is false. Their conduct and such a declaration by no means agree. Would they in that case occasionally visit the town? Would they trust themselves in the environs of it? Could they think themselves safe at *Cambridge* and *Brooklyn*? Could they think themselves safe any where in the province, or indeed in *America*? Must they not know, if any evil were really intended them, it might easily overtake them any where, and every where on this side of the *Atlantic*? Some other reason than their safety must therefore be looked for to account for their retiring, and discontinuing their boards. A similar proceeding of theirs in *June*, 1768, and their Letters and Memorials, lately published, give occasion at least to conjecture what the reason may be. Is it not probable it was to corroborate the said depositions, and thence induce administration to think it necessary, not only that troops already here should be continued, but that a further number should be sent to strengthen and support them? If this measure cannot be effected, and should the Commissioners be so unfortunate as to remain here unattacked in the absence of the troops, it might naturally be thought they could have remained here without them in 1768; and therefore that they had put the nation to a very great expence, for no other purpose than further to alienate the affections of the *Americans*, and to give them an additional reason to wish themselves independent of it: And hence the Commissioners might have cause to expect a national resentment against them.—However injurious to us the effects of such a policy may be, we cannot but applaud it (on the principles of the *Machiavellian* system) as it stands related to themselves. If they thought their own existence in danger, considered as Commissioners, how natural was it to use the means to support it? And what fault could be found with the means, of those principles justified them? Why need they trouble their heads about consequences that would not affect themselves? or, if they would, and such existence appeared precarious without those means, was it not necessary they should be used, and the consequences disregarded?—If the means be successful to the end for which they seem designed, it requires no prophetic spirit to foretell that the consequences may be —— bad enough. Whether the present Commissioners at all (whose appointments are fully equal to any benefit the Nation or Colonies are likely to reap from them, and whose usefulness hitherto may be valued by some of the negative quantities in algebra) are *things* of importance enough to hazard those consequences, or any ill consequence at all, is humbly submitted to the wisdom of administration to determine.

The consequent impossibility of their holding boards—This impossibility was of their own creating. If they had continued in town (from whence they had not the least reason to depart, unless to answer purposes they would choose to conceal) they might have held their boards as usual.

The detriment thence arising to the Revenue, and his Majesty's service—If any such detriment has arisen, the fault is their own. *His Majesty's service* is a cant term in the mouths of understrappers in office. Many of them either do not know the meaning of it, or abuse it to answer their own corrupt purposes. It is used to express something distinct from the service of the people. The King and People are placed by it in opposite interests. Whereas, by the happy constitution we are under, the interest of the King is the interest of the people, and his service is their service: both are one, and constitutionally inseparable. They who attempt to separate them attempt to destroy the constitution. Upon every such parricide may the vengeance both of King and People descend.

Government at an end—This has been the cry ever since the stamp-act existed. If the people saw they were going to be enslaved; if they saw Governor *Bernard* (from whom they had a right to expect that he would do nothing to promote it) was zealous and active to rivet the chains; and that *his* government, in its principles and conduct, tended to the establishment of a tyranny over them, was it unnatural to refuse such an acquiescence in such measures? Did an opposition to them indicate a disregard to government? If government, in the true idea of it, has for its object the good of the governed, *such* an administration could not be called government: and an opposition to it by no means included an opposition to government. From such an opposition has arisen the cry, that government is at an end. The sooner *such* government is at an end the better.

When a people have lost all confidence in government, it is vain to expect a cordial obedience to it. Hence irregularities may arise, and have arisen. But they will cease, when the true ends of government are steadily pursued. Then, and not till then, may it be expected, that men of weight and influence will exert themselves to make government respected. Nay, such exertions will then be needless, for mankind cannot help respecting what is in itself respectable, especially when it is at the same time so promotive of their own good as good government is.

The province in a state of rebellion—Into this state its enemies, on both sides of the *Atlantic*, have been endeavoring to bring it. When they could not make it subservient to their interest and views; and when their measures had raised a spirit of opposition to them, that opposition was made the lucky occasion to represent the province in a state of rebellion, or verging towards it. To justify such a representation the more fully, they endeavoured to drive it into that state: whereby in the end they might hope to gratify both their malice and avarice: their malice, by injuring it most essentially; and their avarice, by the subjection of it to their tyranny and pillage. But nothing can be more false than such a representation: nothing more foreign from this people than a disposition to rebellion. The principles of loyalty were planted in our breasts too deep to be eradicated by *their* efforts, or any efforts whatever: and our interest co-operated with those principles.

It is humbly to be hoped his Majesty will not be influenced, by *such* representations, to think themselves unfavorably of *his faithful subjects of this province*: and *that* hope is grounded upon their innocence: of which they have the highest evidence in their own consciousness; and of which they have given their adversaries no other cause to doubt, than what arises from an opposition to *their* measures. Measures, not only ruinous to the province, but hurtful to *Great Britain*, and destructive of the union, and commercial intercourse, which ought always to subsist between her and her colonies.

The foregoing Observations appeared necessary to vindicate the Town and Province from the aspersions so unjustly cast upon them. The few that follow refer to the present and future state of *Great Britain* and her colonies.

HOW happy is *Britain*, with regard to situation, and many internal circumstances; and in connection with her Colonies!

Separated from the rest of the world, and possessed of so large a naval force, she is secure from foreign invasions: her government (well administered) is the best existing; her manufactures are extensive, and her commerce in proportion. To the two latter the Colonies have in a considerable degree contributed. By these means she has risen to her present opulence and greatness, which so much distinguish her among the powers of *Europe*. But however great and opulent she may be, she is capable of being more so; and so much so, that she may be deemed at present in a state of minority, compared with what she will one day probably be, if her own conduct does not prevent it. The means of this greatness are held out to her by the Colonies; and it is in her power, by a kind and just treatment of them, to avail herself of those means.

The Colonists are husbandmen, and till lately have manufactured but a small part of their clothing, and the other articles with which they had been usually supplied from *Great Britain*. But they have been taught by experience they can supply themselves; and *that* experience (which has been forced upon them) has demonstrated most clearly, that they have within themselves the means of living conveniently, if not with elegance, even if their communication with the rest of mankind were wholly cut off. This, however, could not be an eligible state: but no one intitled to and deserving the liberties of an *Englishman*, can hesitate a moment to say, that it would be preferable to slavery; to which the Colonists have apprehended themselves doomed, by the measures that have been pursued by Administration.

If the Colonists might be permitted to follow their inclinations, with which at the same time their interests coincides, they would be husbandmen still, and be supplied as usual from *Great Britain*. The yearly amount of those supplies (as appears by the exports from Britain) is very considerable, and might in future increase in proportion to the increase of the Colonists. Their increase is rapid: they are daily emigrating from the old towns, and forming new ones; and if they double their numbers every twenty years, as it is said they will continue to do, so long as they can form into families by procuring the means of subsistence at an easy rate, which probably will be the case, till *America* shall be well people, there will be in a short time a prodigious addition to his Majesty's subjects; who, if not compelled to manufactures for themselves, will occasion a proportionable demand for the manufactures of *Great Britain*. If it be considered too, that *America*, from its different soils and climates, can raise perhaps all the productions of other countries in the same latitudes: which being remitted in exchange would most of them be rough materials for *Britain* to manufacture; what a fund of wealth and power will be finding employment, and the consequent means of subsistence, will greatly encrease; and her trade and navigation be in proportion. She might then view with indifference the interdiction of her trade with other parts of the world, though she would always have it in her power, from the superiority of her naval force, which such a trade and navigation would enable her to support, to do herself justice, and command universal respect.

Connected with her Colonies, she would then be a mighty empire: the greatest, consisting of people of one language, that ever existed.

If these observations be not wholly visionary, and a mere reverie, they possibly may not be unworthy the consideration of Parliament: whose wisdom will determine, whether any revenue whatever, even the greatest that *America* could possibly produce, either without or with her good will, would compensate the loss of such wealth and power; or justify measures that had the least tendency to bring them into hazard: or whether for such a revenue it would be worth while to hazard even the present advantages, resulting to *Great Britain* from an union and harmony with her Colonies.

TOWN LEADERS AND THE BATTLE
FOR PUBLIC OPINION[90]

In the letter transcribed below, Boston's town leaders tell Benjamin Franklin that they are pleased with the shaping of public opinion so far, but they could not be complacent. They understood the power of opinion—with the public and on policy-makers, in London as well as Boston. All of the stereotypes notwithstanding, Whitehall and Westminster did not attempt to shape the empire in an informational vacuum. Virtually every debate over imperial policy included a reading into the parliamentary record of papers relating to colonial affairs. But Boston's leaders felt they were at a disadvantage in this setting. Imperial authorities like governors and customs agents sent their reports through official channels; town leaders had to hope that someone friendly to their cause would informally do the same for them. They could send petitions to the king, but he might refuse to receive them or pass them along to Parliament. They could correspond with a lobbyist like Franklin, hoping that he would convey their concerns to the right people, but Franklin depended on ears that might not hear. Whatever petition he and other colonial agents drafted for Parliament's consideration had to be introduced by someone sitting in the Lords or the Commons.

Hence the anxiety expressed by town leaders in their letter to Franklin over the potential impact of Preston's account and their attempt to counter it (see Documents 13 and 14). Thus too their concern that A Short Narrative *act as an effective counter to* A Fair Account *(see Documents 19 and 20). The London press, they feared, was never quite sympathetic enough to make their case fully appreciated, nor were there enough men around the king or in either house of Parliament to defend their rights and protect their interests. There had never been much enthusiasm on either side of the Atlantic for the idea of seating*

Americans in Parliament. What frustrated colonists learned over these years is that any sort of less formal representation—through lobbyists or sympathetic members of Parliament or even merchants in London—proved inadequate to their political needs.

Though the men who signed the town's letter to Franklin were joined in common cause, they were not necessarily of one mind on how to proceed. Take, for example, two of the eight, William Molineux and Thomas Cushing. Molineux was English-born and an Anglican; Cushing was a Boston native and congregationalist. As merchants concerned about the enforcement of the navigation system they shared something in common and both were committed to a defense of what they considered their rights. Protest against the navigation system, then, had brought them together as political allies for nearly a decade. They went together on March 6 with the other town leaders to see Hutchinson and demand that he remove the troops from town. But whereas Cushing was extremely cautious, concerned that being too emphatic in speech or too aggressive in behavior could widen the divide between Boston and London, Molineux stirred crowds with fiery rhetoric and took to the streets to make his point. Although both had supported non-importation as a response to the Townshend Program, Cushing did not approve of the pressure tactics that Molineux thought essential to insure compliance. Cushing, by contrast, worried Samuel Adams and others who felt that he dragged his heels, and yet he kept his prominence in the town meeting long after he was no longer a selectman and he served as speaker of the Massachusetts House at the time of the massacre. Cautious though he may have been, he had chaired the extralegal meeting of town delegates that gathered in September 1768 to protest the sending of troops. Molineux concerned some of his colleagues in the town meeting because he pushed so hard and yet, vehement as he was against having troops in the town, he turned around and rented them warehouse space to use as a barracks once they arrived—though, it is said, at an inflated rate.

The more contentious the issue, the greater the possibility for friends and political allies to differ. Among town leaders like Molineux and Cushing, disagreement over means exposed a difference over ends as well, though neither could predict exactly where his protest might take him. Cushing wanted to avoid confrontation and yet he did not want London trampling American rights. Molineux was not as averse to street action as Cushing and feared the outbreak of revolt far less. Yet even he did not view himself as a revolutionary. He died in 1774, before the fighting erupted in earnest.

*   *   *

Sir,

It affords very great Satisfaction to the Town of Boston to find the Narrative of the horrid Massacre perpetrated here on the 5th of March last which was transmitted to London, has had the desired effect; by establishing truth in the Minds of honest Men, and in some Measure preventing the Odium being cast on the Inhabitants, as the aggressors in it. We were very apprehensive that all attempts would be made to gain this Advantage against us: and as there is [no r]eason to think that the Malice of our Enemies is in the least degree abated, it has been thought necessary that our friends on your side of the Water, should have a true State of the Circumstances of the Town, and of every thing which has Materially occurred, since the removal of the Troops to the Castle. For this purpose we are appointed a Committee: But the time will not admit of our writing so fully by this Conveyance, as we intend by the next, in the mean time we intreat your further friendship for the Town, in your Endeavours to get the Judgment of the Public Suspended, upon any representation that may have been made by the Commissioners of the Customs and others, until the Town can have the Opportunity of knowing what is alleged against it, and of answering for itself. We must confess that we are astonished to hear that the Parliament had come to a determination, to admit garbled extracts from such Letters as may be received from America by Administration and to Conceal the names of the Persons who may be the Writers of them. This will certainly give great Encouragement to Persons of wicked Intentions to Abuse the Nation and injure the Colonies in the grossest manner with Impunity, or even without detection. For a Confirmation hereof we need to recur no further back than a few Months, when undoubtedly the Accounts and Letters carried by Mr. Rob[in]son would have been attended with very Unhappy if not fatal effects, had not this Town been so attentive as to have Contradicted those false Accounts by the depositions of many credible Persons under Oath. But it cannot be supposed that a Community will be so Attentive but upon the most Alarming Events: In general Individuals are following their private concerns; while it is to be feared, the restless Adversaries are forming the most dangerous Plans for the Ruin of the Reputation of the People, in order to build their own Greatness on the Distruction of their liberties. This Game they have been long playing; and tho' in some few instances they have had a losing hand yet they have commonly Managed with such Art, that they have so far succeeded in their Malicious designs as to involve the Nation and the Colonies in Confusion and distress. This it is presumed they never could have accomplished had not those very letters been kept from the View of the Public, with a design perhaps to conceal the falshood of them the discovery of which would have prevented their having any mischievous Effects. This is the Game which we have reason to believe they are now playing: With so much Secrecy as may render it impossible for us fully to detect them on this Side of the Water; How deplorable then must be our Condition, if Ample Credit is to be given to their Testimonies against us, but the Government at home, and if the Names of our Accusers are to be kept a profound Secret, and the World is to See only such parts or parcells of their Representations as Persons, who perhaps may be interested in their favor, shall think proper to hold up. Such a Conduct, if allowed, seems to put into the Power of a Combination of a few designing Men to deceive a Nation to its Ruin. The Measures which have been taken in Consequence of Intelligence Managed with such Secrecy, have already to a very great degree lessened that Mutual Confidence which had ever Subsisted between the Mother Country and the Colonies, and must in the Natural Course of things totally alienate their Affections towards each other and consequently weaken, and in the End destroy the power of the Empire. It is in this extended View of things that our Minds are affected. It is from those Apprehensions that we earnestly wish that all Communication between the two Countries of a public Nature may be unvailed before the public: with the names of the persons who are concerned therein, then and not till then will American affairs be under the directions of honest Men, who are never affraid or Ashamed of the light. And as we have abundant Reason to be jealous that the most mischievous and virulent Accounts have been very lately sent to Administration from Castle William, where the Commissioners have again retreated for no reason that we can conceive but after their former manner to misrepresent and injure this Town and Province, we earnestly intreat that you would use your utmost influence to have an Order passed that *the whole* of the packetts sent by the Commissioners of the Customs and others under the Care of one Mr. Bacon late an Officer of the Customs in Virginia, who took his passage the last Week in the Brigantine Lydia[,] Joseph Wood[,] Commander[,] may be laid before his Majesty in Council. If the Writers of those Letters shall appear to be innocent, no harm can possibly arise from such a Measure; if otherwise, it may be the Means of exploring the true Cause of the National and Colonial Malady, and of affording an easy remedy, and therefore the Measure must be justified and applauded by all the World.

We have observed in the English Papers, the most notorious falsehoods published with an apparent design to give the World a prejudice against this Town, as the Aggressors in the unhappy Transaction of the 5th of March, but no account has been more repugnant to the truth, than a paper printed in the public Advertiser of the 28th of April which is called *The Case of Capt. Preston*. As a Committee of this Town We thought ourselves bound in faithfulness to wait on Capt. Preston to enquire of him whether he was the Author. He frankly told us that he had drawn a state of his Case, but that it had passed thro different hands and was altered at different times, and finally the Publication in the Advertiser was varient from that which he sent home as his own, but he declined Satisfying us herein, saying that the Alterations were made by Persons who he supposed might Aim at Serving him, though he feared they might have a Contrary effect, and that his discrimenating to us the parts of it which were his own from those which had been altered by others might displease his friends at a time when he might stand in need of their essential Service. This was the Substance of the Conversation between us, whereupon we retired and wrote to Capt. Preston a Letter the Copy of which is now inclosed.

The next day not receiving an Answer from Capt. Preston at the time we proposed, we sent him a Message desiring to be informed whether we might expect his Answer to which he replyed by a Verbal Message as Ours was that he had nothing further to add to what he had said to us the day before, as you'l please to observe by the inclosed Certificate.

As therefore Capt. Preston has utterly declined to make good the Charges against the Town in the Paper called his case or to let us know to whom we may apply as the Author or Authors of those parts which he might have disclaimed, and especially as the whole of his Case thus Stated directly Militates not only with his own Letter published under his hand in the Boston Gazette, but with the depositions of others annexed to our narrative which were taken, not behind the Curtain as some may have been, but openly and fairly, after notifying the Parties interested, and before Magistrates to whose Credit the Governor of the Province has given his full Attestation under the Province Seal, we cannot think that the Papers called the case of *Capt. Thomas Preston*, or any other Paper of the like import can be deemed in the opinion of the sensible and impartial part of Mankind as sufficient, in the least degree to prejudice the Character of the Town. It is therefore altogether needless for us to point out the many falsehoods contained in this Paper; nor indeed would there be time for it at present for the reason above mentioned. We cannot however omit taking Notice of the Artifice made use of by those who drew up the Statement in insinuating that it was the design of the People to plunder the Kings Chest; and for the more easily effecting to Murder the Centinel posted at the Custom House where the money was lodged. This intelligence said to have been brought to Capt. Preston by a Townsman, who assured him *that he heard the Mob declare* they would Murder the Centinel. The Townsman probably was one Greenwood a Servant to the Commissioners whose deposition Number 96 is inserted among others in the Narrative of the Town and of whom it is observed in a Marginal Note that "Through the whole of his examination he was so inconsistent, and so frequently Contradicted himself, that all present were Convinced that no Credit ought to be given to his deposition, for which reason it would not have been inserted had it been known that a description relating to this affair, from this Greenwood by Justice Murray and carried home by Mr. Robinson," and further "this deponent is the only person, out of a great number of Witnesses examined, who heard any thing mentioned of the Custom house." Whether this part of the Case of Capt. Preston was inserted by himself or some other person we are not told: It is very much to be questioned whether the information was given by any other than Greenwood himself, and the *Sort of Character* which he bears is so well known to the Commissioners and their Connections some of whom probably assisted Capt. Preston in Stating his Case, as to have made them ashamed if they regarded the truth, to have given the least credit to what he said. Whoever may have helped them to this intelligence, we will venture to say, that it never has been and never can be supported by the Testimony of any Man of a tolerable reputation. We shall only observe upon this occasion, how inveterate our Enemies here are, who, rather than omit what they think a lucky opportunity of Slandering the Town, have wrought up a Narrative not only unsupported by, but contrary to the clearest evidence of facts and have even prevailed upon an unhappy Man under pretence of friendship to him, to adopt it as his own: Though they must have known with a common share of understanding, that its being published to the world *as his own*, must have injured him, under his present circumstances, in the most tender point, and so shocked was Capt. Preston himself, at it appearing in the light on this side the Water, that he was imme-diately apprehensive so glaring a falsehood would raise the indignation of a people to such a pitch as to prompt them to some Attempts that would be dangerous to him, and he accordingly applyed to Mr. Sheriff Greenleaf for special protection on that Account. But the Sheriff assuring him there was no such disposition appearing among the People (which is an undoubted truth Capt. Preston fears at length Subsided: And he still remains in safe Custody, to be tried by the Superior Court of Judicature at the next term in August; unless the Judges shall think proper further to postpone the Trial, as they have done for one whole term, since he was indicted by the Grand Jury).

Before we conclude it may not be improper to observe that the removal of the troops was in the Slowest order, insomuch that eleven days were spent in Carrying the two Regiments to Castle Island, which had before landed in the Town in less than forty eight hours; Yet in all this time, while the Number of the Troops was daily lessening, not the least disorder was made by the inhabitants, tho' filled with a just indignation and horror at the blood of their fellow Citizens so inhumanely Spilt! And since their removal the Common Soldiers, have frequently and even daily come up to the Town for necessary provisions, and some of the officers, as well as several of the families of the Soldiers have resided in the Town and done business therein without the least Molestation. Yet so hardy have our Enemies been as to report in London that the enraged populace had hanged up Capt. Preston.

The strange and irreconcileable conduct of the Commissioners of the Customs since the 5th of March, their applying for leave to retire to the Castle so early in the month, and spending their time making excursions into the Country 'till the 20th of June following, together with other material Circumstances, are the Subject of our present enquiry; the result of which you will be made acquainted with by the next Conveyance. In the mean time we remain with strict truth, Sir Your much Obliged and most Obedient Servants

THOMAS CUSHING	WM. PHILLIPS
R DANA	W MOLINEUX
SAML ADAMS	EBENEZER STORER
JOHN HANCOCK	WM GREENLEAF

DOCUMENT **23**

THE SOLDIERS' APPEAL FOR A SINGLE TRIAL[91]

Of the many documents connected with the massacre, the brief appeal reproduced below is among the most intriguing. It is signed by Hugh White and James Hartigan; Mathew Kilroy, who presumably could not write, made his "mark." Hartigan's name was also rendered elsewhere as "Hartegan," and Kilroy appears in documents variously as "Killroy" and even "Kilroi"—spelling inconsistencies common for the age. The three accused asked that they be tried with Preston, not separately. The petitioners feared that if Preston were found innocent in one trial, that would increase the likelihood of their being found guilty in the next—a not unreasonable assumption. Only these three of the eight signed the appeal. Did the other five object or refuse to be involved? And why did they wait until October 24th, the day that Preston's trial began, to submit it? Had they made the appeal despite the advice of counsel?

A single trial would not necessarily have improved their chances, particularly if they shared attorneys. What was in the best interest of Preston may not have been in the best interests of his men if the defense attempted to argue on behalf of both simultaneously. By the professional standards of that day John Adams, Josiah Quincy Junior, and Robert Auchmuty, who acted for the defense, were not obliged to choose between representing Preston or the enlisted men. There could indeed have been just one trial, with defense counsel pleading for all nine. We do not know the precise date at which the Superior Court decided there would be two trials rather than one, with Preston being tried first, but both their separation and their sequence worked to the advantage of the defense rather than the prosecution—which everyone involved may well have known.

Kilroy's apparent inability to read or write did not disqualify him from pleading benefit of the clergy because the reading requirement—often a biblical passage—had been dropped many years before. Illiteracy is more of a commentary on the plight of the lower class in the British Isles than it is a commentary on the British army. The image of British soldiers being drawn from the dregs of society, many of them criminals pressed into service, is overdrawn. Illiteracy was still widespread among the working-class poor and virtually the only enlisted men whose duties required that they read were sergeants. True, the social divide between men in the ranks and men in the officer corps gaped wide. Gage was the younger son of a viscount and Dalrymple was the nephew of an earl. Many officers of higher rank could claim such social connections; virtually no one among the enlisted men could. Few, though, were habitual criminals; fewer still were dragooned into the army, in the way that the Royal Navy made use of press gangs. Even so, it was difficult to keep the ranks filled and rules on paper about age, height, and health were often ignored. The ideal recruit was roughly twenty, at least five foot seven, and healthy enough to serve a full decade. Most were English, though there was a disproportionate number of Scots and Irish when compared with the total population. That was primarily a function of limited opportunity in an age facing unsettling change in both town and countryside.

Soldiers in the lowest ranks were paid at about the same rate as day laborers and they were regarded as occupying the same lower rung on the class ladder— note, indeed, the characterization of the enlisted men in the indictment (see Document 18). Their lives could be "austere, squalid, harsh,"[92] but that was the condition afflicting the working class throughout much of Britain. And for all the privation facing the men, some did what they could to make the best of it. It is notable that Hartigan brought his wife, and Hugh Montgomery his wife and children, to Boston.

* * *

To the Honourable Judges of the
Superior Court,

May it please Yr. Honours we poor Distressed
Prisoners Beg that ye Would be So good as to lett us have
our Trials at the same time with our Captain, for we
did our Captains Orders & if we don't Obay is command
should have been Confin'd & shott for not doing of it —
We Humbly pray Yr. Honours that you would take it into
yr. serious consideration & grant us that favour for we
only desire to Open the truth before our Captains face
for it is very hard he being a Gentelman should have more
chance for to save his life then we poor men that is
Obadged to Obay his command — we hope that Yr. Honours
will grant this our petition, & we shall all be in duty
Bound ever to pray for your honours

Dated Boston Goal
October ye 24th 1770

Hugh White
James Hartigan
Math his + Killroy
        mark

Document 23 The soldiers' request for a separate trial. Courtesy of the Boston Public
Library/Rare Books.

QUESTIONS ABOUT THE COURT RECORD

John Hodgson took notes at the soldiers' trial that would eventually stand as the formal record. John Adams stated that Hodgson was a "Scottish or English stenographer" who had acted on his own in taking notes at that trial and at Preston's before. As in England, Massachusetts courts did not have clerks to record proceedings. Even the Court of King's Bench in London relied on professional note-takers, whose versions could end up as part of the official record. The only check on their accuracy would be the judges who presided. They had the right to review transcriptions before they were published.

According to Adams, Hodgson showed him his transcript from the soldiers' trial before it went to press. Adams "found so much inaccuracy and so many errors" in taking down his arguments that he "scratched out everything but the legal authorities and the testimonies of the witnesses."[93] But was Hodgson any better on the witnesses? The testimony of Edward Langford during the soldiers' trial serves as a case in point. Langford, one of the town watchmen, came upon the scene when Hugh White, the sentry, faced a growing crowd alone. Langford—unarmed, except for a staff—tried to calm White and put himself between White and the boys taunting him. He stepped back when Preston arrived with the relief party.[94] According to Hodgson's published transcript, Langford said that he was sure Kilroy shot Gray, but he did not claim to have actually seen Kilroy aim at Gray and pull the trigger. Rather, he deduced that Kilroy shot Gray because he heard Kilroy's musket fire, then Gray fell at his feet. When asked if Kilroy shot Gray he responded "it must have been" because "there was no other gun discharged at that time."[95] But another account, sent by Hutchinson to London and quite likely also prepared by Hodgson, differed from the printed version. Here Langford is recorded as saying, "There were two

Figure 14 A lead bullet, one of two bequeathed to the Massachusetts Historical Society in 1940. Their provenance before then is unclear. This one purportedly broke Edward Payne's arm as it passed through and then lodged in the door post behind Payne, who had been watching the scene from the entrance to his own house. The .75-caliber soft lead ball fired by a Brown Bess musket could produce a horrific wound, partic-ularly if it struck bone,  *which would shatter and cause the lead to flatten and spread, tearing tissue as it passed through. For Payne's location in relation to the soldiers and the crowd around them, see Revere's plan of the massacre scene (Document 10), on the lower left. Courtesy of the Massachusetts Historical Society.*

or three men on Kilroys right, 2 Guns were fired before he fired, upon his firing Gray who stood next to me droped at my feet, I don't know his Gun killed him, I heard no other."[96] The deduction made in the first version is absent in the second. Which, if either, recorded Langford's words accurately? It is impossible to say. How many other discrepancies are there? Again, it is impossible to say.

With modern record-keeping techniques it will presumably be easier for scholars in the future to establish what was said in a Massachusetts murder trial now than it has been for students of the massacre to reconstruct the trials that followed then. Nevertheless, the task for jurors remains relatively unchanged, despite improvements in assembling a body of evidence—the use of DNA, for example. The system still depends on Blackstone's notion of citizens "good and lawful" who can decide fairly and reach the best verdict, even in the face of conflicting testimony and fragmentary evidence.

Printed below are various versions of testimony offered by Richard Palmes, who was turned to more than any other witness in the aftermath of the mass-acre. Writing once again as "Vindex," Samuel Adams thought Palmes's version "the clearest account" of Private Montgomery's behavior in particular—crucial, because many thought that Montgomery fired first.[97] Palmes's deposition appears in A Short Narrative; A Fair Account printed either a briefer version of his statement or a second account given to a different justice of the peace.

Palmes testified at both Preston's and the soldiers' trial and was so troubled by what he considered inaccuracies in Hodgson's printed account that he submitted his own renditions to the Boston Gazette, *which in turn printed them. Considering the stakes involved, the differences are notable. Concerned about the record of his testimony during the soldiers' trial, Palmes wanted the public to understand what had happened between him and Montgomery, and to know that Montgomery slipped and fell after he fired, not before.*

A Boston merchant, Palmes obviously considered himself Preston's social equal. He placed his hand on Preston's shoulder; Preston responded respectfully; neither of which would have happened if someone like Attucks or Gray had attempted it. Again we are reminded that class and status mattered that night.

* * *

DEPOSITION IN THE *SHORT NARRATIVE*, 38–40 (NO. 53)

I Richard Palmes of Boston, of lawful age, testify and say, that between the hours of nine and ten o'clock on the 5th instant, I heard one of the bells ring, which I supposed was occasioned by fire, & enquiring where the fire was, was answered that *the soldiers were abusing the inhabitants*; I asked where, was first answered at Murray's barracks, I went there and spoke to some officers that were standing at the door, I told them I was surprized they suffered the soldiers to go out of the barracks after eight o'clock; I was answered by one of the officers pray do you mean to teach us our duty; I answered I did not, only to remind them of it; one of them said you see that the soldiers are all in their barracks, and why do not you go to your homes; Mr. James Lamb and I said, Gentlemen let us go home, & were answered by some, home, home; accordingly I asked Mr. William Hickling if he was going home, he said he was, I walked with him a far as the post-office, upon my stopping to talk with two or three people, Mr. Hickling left me; I then saw Mr. Pool Spear going towards the townhouse, he asked me if I was going home, I told him I was; I asked him where he was going that way, he said he was going to his brother David's. But when I got to the town-pump, we were told there was a rumpus at the custom-house door; Mr. Spear said to me you had better not go, I told him I would go and try to make peace; I immediately went there and saw *Capt. Preston* at the head of six or eight soldiers in a circular form, with guns breast high and bayonets fixed; the said Captain stood almost to the end of their guns. I went immediately to Capt. Preston (as soon as Mr. Bliss had left him) and asked him if their guns were loaded, his answer was they are loaded with powder and ball; I then said to him I hope you do not intend they shall fire upon the inhabitants; his reply was, by no means. When I was asking him these questions my left hand was on his right shoulder; Mr. John Hickling had that instant taken his hand off my shoulder, and stept to my left, then instantly I saw a piece of snow or ice fall among the soldiers, on which the soldier at the officer's right hand stept back and *discharged his gun*, at the space of some seconds the soldier at his left *fired* next, and the others one after the other. After the first gun was fired, I heard the word *Fire*, but who said it I know not; after the first gun was fired the *said officer had full time to forbid the other soldiers not to fire, but I did not hear him speak to them at all*; then turning myself to the left I saw one man dead, distant about six feet; I having a stick in my hand made a stroke at the soldier who fired, and struck the gun out of his hand. I then made a stroke at the officer, my right foot slipt, that brought me on my knee, the blow falling short, he says I hit his arm; when I was recovering myself from the fall I saw the soldier that fired the first gun endeavouring *to push me through with his bayonet*, on which I threw my stick at his head, the soldier starting back, gave me opportunity to jump from him into exchange-lane, or I must been inevitably run thro' my body. I looked back and saw three persons laying on the ground, and perceiving a soldier stepping round the corner as I thought to shoot me, I ran down Exchange Lane, and so up the next into Kingstreet, and followed Mr. Gridley with several other persons with the body of Capt. Morton's apprentice up to the prison house, and saw he had a ball shot through his breast; at my return I found that the officer and soldiers were gone to the main guard. *To my best observation there were not seventy people in King Street at the time of their firing, and them very scattering*, but in a few minutes after the firing there were upwards of a thousand; finding the soldiers were gone I went up to the main-guard and saw there the soldiers were formed into three divisions, the front division in the posture of platoon firing, and I expected they would fire. Hearing that his Honor the Lieutenant Governor was going to the Council-chamber, I went there, his Honor looking out of the door desired the people to hear him speak; he desired them to go home and he would enquire into the affair in the morning, and that the law should take its course, and said, I will live and die by the law. A gentleman desired his Honor to order the soldiers to their barracks, he answered it was not in his power, and that he had no command over the troops and it lay with Col. Dalrymple and not with him, but that he would send for him, which after some time he did; upon that a gentleman desired his Honor to lookout the window facing the main-guard, to see the position the soldiers were in, *ready to fire on the inhabitants, which he did after a good deal of persuasion*, and called for Col. Carr and desired him to order the troops to their barracks in the same order they were in; accordingly there ordered to should their guns, and were marched off by some officers, and further saith not.

DEPOSITION IN THE *FAIR ACCOUNT,* APPENDIX, 13–14 (NO. 112).

I Richard Palms, of lawful age, testify and say that between the hours of nine and ten o-clock last Monday evening, the 5th instant, I heard one of the bells ring, which I thought was for fire; I went towards where I thought it was, and was told that the soldiers were abusing the inhabitants; I asked where the soldiers were, and was answered in King street, and that there was a rumpus at the custom-house door; as soon as I got there I saw Capt. Preston at the head of six or eight soldiers; the soldiers had their guns breast high, with their bayonets fixed. I went immediately to Capt. Preston, and asked him if the soldiers guns were loaded; his answer was, "They were loaded with powder and ball;" I then asked him if he intended they should fire on the inhabitants, his answer was, "By no means." I did not hear him tell the soldiers not to fire, nor did I hear him speak to them. I saw a piece of ice fall among the soldiers; immediately upon this the soldier upon his right hand fired his gun, that instant I heard the word "Fire," but by whom I know not; the soldier at his left hand fired next, and the others one after another, as fast as they could. I turned myself to my left, and saw one man dead, upon which I struck the soldier who first fired the gun, and hit his left arm or hand, which made his gun fall; I then struck at Capt. Preston, and thought I hit his head, but he says I hit his arm; on my making the stroke at him I fell on my right knee. I saw the soldier that had fired the first going to push his bayonet at me, upon which I threw my stick at his head; he gave back, and gave me an opportunity to jump out of his way, or must have been run through the body. I directly passed through Exchange-lane, and so up the next by Mr. Kent's office, and saw three people on the ground, and saw Mr. Gridley, with several other persons, carrying Mr. Morton's apprentice up to the prison house. I followed him, and saw he had a ball shot through his breast; at my return, found the soldiers were gone to the main guard, &c.

TESTIMONY IN PRESTON'S TRIAL, FROM AN UNPUBLISHED SOURCE, PRO/CO/5/759, FOS. 361–362

Being at the Coffee House afer I heard the Bells—went up King Street—saw the Centinel walking quietly—went up by the Town House—people told me the Soldiers at Murray's barracks were abusing the People—I went there saw a number of Officers at the Gate with Guns and People before them about 20 or 30—I ask'd the Officer why they suffered the Men to be out after eight oClock—Do you mean to teach me my duty—no but to remind of it —One of the Officers said the Soldiers are gone into the Barracks, let the People go home—Mr. Lamb said home, home—they went off—I came through the alley with Mr. Hickling—I saw Mr. Pool Spear—I walked with him to the Pump—somebody there said there was a Rumpus in Kingstreet—I went down—when I had got there I saw Capt. Preston at the head of 7 or 8 soldiers at the Custom house drawn up, their Guns breast high & Bayonets fixed—found Theodore Bliss talking with the Captain—I heard him say why don't you fire or words to that effect—the Captain answered I know not what and Bliss said God damn you don't you fire—I was close behind Bliss—they were both in the front—then I step'd immediately between them and put my left hand in a familiar manner on the Captain's right shoulder to speak to him—Mr. John Hickling then looking over my shoulder I said to Preston are your Soldiers Guns loaded—he answered with powder & ball—Sir I hope you don't intend the Soldiers shall fire on the Inhabitants—he said by no means—the instant he spoke I saw something resembling Snow or Ice strike the Grenadier on the Captains right hand being the only one then at his right—he instantly stepd one foot back and fired the first Gun—I had then my hand on the Captains shoulder—after the Gun went off I heard the word fire—the Captain and I stood in front about half between the breech and muzzle of the Guns—I dont know who gave the word fire—I was then looking on the Soldier who fired—the word was given loud—the Captain might have given the word and I not distinguish it—after the word fire in about 6 or 7 seconds the Grenadier on the Captains left fired and then others one after another —The Captain stood still till the second Gun was fired—after that I turned and saw the Grenadier who fired first attempting to prick me by the side of the captain with his Bayonet—I had a large Stick in my hand—I struck over hand and hit him on his left arm—knocked his hand from his Gun— the Bayonet struck the Snow and jarr'd the breech out of his hand—I had not before struck at anybody—Upon that I turnd, thinking the other would do the same and struck at anybody at first and hit Preston—in striking him my foot slip'd and my blow fell short and hit him, as he afterwards told me, on the arm—When I heard the word fire the Captains back was to the Soldiers and face to me—Before I recovered the Soldier who fired the first Gun was attempting again to push me through—I tossed my Stick in his face—he fell back and I jump'd towards the lane—he push'd at me there and fell down—I turn'd to catch his Gun—another Soldier pushed at me and I ran off—returned soon and saw the dead carrying off and the party was gone—The Gun which went off first had scorched the nap of my Surtout at the elbow—I did not hear the Captain speak after he answered me—was there but about 3/4 of a minute in the whole—There was time enough between the first and second Gun for the Captain to have spoke to his Men—He stood leaning on the dagger in the scabbard—At the time of the firing there was between 50 & 80 people at some distance not crowding upon the Soldiers & thin before them.

Testimony in the Soldiers' Trial, Same Source, fos. 383–384

I know Montgomery I saw him with the party after 9 oclock heard, Saw a piece of Ice or Snow strike Montgomery's Gun, it made a noise, whether it staggered him back or he only stepd back I cant tell which I then thot he stepd he immediately recovered and fired, as soon as he fired I heard the word fire and in 6 or 8 seconds another Gun was fired and then the next, the last was fired 2 seconds after the rest, just as this last Gun was fired I made a stroke with a stick at Montgomery, hit his arm, his Gun drop'd with the Bayonet to the Ground, and before he recovered I struck at the next, Montgomery then pushed at me again and dropd his Gun. I attempted to take it up but another Soldier pushing at me I turned & run. I am sure Montgomery did not fall before he fired, the thing thrown struck his Gun and body. I saw no other blow or anything else thrown save what I have mentioned. I had a Surtout on and the powder from Montgomery's gun scorched the Nap off my Surtout elbow. I was in close conversation with Capt. Preston when the first Gun was fired as soon as this Gun was fired there was a general running every way.

Testimony in the Soldiers' Trial, from Hodgson's Printed Record

Q. Do you know any of the prisoners?

A. I know *Montgomery*, I saw him in *King-street* with the party on the evening of the 5th of *March* last. I was with some gentlemen in company, I heard the bells ring after 9 o'clock; I went into *King-street*, and saw the Sentry at the *Custom-house* door as usual, and no body with him: when I came to the *Town-house*. I was told the soldiers were abusing the inhabitants; I asked where, and was told at *Murray's* barracks. I went down there, and saw four or five soldiers, with their guns and bayonets; I told the officers who stood by, I was surprised they suffered the soldiers to be out at that time of night; an officer said, do you pretend to teach us our duty Sir, I said no, only to remind you of it: You see, says he, the soldiers are in their barracks, why do not you go home. I saw Mr. *Hickling*, he was my neighbour, he said he was going home, we came up as far as the post-office, where he left me; then I saw Mr. Spear, he said he was going to his brother *David's*; when I got to the Town pump, I heard a noise, and was told there was a rumpus at the *Custom house*; I said, I will go down and make peace, he said, you had better not go. I left Mr. *Spear*, and went down, and saw Capt. *Preston* at the head of seven or eight soldiers, with their guns, and bayonets fixed; I went to Capt. *Preston*, and saw Mr. Theodore Bliss talking with him, who said to

Capt. *Preston*, "Why do you not fire," "God damn you fire." I stept between them and asked Capt. *Preston* if the soldiers were loaded, he said yes, with powder and ball: I said, I hope Sir you are not going to fire upon the inhabitants, he said by no means: That instant I saw a piece of ice strike *Montgomery*'s gun, whether it sallied him back, or he stept one foot back, I do not know, but he recovered himself, and fired immediately. I thought he stept back and fired, he was the next man to Capt. *Preston*, the only soldier that was betwixt the *Captain* and the *Custom house*. When he fired, I heard the word fire, who gave it I do not know. Six or eight seconds after that, another soldier on the *Captain's* right fired, and then the rest one after the other, pretty quick; there was an interval of two or three seconds, between the last gun but one, and the last.

Q. How many guns were fired?

A. I do not know for certain, seven or eight I believe, I did not count them. Before the last gun was fired, *Montgomery* made a push at me with his bayonet, I had a stick in my hand, as I generally walk with one, I struck him, and hit his left arm, and knocked his gun down; before he recovered I aimed another stroke at the nearest to me, and hit Capt. *Preston*, I then turned and saw *Montgomery* pushing at me again, and would have pushed me through, but I threw my stick in his face, and the third time he ran after me to push at me again, but fell down, and I had the opportunity to run down *Royal-exchange lane*.

Q. Did you take notice of the situation of the soldiers?

A. I saw the form they were in, they were formed in a half circle.

Q. Which way did *Montgomery* front?

A. He fronted the watch house.

Q. Did you stand in a range with the watch house and corner of the *Custom-house*?

A. Yes.

Q. Are you certain that *Montgomery* was struck and sallied back before he fired?

A. Yes.

Q. Do you know whether it was a piece of ice or a club?

A. No.

Q. Do you know whether it hit his body, or his gun, or both?

A. It struck both, I suppose.

Q. Did you see any other violence offered, except that which struck *Montgomery*, and the blows that you aimed and gave?

A. No, no other.

Q. Are you sure *Montgomery* did not fall, just before he discharged his gun?

A. Yes.

Q. Upon the firing the first gun did the people seem to retire?

A. Yes, they began to run, and when the rest were firing they were a running.

Q. Did you see any of the deceased fall?

A. No, I did not, but afterwards I saw Gray and Attucks lying.

Q. Did you see all the rest of the soldiers discharge their pieces?

A. I saw the smoke, and it appeared to me at that time they all fired.

Q. When the last gun was fired, where were the people?

A. They were running promiscuously about every where.

Testimony from Both Trials, as Palmes Recalled it, *Boston Gazette*, March 25, 1771

As the sentiments of the People seems various concerning the Testimony I gave relating to the Concern of Capt. Preston and the Soldiers, in the horrid Massacre of the 5th of March, 1770, I beg your Favour, to communicate thro' the Channel of your important Paper, my whole Evidence, which without Favor or Affection, take as follows.

At PRESTON's Trial

Court. PLEASE to relate to the Court what you know concerning the 5th of March.

A. Between the hours of nine and ten o'clock, &c. as per Narrative p. 38 No. 53.

Q. Did you hear Mr. Bliss say any thing to Captain Preston?

A. I did.

Q. Inform the Court what he said to him.

A. He said to Capt. Preston, "*Why don't you fire?*" Capt. Preston made him some answer, but what it was, I cannot say.—Then Mr. Bliss returned, God damn you, why don't you fire? Upon this, I stept in between him and Capt. Preston, as related above.

Q. At the time the soldiers fired, did you see a number of things thrown at them?

A. I saw nothing thrown, or touch them, excepting that which struck Montgomery.

Q. Did you situate yourself before Capt. Preston, in order that you might be out of danger, in case they fired?

A. I did not apprehend myself in any danger.

Q. Did you hear Captain Preston give the word *Fire*?

A. I have told your Honours, that after the first gun was fired, I heard the word *fire!* But who gave it, I know not.

Q. Do you think it was possible Capt. Preston should give the word *fire*, and you not be certain he gave it.

A. I think it was.

At the SOLDIERS' Trial

Court. Do you know any one of the prisoners at the bar?

A. I know Montgomery: I saw him with the party in King-street the 5th of March.

Q. Please to relate what you saw of him.

A. I then repeated the same as I did in at the trial of Captain Preston.

Q. In what manner were the soldiers situated?

A. They were in a circular form.

Q. Which way did Montgomery front?

A. He fronted the Watch-House.

Q. Did you stand in range with the Watch-House, and corner of the custom-house?

A. In a range from Montgomery's left, with the watch-house.

Q. Are you sure Montgomery was struck and sallied back before he fired?

A. I tho't he stept back when it hit him.

Q. Do you know whether it was a piece of ice, or a club?

A. It was something resembling ice.

Q. Do you know whether it hit his body, or his gun, or both?

A. I think it struck both.

Q. Did you see any other violence offered, except to Montgomery, & the blows that you gave?

A. I saw no other.

Q. Are you sure Montgomery did not fall just before he fired?

A. Yes, I am sure of it.

Q. Upon firing the first gun, did the people seem to retire?

A. Yes, they appeared to me to run, promiscuously, from the first gun's being fired to the last.

Q. Did you see any of the deceased fall?

A. I did not; my back was towards them; at that time I ran into royal-exchange-lane; and as I turned, I saw Gray & Attucks lying in the snow.

Q. Did you see all the rest of the soldiers discharge their pieces?

A. I saw the smoke, and at the time it appeared to me they all fired.

Court. Call James Bailey [Palmes essentially follows Hodgson's *Trial* here].

Q. Have you heard Mr. Palmes?
A. Yes.
Q. Are you satisfied notwithstanding what Mr. Palmes says, that Montgomery was knocked down by a blow given him immediately before he fired?
A. Yes.

I imagine this evidence was bro't to invalidate my declaration in court; but I assure the world upon the oath I then took, that Montgomery did not fall until he attempted to push his bayonet thro' my body; which was about the time the last gun went off.

A JUDGE'S DIRECTIONS TO JURORS[98]

Three of the four judges who presided at Preston's and the soldiers' trials attended Harvard College; none of the four attended law school. Indeed, there was no law school for them to attend. Colonial American lawyers learned the law under an apprenticeship system that is now little understood and too easily dismissed as inferior to the formal schooling now required before an aspiring attorney can become a member of the Bar in most states. Apprenticeships could be as inexact as they were informal, lacking method or substance. But as Professor Dan Coquillette has argued, for a privileged few the apprentice-ship approach had much to recommend it and it was not inherently inferior because young lawyers learned their trade in an office rather than a classroom. It is clear that at least in some instances they did not simply perform mundane tasks as clerks for the lawyers who took them on; they read in legal philosophy as well as court procedure and learned as much about the principles of justice that undergird the rule of law as students learn now through the case study approach.[99]

Edmund Trowbridge, whose directions to jurors in the soldiers' trial follow, was born in 1709. He was a practicing attorney by the 1730s in his home-town of Cambridge and involved in provincial politics by the 1740s, first as a member of the Massachusetts House and then as a member of the governor's Council. He served briefly as attorney general, and Francis Bernard appointed him to the Superior Court in 1767. Although he was no slavish government man, he did not hide his disdain for popular politics and mob action. In the years following the massacre he and Thomas Hutchinson would have a falling out. Trowbridge decided against taking a loyalist stand, even if he was not particularly attracted to the patriot cause. At the time of the massacre trials, however, he and Hutchinson were allied and they were generally perceived by their critics as being part of an elitist element too far removed from the people. Technically speaking, Hutchinson was still chief justice as well as lieutenant governor, though he did not take the bench in controversial cases like those that resulted from the massacre. His multiple office-holding was common on the provincial level, decried though it would be by his political opponents. Benjamin Lynde stood in as acting chief justice, joined on the bench by Trowbridge, Peter Oliver, and John Cushing.

Though junior-most of the four in age and years served on the Court, Trowbridge was regarded by many as the best legal scholar among them, a stickler for detail who reveled in mastering the arcane. He was the only one of the four who had practiced law; Lynde had studied law but did not earn a living from it. Neither Oliver nor Cushing—nor Hutchinson, for that matter— had studied the law or joined the Bar before they became judges.

Trowbridge gave some sense of his attachment to legal detail in his instructions to jurors in the soldiers' trial. That he attempted to guide jurors in interpreting the evidence, not just make sure they understood points of law and the legal issues involved, was common practice. He and his "brothers" on the bench routinely sought to direct jurors toward what they considered the correct verdict—and in that they imitated English judges, as they did in most things legal. Their jury directions consequently often acted as a closing argument. Done well, their commentary could easily overshadow the points made by the prosecutors and defense counsel.

Despite there being a certain amount of pedantry in Trowbridge's instructions to jurors at the soldiers' trial, his didactic style served a purpose. Trowbridge endeavored to lay a strong legal foundation for the verdicts he thought the jurors should reach. Thus his distinguishing between murder and manslaughter, and his setting aside treason as irrelevant. He also insisted that the King had the authority to station soldiers among civilians, in peacetime as well as war. He concentrated on those witnesses whose testimony supported the position he thought jurors should take, although he did so artfully, in the form of suggestions rather than instructions, an "if you believe this, then you ought to conclude that" approach. The other judges did much the same. No doubt some Court watchers thought the jury's subsequent verdicts reasonable. No doubt others thought that all four judges took the soldiers' side and attempted to sway any wavering jurors with their one-sided recapitulation of the evidence. Yet no notable public protest followed the verdicts. The jurors afterward went home; the soldiers—Kilroy and Montgomery included, after their sentencing and branding—went free.

* * *

Gentlemen of the Jury,

William Wemms, James Hartegan, William McCauley, Hugh White, Matthew Killroy, William Warren, John Carrol and *Hugh Montgomery,* prisoners at the bar, are charged by the Grand Jurors for the body of this county, with having feloniously and of their malice aforethought, shot and thereby killed and murdered *Samuel Maverick, Samuel Gray, James Caldwell, Patrick Carr,* and *Crispus Attucks,* against the peace, crown and dignity of our Sovereign Lord the King; altho' it is laid in each indictment that some one of the prisoners in particular gave the mortal wound, yet as all the rest of them are charged as principals in the murder; and therefore, if upon consideration of the evidence given in this case, it should appear to you that all the prisoners gave the mortal wound, or that any one of them did it, and that the rest were present aiding and abetting him to do it, the indictment will be well maintained against all the prisoners, so far as respects the killing, because in such case, the stroke of one is, in consideration of law, the stroke of all. And as the crime whereof the prisoners are accused is of such a nature as that it might have been committed by anyone of them, though the indictments purport a joint charge, yet the law looks on the charge as several against each of the prisoners. To this charge they have severally pleaded Not Guilty, and thereby thrown the burden of proof on the Crown.

Considering how much time has already been taken up in this case, and the multiplicity of evidence that has been given in it, I shall not spend any time in recapitulating what each witness has testified, especially as your Foreman has taken it in writing from the mouths of witnesses, but shall endeavour to point out the manner in which the various testimonies are to be considered, and how the evidence given is to be applied, still leaving it to you to determine how far that which has been testified by each witness is to be believed. But before I do this, it may not be improper, considering what has in the course of this year been advanced, published, and industriously propagated among the people, to observe to you that none of the indictments against the prisoners are founded on the act of this province, or the law given to the *Jews,* but that, all of them are indictments at common law.

The prisoners are charged with having offended against the common law, and that only; by that law therefore they are to be judged, and by that law condemned, or else they must be acquitted. This seems to be make it highly proper for me to say something to you upon the common law, upon homicide and the several kinds and degrees of it, and the rules for trial of homicide as settled and established by the common law.

The laws of *England* are of two kinds, the unwritten or common law, and the written or statute law. The general customs or immemorial usage of the *English* nation, is properly the common law. And the evidence thereof are the Records of the several Courts of Justice, the Books of Reports and Judicial Decisions, and the Treatises of the Sages of the Law, handed down to us from the times of the highest antiquity. The common law is the law by which the proceedings and determinations in the King's ordinary Courts of Justice, are guided and directed.

This law is the birth right of every Englishman.—The first settlers of this country brought it down from *England* with them.—It was in force here when the act of this province against common murder was made. Murder here was then a felony by common law, and excluded Clergy by, 23 Henry VIII c. 1 and 1 Edward VI c. 12.—So that, that province act created no *new* Felony. It was in affirmance of the common law.—If murder by that act had been made a *new* felony, a murderer would not be intitled to the benefit of clergy by force of 25 Edward III c. 4 because it is not taken away by that province act or any other made since.

Homicide is of three kinds, justifiable, excusable, and felonious—The first has no share of guilt at all—the second very little, but the third is the highest crime against the law of nature. There are also degrees of guilt in felonious homicide, which divide the offence into manslaughter and murder. I shall give some instances under each head, proper to be considered in this case, *and known to this day.*

And first of justifiable homicide.—Killing him who attempts to rob or murder me, to break open my dwelling-house in the night, or burn it, or by force to commit any other felony on me, my wife, child, servant, friend, or even a stranger, if it cannot otherwise be prevented, is justifiable. By common law it was, and still is, the duty of peace officers, such as Justices of the Peace, Sheriffs, Under-sheriffs, and Constables, to suppress riots, routs, and unlawful assemblies.—The Statute 13 Henry IV c. 8 subjected Justices of the Peace, Sheriffs, and Under-sheriffs to the penalty of £100, if they neglected their duty therein. And as the common law obliges the peace officers to suppress riots, &c. so it empowers them to raise a sufficient force to enable them to do it.—A Justice of the Peace, Sheriff, or Under-sheriff may raise the power of the county, and the Constable of a town, the people of a town, to aid and assist him in suppressing a riot and apprehending the rioters, and if they stand in their defence, resist the officer, and continue their riotous proceedings in pulling down a house, assaulting and beating, or abusing any person or persons, such rioters may lawfully be killed, if they cannot otherwise be prevented. It is the duty of all persons (except women, decrepid persons, and infants under sixteen) to aid and assist the peace officers to suppress riots &c. when called upon to do it.— They may take with them such weapons as are necessary to enable them effectually to do it, and may justify the beating, wounding, and even killing such rioters as resist, or refuse to surrender, if the riot cannot otherwise be suppressed, or the rioters apprehended. So in case of a sudden affray, if a private person interposing to part the combatants, and giving notice of his friendly design, is assaulted by them, or either[100] of them, and in the struggle he happens to kill, he may justify it, because it is the duty of every man to interpose in such cases to preserve the public peace. *A fortiori*[101] private persons may interpose to suppress a riot.

Homicide excusable in self-defence is where one is engaged in a sudden affray, quits the combat before a mortal wound could be given, retreats as far as he safely can, and then urged by mere necessity, kills his adversary in the defence of his own life. This differs from justifiable self defence, because he was to blame for engaging in the affray, and therefore must retreat as far as he can safely; whereas in the other case aforementioned neither the peace officers, nor his assistants, nor the private person, is obliged to retreat, but may stand and repel force by force.

Manslaughter is the unlawful killing another without malice express or implied:—As voluntarily upon a sudden heat, or involuntarily in doing an unlawful act. Manslaughter on a sudden provocation differs from excusable homicide in self defence, in this; that in one case there is an apparent necessity for self-preservation to kill the aggressor, in the other there is no necessity at all, it being a sudden act of revenge. As where one is taken in the act of adultery, and instantly killed by the husband in the first transport of passion. So if one, on angry words assaults another by wringing his nose, and he thereupon *immediately* draws his sword and kills his assailant, it is but Manslaughter, because the peace is broken, with an indignity to him that received the assault, and he being so affronted, might reasonably apprehend the other had some further design on him.

Where one happens to kill another in a contention for the wall, it is but manslaughter. So where H and A came into *Buckner*'s lodging, A takes down a sword in the scabbard hung there, stood at the chamber door with the sword undrawn to prevent *Buckner* from going out before they could bring a Bailiff to arrest him for a debt he owed H; and upon some discourse between *Buckner* and H, *Buckner* takes a dagger out of his pocket, stabs and kills H with it. This was adjudged only manslaughter at common law, and not to come within the statute of 1 James I against stabbing, because *Buckner* was unlawfully imprisoned. So where an officer abruptly and violently pushed into a gentleman's chamber, early in the morning to arrest him, without telling him his business, or using words of arrest, and the gentleman not knowing him to be an officer, in his first surprise, *took down a sword and stabbed him.* This also was ruled to be but manslaughter at common law, because the gentleman might reasonably conclude from the officer's behaviour, that he came to rob or murder him. So where *Marshal* and some other Bailiffs, came to *Cook*'s dwelling house about eight o'clock in the morning, called upon him to open his doors and let them enter, because they had a warrant, on such and such writs, at the suit of such persons, to arrest him, and required him to obey them, but he told them they should not enter, and bid them depart, and thereupon they broke a window, and then came to the door of the house, and in attempting to force it open, broke one of the hinges, where upon *Cook* shot *Marshal* and killed him; it was adjudged not to be murder, because though *Marshal* was an officer, yet he was not in the due execution of his office, but was doing an unlawful act in attempting to break open the house to execute such a civil process; and every one has a right to defend his house in such cases; but to be manslaughter, because *Cook* saw *Marshal*, knew him, shot and killed him voluntarily, when he might have resisted him without killing him. Though no words of reproach, nor actions, or gestures expressive of reproach or contempt, without an assault, will by common law free the party killing from the guilt of murder, yet words, of menace of bodily harm, may amount to such a provocation, as to make the offence to be but manslaughter.

If these determinations appear new and extraordinary to you, it is not to be wondered at, considering the doctrines that of late have been advanced and propagated among you. In the course of this year you doubtless have heard much of the law given to the *Jews*, respecting homicide, as well as of the precept given to *Noah*, that "Whoso shedeth man's blood, by man shall his blood be shed." Whence it has been inferred, that whoever *voluntarily* kills another, whatever the inducement, or provocation may be, is a *murderer*, and as such ought to be put to death. But surely not only the avenger of blood, and he who killed a thief breaking up an house in the night, were exceptions to that general precept, but also he who killed another in his own defence. Even the Jewish Doctors allowed for this and that justly; because the right of self-defence is founded in the law of nature. The *Jews* indeed suppos'd their law equally subjected to death, him who killed another, whether of malice aforethought, or on a sudden falling out: but it seems the early christian divines did not, for the Clergy in the reign of *Canute*, the beginning of the eleventh century, so construed the *Mosaical* law as to deem him a murderer, who in time past had conceived hatred against his neighbour and him in wait for him and killed him, and him guilty of manslaughter only who killed another on a sudden provocation; and it is ordained by one of the laws of *Canute*, that if any person shall with premeditation kill another he shall be openly delivered up to the kindred of the slain, but if the killing be not with premeditation the Bishop shall take cognizance of it. And as homicides have since happened, and been tried in the King's Courts, the Judges have from time to time, determined them to be either justifiable, excusable, or felonious: and if felonious, to be murder or manslaughter, according to the particular circumstances that attended the killing.

These determinations of the King's Courts, for so many ages past, shew, not only what the common law in cases of this kind is, but that these rules of the common law, are the result of the wisdom and experience of many ages.—However it is not material in the present case, whether the common law is agreeable to, or variant from, the law given to the *Jews*, because it is certain, the prisoners are not in this Court to be tried by *that* law, but by the common law, that is according to the settled and established rules, and antient customs of the nation, approved for successions of ages.

Murder, by the common law, is the unlawful killing [of] a reasonable creature, under the King's peace, of malice aforethought, by a person of sound mind and discretion. Malice is the grand criterion that distinguishes murder from all other homicide. Malice aforethought, is not confined to an old grudge, or fixed, settled anger against a particular person, but it extends to a disposition to do evil. It is the dictate of a wicked, depraved, and malignant spirit. As when one with a sedate, deliberate mind, and formed design kills another. Not where the killing is owing to a sudden transport of passion, occasioned by any considerable provocation. For the law pays such regard to human frailty, as not to put a hasty act, and a deliberate one, upon the same footing with regard to guilt.

In the case of duelling, when two, upon a sudden quarrel, instantly draw their swords and fight, and one kills the other, it is manslaughter; but if on such a quarrel in the morning, they agree to fight in the afternoon, or so long after as that there is sufficient time for the blood to cool, the passions to subside, and reason to interpose, and they meet and fight accordingly, if one kills the other, it is murder. So if a man resolves to kill the next man he meets, and does it, it is murder, although he knew him not, for this shews the malignity of his heart, and his universal malice. So where one maliciously strikes or shoots another, but misses him and kills a third person, whom he did not intend to hurt, it is nevertheless murder, because he is answerable for all the consequences of his malicious act; but if the blow intended against A, and lighting on B, arose from a sudden transport of passion, which in case A had died by it, would have reduced the offense to manslaughter, the fact will admit of the same alleviation if B should happen to fall by it.

If two or more come together to do an unlawful act against the King's peace, of which the probable consequence might be bloodshed, as to beat a man, or commit a riot, and in the prosecution of that design, one of them kills a man, it is murder in them all. So where one kills another willfully without a considerable provocation, it is murder, because no one unless of an abandoned heart, would be guilty of such an act upon a slight or no apparent cause. So if one kills an officer of justice, either civil or criminal, in the execution of his duty, or any of his assistants endeavouring to conserve the peace, or any private person endeavouring to suppress an affray, or apprehend a felon, knowing his authority, or the intention with which he interposes, it is murder.

As to the rules settled and established by common law, for the trial of homicide, it is observable, That no person can by common law, be held to answer for any kind of homicide, at the suit of the king only, unless he first be accused thereof by a jury of the country where the fact was done.—That he who is so accused, may on the plea of Not Guilty, not only put the council for the King upon the proof of the fact, but when it is proved, may give any special matter in evidence to justify or excuse it, or to alleviate the offence.— That the facts are to be settled by another Jury of the same county, who are supposed to be best knowing of the witnesses and their credibility, and their verdict must be founded on the evidence given them in Court.—That if any of the jurors are knowing of the facts, they ought to inform the Court if it, be sworn as witnesses, and give their testimonies in Court, to the end it may be legal evidence to their fellows, and the Court may know on what evidence the jury's verdict is founded.—That the Court are to determine the law arising on the facts, because they are supposed to know it.—That the Jury, under the direction of the Court in point of law, matters of fact being still left to them, may give a general verdict conformable to such direction; but in cases of doubt, and real difficulty, the Jury ought to state the facts and circumstances in a special verdict, that the Court upon farther consideration thereof, may determine what the law is thereon.—That although malice is to be collected from all circumstances, yet the Court, and not the Jury, are the proper Judges thereof; as also, if the quarrel was sudden, whether there was time for the passions to cool, or whether the act was deliberate or not. The judge ought to recommend to the Jury to find the facts specially, or direct them hypothetically, as—if you believe such and such witness, who have sworn so and so, the killing was malicious, and then you ought to find the prisoners guilty of murder; but if you do not believe these witnesses, then you ought to find them guilty of manslaughter only. And according to the nature of the case,—if you on the evidence given, believe the facts to be so, then the act was deliberate, or if you believe the facts to be so, then it was not deliberate, and according as you believe, so you ought to find one or the other.

To what has been said under this head I must add, that in the trial of this case, both the Court and jury are as much obliged to observe these rules, as Court and Jury in *England* would be in the trial of a like case there; the law in these respects is the same here, as there. A Juror's oath in this case is also the same here, as there. Therefore by law, you are to settle the facts in this case, upon the Evidence given you *in Court*: you must be sensible, that in doing it, you ought not to have any manner of regard to what you have read or heard of the case *out of Court*. And as it is the proper business of the Court, to determine the law arising upon the facts, you must also be sensible, that you are to take the law from the Court, and not collect it from what has been said by people out of Court, or, published in the news-papers, or delivered from the pulpits.

Having premised these things, I shall observe to you, the several questions that arise in this case; and point out to you the manner in which I think they may be best considered and determined.

The principal questions are these, *viz.*

    I. Whether the five persons said to be murdered, were in fact killed? And if so,

    II. Whether they, or either[102] of them were killed by the prisoners, or either of them? And if they were, then

    III. Whether such killing was justifiable, excusable, or felonious? And if the latter,

    IV. Whether it was manslaughter or murder?

As to the first, you have not only the coroner's inquest, but the testimony of so many witnesses, that the five persons were shot and thereby mortally wounded in the night of the 5th of *March* last, and some of them died instantly, and the rest in a few days after, that you doubtless will be satisfied they were all killed. And the same evidence must I think, also convince you, that they were all killed by the party of soldiers that were at the *Custom-house* that night, or by some of them.

Whether the prisoners were there, will therefore be your next enquiry. For if either of them was not, he must be acquitted. You have the testimony of *Bridgham* and *Simpson* as to *Wemms*; of *Danbrooke* and *Simpson* to *Hartegan*, of *Austin* as to *McCauley*; of *Simpson, Langford, Bailey* and *Clark* as to *White*; of *Archibald, Langford,* and *Brewer* as to *Killroy*; of *Dodge* and *Simpson* as to *Warren*; and of *Bailey, Bass, Palmes, Danbrooke* and *Wilkinson* as to *Montgomery*'s being at the *Custom house* that night, and of the party of soldiers that was there; and this is not contested with any opposite proof.—The law doth in this case make the testimony of two witnesses necessary for the Jury to settle a fact upon: If one swears it, and upon his testimony you believe it, that is sufficient evidence for you to find the fact. But if you are satisfied upon the evidence, that all the prisoners were there, yet, as each prisoner is severally charged with having killed these five persons, and by his plea has denied the charge, you must be fully satisfied upon the evidence given you, with regard to each prisoner, that he in particular, did *in fact*, or *in consideration of law*, kill one or more of these persons that were slain, or he must be acquitted.

The way therefore to determine this, will be for you to name some one of the prisoners, and then consider, whether it appears upon the evidence in the case, that he did *in fact* kill *Maverick*? And then, when upon the evidence it appears, he *in fact* killed Gray? And so enquire in the same manner, whether he did *in fact* kill either of the other three persons? And having noted how it appears upon the evidence with regard to him; you must then proceed in like manner with each of the other prisoners; and if upon a full consideration of the evidence in the case, you should be in doubt, as to any one of the prisoners having *in fact* killed either of the persons that were slain, you must consider whether he did it *in consideration of law*? Now all that are present, aiding and abetting one person in killing another, do, in judgment of law, kill him. The stroke of one is, in consideration of law, the stroke of all. When a number of persons assemble together to do so an unlawful act, and in prosecution of that design, one of them kills a man, all the rest of the company are in law considered as abetting him to do it.

You must therefore enquire how, and for what purpose, the prisoners came together at the *Custom house*, and what they did there before these persons were killed?

The Council for the prisoners say, that, if they were at the *Custom house* that night, they went there by order of the *Captain* of the *Main-guard* to support and protect the Sentry, who was insulted, assaulted and abused by a considerable number of people, assembled for that purpose; but as this is denied by the Council for the Crown, it will be proper to consider whether he was attacked? And if so, whether the prisoners went by order of the *Captain*, to support and protect him?

That a Sentry was in fact then placed at the *Custom house*, by order of Colonel *Dalrymple*, the Commanding Officer, as also that one had been placed there for a long time before, is testified by Capts. *O'Hara*, and *Mason*, and indeed the right to place Sentries, (it being in time of peace) is the only thing that has been questioned. Upon this, therefore I would observe, that as the main design of society, is the protection of individuals by the united strength of the whole community; so for the sake of unanimity, strength and dispatch, the supreme executive power is by the British constitution vested in a single person, the King or Queen. This single person has the sole power of raising fleets or armies; and the Statute of 13 Charles II c. 6 declares, That within all his Majesty's realms and *dominions*, the sole supreme government, command and *disposition* of the militia, and of *all forces* by sea and land, and *all forts* and *places of strength* is, by the law of *England* ever was, the undoubted right of his Majesty and his royal Predecessors, Kings and Queens of *England*. And as *Charles* the Second had this right as King of *England*, it of course comes to his successors, and our present Sovereign Lord the King, now hath it.

Indeed the Bill of Rights declares among other things, That the raising or keeping a standing army, within the kingdom, in a time of peace, unless with the consent of Parliament, is against law. And it is said, that upon the same principles whereon that declaration was founded, it is alike unlawful to be done in any other part of the King's dominions. But be that as it may, the Mutiny Acts annually made, shew the consent of Parliament, that the King in time of peace should keep up a standing army not only in the Kingdom, but in *America* also. They not only ascertain the number of troops that shall be kept up, but provide for the regulation of such of the King's troops as are in *America*. And therefore as by these acts the King is impowered to keep up these troops, and he, by common law, has the command and disposition of all forces by sea and land within his dominions, and is the principal conservator of the peace, he doubtless, well might send such part of those troops to this part of his dominions, in order to restore the public peace, or to aid and assist the civil Magistrate in preserving of it, as he judged necessary for the purpose; and if you should think there was no occasion for sending any troops here, for either of those purposes, that will not alter the case, because the King being the proper judge in that matter, the validity of his order will not depend upon the truth of the representations whereon it is founded.

The acts not only fix the number of troops to be kept up, but also establish a law martial for their government. Among other things, the acts subject every officer or soldier that keeps his post, or leaves before being relieved, or disobeys the *lawful* command of his superior officer, to such punishment as a Court Martial shall inflict,—though it extend to death itself. These troops are, and ever since they came here, have been under this martial law, and subject to as strict regulation, as in time of war. Placing Sentries is a necessary part of the regulation of our army, accordingly a Sentry hath in fact been kept at the *Custom house*, ever since the troops have been here; and it is sworn, by the Captains *O'Hara* and *Mason*, that it was done by order of the Commanding Officer. If so, you have no reason to doubt but that it was legally done.

Your next enquiry then will be, whether the Sentry so placed at the *Custom house* was attacked? Many witnesses have sworn that he was. But the Council for the Crown say, the contrary appears by the testimony of Col. *Marshall* and others.

It is with you to determine this matter upon the whole of the evidence given you. In doing it you ought to reconcile the several testimonies, if by any reasonable construction of the words it may be done.—Where some witnesses swear they saw such a thing done, and others swear they were present and did not see it: if the thing said to be done by such as it may be reasonably supposed some might see and others not, by reason of their want of observation, or particular attention to other matters there, as both may be true, you ought to suppose them to be so, rather than presume that any of the witnesses swear falsely. But if witnesses contradict each other, so that their testimonies cannot be reconciled, you must then consider the number of the witnesses on each side, their ability, integrity, indifference as to the point in question, and the probability or improbability arising from the nature of the thing in question, and upon the whole settle the fact as you verily believe it to be.

If you find the Sentry was attacked, the next thing to consider is, whether the prisoners went to protect him, and if so, whether it was lawful for them to do so. There is a great difference between a common affray, and attacking the King's forces. I think the law in that regard ought to be more generally known here than it seems to be. If upon a sudden quarrel from some affront given or taken, the neighborhood rise and drive the King's forces out of their quarters, it is a great misdemeanor, and if death ensues it may be felony in the assailants, but it is not treason, because *there was no intention against the King's person or government*: But attacking the King's forces *in opposition to his authority*, upon a march or in quarters, is levying war against the King. And resisting the King's forces, *if sent to keep the peace, may* amount to an overt act of high treason. Though it may be attended with great inconveniences for private persons, without a peace officer, to make use of arms for suppressing an ordinary riot, yet if the riot be such an one as savours of rebellion, it doubtless may lawfully be done.

You have heard what the witnesses deposed respecting the resolution taken to drive the soldiers out of town, *"because they had no business here."* You have also heard what has been testified of the proposals to *attack* the *Main-guard*—of the assembling of the people especially in *Dock square* —of the huzzaing for the *Main-guard* and *Kingstreet*—and of the attacking of the Sentry. Now if this was done in pursuance of a resolution taken "to drive the soldiers out of the town, *because they had no business here,*" I will not now determine whether it was treason or not; but it certainly was a riot that savoured of rebellion; for the suppressing whereof, private persons might not only *arm* themselves, but make use of their arms, if they could not otherwise suppress it. Much more might the *Captain* of the *Main guard* take the part of the *guard*, armed as usual, and go with them to protect the Sentry. By what *Crookshank, Benjamin Davis, Whittington*, and others have sworn, it seems the Sentry not only called to the *Main guard* for assistance, but two men went and told them they must send assistance directly or the Sentry would be murdered. Whereupon the *Captain* gave orders that a party should go to the assistance of the Sentry, and they were drawn out accordingly, led down to the *Custom house* by a *Corporal*, and followed by the *Captain*. Now as this party did not assemble, or go there, of their own accord, but were sent by their *Captain* to protect the Sentry, it must be supposed *that* was their design in going until the contrary appears. And although upon the evidence you should not be satisfied that the Sentry was attacked in pursuance of a resolution taken *to drive the soldiers out of town, because they had no business here,* yet considering the notice given by the two men to the *Captain*, of the danger the Sentry was in, and what the *Captain* himself might then see and observe of the attack upon the Sentry, (if any regard is to be had to what a great number of the witnesses have sworn) he well might order out such a party, and go with them to protect the Sentry: And it seems to be agreed that if the prisoners were at the *Custom-house* that night, all of them, except the Sentry, were of that party.

It has been said that this party of soldiers, when on their march, pushed *Fosdick* with a bayonet while he was standing peaceably in the street, and struck *Brewer* as soon as they got to the *Custom-house*, which shewed their design was to disturb the peace, and not to preserve it. But as *Fosdick* himself says, that, upon his refusing to move out of his place, they parted and went by him, you will consider whether it is not more reasonable to suppose, that what he calls a push was an accidental touch owing to the numbers in the street, rather than any thing purposely done to hurt him; and so with regard to the blow said to be given by one of the party, and the blow by him or another of them, it will by no means be sufficient to prove a design in the whole party, to disturb the peace, nor will all of them be involved in the guilt of one or more of them that broke the peace, unless they *actually* aided or abetted him or them that did it; because they were assembled and sent forth for a different purpose, and a lawful one. But if they were a lawful assembly when they got to the *Custom house*, yet if afterwards they all agreed to do an unlawful act to the disturbance of the peace, and in the prosecution of that design *Maverick* and the rest were killed, all that party will by law be chargeable with each mortal stroke given by either of them, as though they all had in fact given it.

And it is said, that while they were at the *Custom-house*, before they fired, some of them attempted with their bayonets to stab every one they could come at, without any reason at all for so doing. Such conduct to be sure can neither be justified nor excused. But as the time was so very short, and some of the witnesses declare the people were crouding upon the soldiers, and they were moving their guns backwards and forwards crying stand off, stand off, without moving from their station, you will consider whether this may not be what other witnesses call an attempt to stab the people. But, be that as it may, if the party was a lawful assembly before, this not being the act of the whole, would not make it unlawful. The Council for the Crown insist that the firing upon the people was an unlawful act, in disturbance of the peace, and as the party fired so near together, it must be supposed they previously agreed to do it; that agreement made them an unlawful assembly, if they were not so before, and being so when they all fired, all are chargeable with the killing by any one or more of them.

However just this reasoning may be, where there is no apparent cause for their firing, yet it will not hold good where there is. If each of the party had been at the same instant so assaulted, as that it would have justified his killing the assailant in defence of his own life, and thereupon each of them had at the same instant fired upon and killed the person that assaulted him, surely it would not have been evidence of a previous agreement to fire, or have been evidence of such agreement if the attack was no such as would justify the firing and killing. Though it was such an assault as would alleviate the offence, and reduce it to manslaughter, since here would be *as apparent* a cause of the firing in one case as in the other, and though not *so good* a cause, yet such an one as the law, in condescension to human frailty greatly regards.

You will therefore carefully consider what the several witnesses have sworn. With regard to the assault made upon the party of soldiers at the *Custom house,* and if you thereupon believe they were, before, and at the time of their firing attacked by such numbers, and in such violent manner, as many of the witnesses have positively sworn, you will be able to assign a cause for their firing near together, as they did, without supposing a previous agreement so to do. But it is said that if their firing as they did, don't prove a previous agreement to do it, yet it is good evidence of an actual abetment to fire, as one by firing encourages the others to do the like. As neither[103] of the soldiers fired more than once, it is evident that he who fired last, could not thereby in fact, abet or encourage the firing of any of those who fired before him, and to it cannot be evidence of such abetment.

And if he who fired first and killed, can justify it, because it was lawful for him to do so, surely that same lawful act cannot be evidence of an unlawful abetment. And though he who fired first and killed, may not be able to justify the doing it, yet if it appears he had such a cause for the killing as will reduce it to Manslaughter, it would be strange indeed if that same act should be evidence of his abetting another who killed without provocation, so as to make him who fired guilty of murder. The same may be said as to all the intermediate firings: and, as the evidence stands, I don't think it necessary to say how it would be in case the first persons fired with little or no provocation. If therefore this party of soldiers, when at the *Custom house*, were a lawful assembly and continued so until they fired, and their firing was not an actual *unlawful* abetment of each other to fire, nor evidence of it, they cannot be said to have *in consideration of law* killed those five persons or either of them, but it must rest on the evidence of the actual killing: and, if so, neither of the prisoners can be found guilty thereof, unless it appears not only that he was of the party, but that he in particular *in fact* did kill one or more of the persons slain. That the five persons were killed by the party of soldiers or some of them, seems clear upon the evidence, and indeed is not disputed.

Some witnesses have been produced to prove that *Montgomery* killed *Attucks*; and *Langford* swears *Killroy* killed *Gray*, but none of the witnesses undertake to say that either of the other prisoners in particular killed either of the other three persons, or that all of them did it. On the contrary it seems that one of the six did not fire, and that another of them fired at a boy as he was running down the street, but missed him (if he had killed him, as the evidence stands, it would have been murder) but the witnesses are not agreed as to the person who fired at the boy, or as to him who did not fire at all. It is highly probable, from the places where the five persons killed fell and their wounds, that they were killed by the discharge of five several guns only. If you are upon the evidence satisfied of that, and also that *Montgomery* killed *Attucks*, and *Killroy Gray*, it will thence follow that the other three, were killed, not by the other six prisoners, but by three of them only: and therefore they cannot all be found guilty of it. And as the evidence does not shew which three killed the three, nor that either of the six in particular killed either of the three, you cannot find either of the six guilty of killing them or either of them. If you are satisfied, upon the evidence given you, that *Montgomery* killed *Attucks*, you will proceed to inquire whether it was justifiable, excusable, or felonious homicide, and if the latter whether it was maliciously done or not. As he is charged with murder, if the fact of killing is proved, all the circumstances of *necessity* or *infirmity* are to be satisfactorily proved by him, unless they arise out of the evidence produced against him, for the law presumeth the fact to have been founded in malice untill the contrary appears.

You will therefore, carefully consider and weigh the whole of the evidence given you respecting the attack, made upon the party of soldiers *in general*, and upon *Montgomery* in particular. In doing it, you will observe the rules I have before mentioned, and not forget the part that some of the witnesses took in this unhappy affair, and if upon the whole it appears to you, that *Montgomery* was attacked, in such a violent manner, as that his life was in immediate danger, or that he had sufficient reason to think it was, and he thereupon fired and killed *Attucks*, for the preservation of his own life, it was a justifiable homicide; and he ought to be acquitted.—If you do not believe that was, the case, but upon the evidence are satisfied, that he was by that assembly, assaulted with clubs and other weapons, and therefore fired upon the rioters and killed *Attucks*: then you ought to find him guilty of manslaughter only. But if upon the evidence you believe, that *Montgomery*, without being previously assaulted, fired, and killed *Attucks*: then you will find him guilty of murder. But you must know, that if this party of soldiers *in general* were pelted, with snow-balls, pieces of ice and sticks, *in anger*, this, without more, amounts to an assault, not only upon those that were in fact struck, but upon the whole party; and is such an assault as will reduce the killing to manslaughter. And if you believe, what some of the witnesses have sworn, that the people around the soldiers, and many of them armed with clubs, crouded upon the soldiers, and with the cry of, "Rush on, Kill them, Kill them, Knock them over," did in fact rush on, strike at them with their clubs, and give *Montgomery* such a blow, as to knock him down, as some of the witnesses say, or to make him sally, or stagger, as others say— it will be sufficient to show, that his life was in immediate danger, or that he had sufficient reason to think so.

It seems, a doctrine, has of late been advanced, "that soldiers while on duty, may upon *no occasion whatever* fire upon their fellow subjects, without the order of a civil magistrate." This may possibly account, for some of those who attacked the soldiers, saying to them, "You dare not fire, we know you dare not fire."—But it ought to be known, that the law doth not countenance such an absurd doctrine. A man by becoming a soldier, doth not thereby lose the right of self-defence which is founded in the law of nature. Where any one is, without his own default, reduced to such circum- stances, as that the laws of society cannot avail him, the law considers him, "as *still in that instance* under the protection of the law of nature." This rule extends to soldiers as well as others; nay, while soldiers in the immediate service of the King, and the regular discharge of their duty, they rather come within the *reason*, of civil officers and their assistants, and so are alike under the *peculiar* protection of the law.

If you are satisfied upon the evidence, that *Killroy* killed *Gray*, you will then enquire, whether it was justifiable, excusable or felonious homicide, and if the latter, whether it was with, or without malice. If the blows with clubs were, by an enraged multitude, aimed at the party *in general*, each one might reasonably think his own life in danger; for though he escaped the first blow, he might reasonably expect more would follow, and could have no assurance, that he should be so fortunate as to escape all of them.

And therefore, I do not see but that *Killroy* is upon the same footing as *Montgomery*; and your verdict must be the same as to both, unless what *Hemmingway* swears *Killroy* said, of the affray at the Rope-walk, or both, materially vary the case. *Hemmingway* swears, that he and *Killroy* were talking about the town's people and the soldiers, and that *Killroy* said, "He never would miss an opportunity, when he had one, to fire on the inhabitants, and that he had wanted to have an opportunity, ever since he landed." But he says he cannot remember what words immediately preceded or followed, or at what particular time the words were uttered, nor does he know whether *Killroy* was jocular, or not. If the witness is not mistaken as to the words, the speech was at least, very imprudent and foolish. However, if *Killroy*, either in jest or in earnest, uttered those words, yet if the assault upon him was such, as would justify firing and killing, or alleviate it so as to make it but manslaughter, that will not inhance the killing to murder. And though it has been sworn that *Killroy* and other soldiers had a quarrel with *Gray* and others, at the Rope-walk, a few days before the 5th *March*, yet it is not certain that *Killroy* then knew *Gray*, or aimed at him in particular: But if *Gray* encouraged the assault by clapping the assailants on their backs, as *Hinkley* swears he did, and *Killroy* saw this and knew him to be one of those that were concerned in the affray at the Rope walk, this very circumstance would have a natural tendency, to raise *Killroy*'s passions, and throw him off his guard, much more than if the same things had been done by another person.

In the tumult of passion the voice of reason is not heard. And it is owing to the allowance the law makes for human frailty, that an unlawful voluntary homicide is not deemed murder. If there be "malice between A and B, and they meet casually, A assaults B, and drives him to the wall, B in his own defence kills A, this *se defendendo*,[104] and shall not be heightened by the former malice, into murder or homicide at large, for it was not a killing upon the account of the former malice, but upon a necessity imposed upon him by the assault of A." So upon the same principle, where the assault is such as would make the killing but manslaughter, if there had been no previous quarrel, the killing ought to be attributed to the affair, unless the evidence clearly shews the contrary: an *assault* being known and allowed by law to be a *provocation* to kill, that will free the party from the guilt of murder; whereas neither words of reproach, nor actions expressive of contempt, "are *a provocation* to use such violence," that is, the law doth not allow them to be, *without an assault*, such *a provocation* as will excuse the killing, or make it anything less than murder.

Upon the same principle, where the assault is such, as makes the killing manslaughter, the killing ought to be attributed to the assault, unless the evidence clearly shows the contrary.

This meeting of *Killroy* and *Gray* was casual upon the part of *Killroy* at least; he was lawfully ordered to the place where he *was* and had no right to quit his station without the leave of Capt. *Preston*; nor were any of the party obliged to retreat and give way to the rioters, but might lawfully stand, and repel force by force.

It is needless for me to say what you ought to do with regard to the other six prisoners, in case they had gone to the *Custom-house*, not to protect the Sentry, but to disturb the peace, or after they got there and before the firing had agreed to do so; or in case they had *actually* unlawfully abetted the killing: because none of these things have been testified, nor can any of them be deduced from any thing which has been give to you in evidence.

Having already said much more upon this occasion, than I should have thought necessary in a like case, at any other time, I shall add no more.

THE *SHORT NARRATIVE*
VIEW REAFFIRMED¹⁰⁵

Samuel Adams apparently once again took up his pen and put on the guise of "Vindex" in the aftermath of the massacre. As in 1768 he turned to Edes and Gill's Boston Gazette *for his public outlet. The first essay in this new series appeared on December 10, 1770, before Manwaring and the other civilians were tried and before Kilroy and Montgomery were branded, then released. The last installment was printed six weeks later, on January 28, 1771.*

The first number in the series serves as a reminder that the sarcasm that marks our own age was common then, too. Offering mock compliments to judges, jurors, and counsel for both the prosecution and the defense, "Vindex" called for clarification on what the people could lawfully do the next time the king decided to send soldiers among them. He took a more direct approach when criticizing Bernard, because the troops had come at his behest, and Hutchinson, who had done nothing to lessen the danger of a confrontation until it was too late. He was emphatic: the soldiers should not have been stationed among civilians in the first place—a return to the argument he had made two years before. Furthermore, they had had no justification whatsoever to fire on the crowd. They panicked, just like the sentry who cried out for aid. And why, he chided, if the crowd had become a mob, did the soldiers not seek a civil magistrate to read the Riot Act?

He accused the soldiers in general of looking for an excuse to revenge themselves on the townsmen. The soldiers, he insisted in one of the essays, had been the real mob, not the civilians. Groups of them had been roaming about since the ropewalk scuffle on March 2, looking for a fight, their officers incapable of keeping them in their barracks. He settled on Kilroy as proof of his charge, as can be seen in the second number, printed below. Kilroy, he contended, had been heard to say that he hoped for just such an opportunity to revenge himself. Kilroy should have been convicted of murder, not manslaughter, "Vindex" complained, because he shot Gray deliberately and most likely ran his bayonet through the fallen man's head after he had crumpled to the ground.

As "Vindex," Adams took his evidence primarily from the Short Narrative, not the testimony presented at trial. The prosecutors, he complained, did not want convictions so they avoided calling those who had presented the most damning testimony in their depositions to appear in court. No wonder, then, that justice had been denied; the prosecution had not really sought it. "In ordinary cases, the publick ought to rest satisfied, with the verdict of a jury; a method of trial, which an Englishman glories in as his greatest security," he conceded—paraphrasing Blackstone; but alas, "in times when politicks run high, we find by experience of past ages, it is difficult to ascertain the truth even in a court of law."[106] A Short Narrative had tried to tell the truth; the court proceedings had been designed to conceal it. He reminded the people of which version they should believe. He wanted Bostonians to remember and refer to the event as a massacre, a mantra they had already begun to chant.

* * *

THAT the trial of the soldiers concern'd in the carnage on the memorable 5th of March was the most solemn trial that ever was had in this country, was pronounc'd from the bench. To see eight prisoners bro't to the bar together, charg'd with the murder of five persons at one time, was certainly, as was then observ'd, affecting: But whoever recollects the tragedy of that fatal evening, will I believe readily own that the scene *then* was much more affecting—There is something pleasing and solemn when one enters a court of law—*Pleasing*, as *there* we expect to see the scale held with an equal hand—to find matters deliberately and calmly weigh'd and decided, and justice administered without any respect to persons or parties, and from no other motive but a sacred regard to truth—And it is *solemn* as it brings to our minds the tribunal of GOD himself! before whose judgment-seat the scriptures assure us all must appear: And I have often tho't that no one will receive a greater share of rewards at that decisive day, than he who has approv'd himself a faithful upright judge.

Witnesses who are bro't into a court of justice, while their veracity is not impeach'd, stand equal in the eye of the judge: unless he happens to be acquainted with their different characters, which is not presum'd—The jury who are taken from the vicinity, are suppos'd to know the credibility of the witnesses: In the late trials the witnesses were most if not all of them either inhabitants of this town or *transient* persons residing in it, and the jurors were all from the country: Therefore it is not likely they were acquainted with the characters of *all* the witnesses; and it is more than probable that in so great a number of witnesses, there were different characters, that is, that some of them were more, others less credible. If then the judge, whose province it is to attend to the law, and who, not knowing the characters of the witnesses, presumes that they are all good, & gives an equal credit to them, it is the duty of the jurors who are sovereign in regard to facts, to determine in *their own* minds the credibility of those who are sworn to relate the facts: And this in a trial for murder requires great care and attention. I would just observe here, that in the late trial there were not less than eighty-two witnesses for the jury to examine and *compare*, which was an arduous task indeed! And I will venture further to observe, that some of these witnesses who swore very *positively* were not so creditable as others, and the testimony of one of them in particular, which was very *precisely* related & very *peremptory* might have been invalidated in every part of it. I shall not at present suggest what I take to be the reason why it was not done. These matters will no doubt have their place in the history of the *present times* in some future day, when the *faithful* recorder it is to be hoped will, to use the language of our courts of justice, relate the whole truth, and nothing but the truth.

It is enough for the jury to receive the law from the bench: they *may* indeed determine this for themselves; but of facts they are ever the uncontroulable judges. They ought, therefore to receive the facts from the mouths of the witnesses themselves, and *implicitly* from no other: Unless the jury particularly attend to this, they may be in danger of being misled by persons who would be far from doing it *with design.* For instance, if one should swear that A being forewarn'd against it, level'd his gun and kill'd B: and afterwards it should be forgot that the witness also swore that A immediately advanc'd & push'd his bayonet at C, which pass'd between his waistcoat and his skin; if this I say should be *forgot* and should be overlook'd by the jury when they are together, perhaps instead of bringing it in murder according to the rules of the law laid down by the bench, they would bring it manslaughter—I do not *here* affirm that this has ever been a fact: I mention it as what may hereafter be a fact and to show the necessity of a jury's relying upon *facts* as they receive them from the witnesses themselves, and from them *alone.*

The *furor brevis*[107] which we have heard much of, the fury of the blood which the *benignity* of the law allows upon for upon sudden provocation, is suppos'd to be of *short* duration—the shooting a man dead upon the spot, must have stopp'd the current in the breast of him who shot him, if he had not been beat upon killing—and attempt to stab a second person immediately after infers a total want of remorse at the shedding of human blood; and such a temper of mind afterward discovers the rancorous malice before, especially if it be proved that the same man had declared that he would never miss an opportunity of firing upon people, and that he had long'd for an opportunity so to do: If this does not imply malice at first, I do not see but he might have gone on stabbing people in his *furor brevis*, till he had kill'd an hundred; and after all, it might have been adjudg'd, in indulgence to the human passions, *excusable* homicide.

The law in its *benignity* makes allowance for human passions: But the law is *just*; and makes this allowance upon the principle of *justice*: It gives no indulgence to malice and rancour against any individual; much less against a *community* or the human species—He who threatens or *thirsts* for the blood of the community is an enemy to the publick; and *hostis humani generis*,[108] the enemy of mankind consummates the villain. I will not take upon myself to say that either of these characters belong to any of the late prisoners—There are two remaining yet in gaol, convicted of *manslaughter*. And waiting for the judgment of the court. With regard to one of these, namely *Kilroi*, it was sworn about a week or a fortnight before (the 5th of March, which must be before the affray at the ropewalks, that happening on the 2d) he said he would *never miss an opportunity of firing upon the inhabitants*, and that *he had wanted such an opportunity ever since he had been in the country*—It is said that these might be words spoken *in jest*, or without any intention, when they were spoken, of acting according to their true import & meaning: But the witness said, *he repeated the words several times*: And that after he had told him he was a very great fool for saying so, he again declared he would never miss an opportunity.—It appears that the witness himself, as any one might, tho' him to be in *earnest*, and rebuked him for saying so; and in truth none but a madman, or one whose heart was desperately wicked, would repeatedly, especially after such wholesome reproof, have *persisted* in such a threat; It discovered, to borrow the expression of a very polite & humane gentleman, upon *another late* occasion, a *malignity* beyond what might have been expected from a *Barbarian*.

It was also sworn, that this same *Kilroi* was with a party of soldiers in the affray at the Ropewalks a few evenings before the 5th of March—and that they had clubs & cutlasses.—That *Kilroi* was of the party of soldiers that fired in Kingstreet—that as the party came round before they form'd, *Kilroi* struck a witness upon his arm—and after the firing began, *Kilroi* struck at the same witness, tho' he had hear'd nothing said, nor seen any thing done to provoke the soldiers.—Another witness declared, that he saw *Kilroi* there, that he *knew him well before*, and was positive it was he—that he heard the word fire, twice upon which he said to the soldiers, *damn you, don't fire*, and *Kilroi* alone fired at once, and killed Gray, who had no weapon, and his arms were folded in his bosom. Gray fell at the feet of this witness, and immediately *Kilroi* pushed his bayonet at the witness, which pass'd thro' all his clothes, and came out at his surtuit behind, and he was obliged to turn round to quit himself of the weapon—the witness suppos'd he designed to kill them both:—How long is this *furor brevis*, this small hurricane of passion to last in the breast of a soldier, when called, not by the *civil magistrate*, but by his *military officer*, under a pretence of protecting a Centinel, and suppressing a Riot, who had taken with him weapons not properly of *defence*, but of *death*, and was *calm* enough in this *impetuosity* of anger, to load his gun, and perhaps *with design*, to level it, for it killed one of the very men with whom he had had a quarrel but a few evenings before: He had now a fair opportunity, which he had wished for, and resolved never to miss, of firing upon the inhabitants. It was said upon the words he uttered, that if all the unjustifiable words that had been spoken by the inhabitants of this town were to be bro't in judgment against them, they would have much greater to answer for.—Those who believe the letters of governor Bernard, the Commissioners of the customs, and some others whom I could name, and will name in proper time, may think so. I dare say if Bernard could have proved one overt act of rebellion or treason, after the many things he *pretended* had been said, and he or his tools could have had any *influence*, the words if prov'd, would have been adjudg'd to have been said in sober earnest, and would have been considered as material to have shown the *malignancy* of the heart.

This *Kilroi*'s bayonet was prov'd to be the next morning bloody five inches to the point. It was said to be possible that this might be occasion'd by the bayonet's falling into the human blood, which ran plentifully in the street, for one of their bayonets was seen to fall. It is *possible*, I own; but much more likely that this very bayonet was stab'd into the head of poor Gray, after he was shot, and that this may account for its being bloody five inches from the point.—Such an Instance of Savage barbarity there undoubtedly was.—It was sworn before the Magistrate who first examined into this cruel tragedy, though the witness who then swore it, being out of this province, could not be produced in Court upon the trial. It is not to be wonder'd at that any material witness was out of the way, when it is consider'd that the trial did not come on till the *second* term, and *nine months* after the facts were committed. I shall continue upon the subject at my leisure.

Dec. 11th   VINDEX

DOCUMENT **27**

THE TRIAL OUTCOMES DEFENDED[109]

"Vindex" did not have the local press to himself. "Philanthrop" came right back at him in the pages of the Boston Evening-Post, *the first counter-punch being thrown on December 17, 1770, the last on February 18, 1771. The author, Jonathan Sewall, had written as "Philanthrop" before, during the Stamp Act crisis. Coming to Francis Bernard's defense, he contended that the governor had had no choice but to support legislation with which he personally disagreed because it was the law and he served as the king's representative to the people. In so arguing he probably did not help Bernard's case with opposition leaders; he also ran the risk of damaging his own reputation, which to then had been as a lawyer who put principle above politics and who counted John Adams among his closet friends.*

Sewall had risen with the right combination of talent and family connections: it was good to be a Sewall if one aspired to be among the province's elite, in a society that still put a premium on personal and familial connections, with deference duly accorded to those who had reached the top.[110] But those older ways were being threatened by social dislocations exacerbated by the contentious politics of empire. They ushered in changes that caught up Sewall and others of his generation who preferred not having to choose between rivals for power.

Appointed attorney general in 1767, Sewall was uncomfortable with the pressure, as he saw it, to subordinate "professional integrity and personal judgment to political considerations."[111] Not only did he find himself caught between the governor and his Council and the Massachusetts House, but between the governor and customs commissioners. Hutchinson, like Bernard before him, wanted Sewall to be cautious in pursuing cases against merchants like Hancock accused of violating the navigation acts. The customs commission, predictably, pressed for more vigorous prosecutions. Serving also as a vice-admiralty justice in Halifax, it was almost easier for Sewall to stay in Nova Scotia if that meant avoiding involvement in the political disputes dividing Boston. Convinced that there was no case against Preston or the soldiers, he simply refused to lead the prosecution and stayed at home. Thus the job fell to Samuel Quincy.

He did not resign as attorney general, however, and as "Philanthrop" defended the legal proceedings that he had avoided. He complimented the judges and jurors for their behavior in the trials—sincerely rather than in the mocking tones of "Vindex." "I apprehend VINDEX to be of the number of those who did not hear the trials, and whose former prejudices still remain." "Vindex," he complained, was stirring up the people needlessly, attempting to promote the accounts printed in the Short Narrative as more reliable than the testimony offered in court. He was against accepting such an "ex parte" record—that is to say, a one-sided, inherently biased account. The public should instead rely on the sworn testimony offered in court, which was subject to examination before judges and jurors, unlike the depositions given to justices of the peace that comprised the Short Narrative.

Sewall knew that the odds were against him, that for many the battle for public opinion had already ended. He may have had the literal last word in his exchanges with "Vindex," but, effectively, the last word had already been spoken before he put pen to paper: "massacre." A disillusioned Sewall would leave Massachusetts in 1775, soon afer the shooting war started. After living in England he moved to Canada, where he died in 1796—of a broken heart, thought his old friend, John Adams.

* * *

IN the Boston Gazette for last Monday, VINDEX has taken occasion from the late solemn and affecting Trials, to lead our reflections to that dread tribunal at which we all expect one day to appear, there to give an account, before the omniscient Judge of all, of the deeds done in the body—when the inmost recesses of our souls will be searched, and the very thoughts & designs of our hearts, while in this state of probation, must be subject to the strict impartial scrutiny of the all-seeing eye.—The reflection is awful, and the transition is natural and pertinent.—Happy is the Man who realizes, whose mind is possest with an habitual sense of this important truth, that, however he may, at present, *disguise* or *conceal* the real purposes of his soul and the true motives of his actions, yet a day is coming when they will, most assuredly, be made *manifest.* Such is the imperfect state of things here, that, from our own *ignorance* and *prejudices,* as well as from the *ignorance, prejudice & wickedness* of others, we are liable to continual deception, in innumerable instances—*Truth* often lies concealed from her sincerest followers—Error assumes *her* comely form, and is frequently mistaken for her by deluded Man: and when human Courts of Judicature are able, in cases of importance, to *separate* and *distinguish* the one from the other, to pervade the mists which *passion, party-spirit, prejudice* and *iniquity* have raised, to strip Error and Falshood of their delusive appearances, and to judge and determine agreeable to the unalterable truth of things, then it is, that their proceedings bear the nearest resemblance to the equitable decisions of that August future Day of Judgment and retribution to which VINDEX, with *great propriety,* has carried our ideas. I say with great propriety; for whoever attended the late trials and observed the great *care,* the unwearied *patience,* the unbyassed *impartiality,* the unshaken *integrity,* and the penetrating *discernment* of the *Judges;* the *patience* and *attention of the Jurors,* and the ingenuous *candour* of most of the *witnesses;* whoever, I say, has attended to these things, and at the same time reflects on the *prejudice* which had almost universally taken hold of the causes, in publick *prayers, sermons, newspapers, prints, narratives* and *depositions* taken *extrajudicially* and *ex parte,* will see in a striking light, the resemblance above-mentioned. There was a time when, from the foregoing causes, I suppose, a very great majority of the good people of this province were ready, had they been called upon, to give their voices for condemning all the supposed *Murderers,* whereas now, I cannot suppose a single person can be found, who heard the trials, and is not, in his conscience, clearly satisfied with the Justice of the *Court* and *Juries* in their determinations; and, when the trials are published, I have no doubt but all will receive the same satisfaction. I apprehend VINDEX to be of the number of those who did not hear the trials, and whose former prejudices therefore still remain; for if I understand his *obscure hints,* he discovers a dissatisfaction at the *event* of the trials, and a *jealousy* of the *integrity* of the *Judges,* and of the due *care* and *attention* of the *Jurors;* which dissatisfaction & jealousy VINDEX seems desirous of communicating to others.—*Kilroi* seems to be principally pointed out by him, as one whose acquittal of *murder,* he suggests was not agreeable to the *rules* of law as laid down by the *Bench,* and the *evidence* produced upon the trial. As I would willingly consider VINDEX an honest inquirer after the truth, I shall have no objection against arraigning and trying *Kilroi* over again in the *newspapers;* but I think this will better be done after the *publication* of the trial in *court,* when in case of any dispute between us, respecting any part of the *evidence,* we may both recur to *the book;* and I flatter myself I shall be able to remove all dissatisfaction and *jealousy* from the mind of VINDEX: or, *at least,* to vindicate the characters of the *Court* and *Jurors* against any aspersions in point of *integrity, knowledge, care* or *attention.* In the mean time, I cannot help asking VINDEX whether he conceives it to be perfectly consonant to the rules of *justice* and *equity,* to publish the *only* material piece of evidence produced against *Kilroi,* and to argue upon that *alone,* without taking any notice of the *great variety* of evidence produced in his *favour?* or whether it is decent or right to suspend the characters of the *Court* and *Jurors* upon such a *partial* representation? That VINDEX has done this, will appear hereafter; and if he does not know it, it is truly extraordinary—if he is conscious of it, he will do well to pursue the suggestion of his *own mind,* and consider what account he can give of such disingenuous conduct, at the tremendous *Bar* where the truth can, by no other art or artifice, be obstructed or evaded. From the repeated instances of *indecent freedom* and *barefaced injustice* with which the most *amiable* and *respectable* characters have of late years been treated, it is not much to be wondered at, if, with any, it should be thought a light matter now to villify and abuse the character of *Judges,* whose *integrity,* during a course of many years administration, has never been *impeached,* but on the contrary has always been *revered*—but, if there is a difference between *truth* and *falshood, justice & injustice, right & wrong,* most surely these things ought not to be, and the authors of them must, as the righteous Lord liveth, one day be called to *judgment.* Who is the *hostis humani generis,* but he who wantonly destroys the *publick peace?* Who does his endeavour to sap the foundation of *good government* and *order,* and to introduce general *discontent, anarchy and confusion?* That such are the natural consequences of a *licentious, indiscriminate, open* abuse of *all* publick characters, must be evident to every one who has any competent knowledge of mankind; and that such abuse has abounded of late, our publick *news-papers* too, too plainly evidence. I do not charge VINDEX with such designs; his own conscience will *condemn* or *acquit* him as the *truth* is—but that his performance has a *direct tendency* to produce consequences destructive of *publick peace* and *confidence,* is certain. Besides what I have already observed upon, there is another circumstance related by VINDEX which ought never to have been mentioned to the prejudice of the *Court* or *Jury*—I mean that of the *bloody bayonet* and the wound in *Gray's* head; such an instance of savage barbarity, he says, there undoubtedly was—but it is certain no such *evidence* was given in *Court;* and it is, in the highest degree, unjust to blame the *Court* and *Jury* for not regarding *evidence* which they never *heard*—and indeed the fact may well be doubted, notwithstanding its having been *sworn* to before a *magistrate;* for little credit can be given to *such oaths,* when it is considered how materially different many of the *printed* depositions are from the testimonies of the *same witnesses* when they testified in *open Court*—and further the impossibility of the bayonet's being bloody the *next morning,* is demonstrable from this, that every gun and bayonet of the party were scowered clean that *very night* the melancholy affair happened, agreeable to the constant practice of the army after firing. We cannot therefore be too cautious in giving credit to loose declarations, or *ex parte* depositions.

When VINDEX is at leisure to continue the subject, perhaps it may likewise be continued by,

Philanthrop

ANNUAL COMMEMORATION[112]

The question of whether Boston would "take any measures, that a Public Monument may be Erected on the spot where the late Tragical Scene was acted, as a Memento to Posterity of that horrid Massacre, and the destructive Consequences of Military Troops being quartered in a well regulated City" was raised less than two weeks after the event.[113] The town meeting decided that something on that scale would have to be considered by the General Court as well. But town leaders did not drop the subject of a commemoration. The meeting adjourned in October 1770 and did not reconvene until March 1771, after the 5th had already passed. Deciding on an appropriate public observance became an order of business soon after. A committee that included Samuel Adams and John Hancock recommended an annual oration, which the town meeting approved. Beginning the next month and repeated each March 5 or 6 (if the 5th fell on a Sunday) thereafter for the next twelve years, there would be a massacre oration.

For the first few years the town meeting followed a fairly steady routine. The "inhabitants" at large chose a speaker during a town meeting, the meeting convened on that date for its regular business at Faneuil Hall, then adjourned and reassembled at the more capacious Old South Meeting House. Edes and Gill subsequently published the oration. Either they or the individual authors added aphoristic Latin epigraphs from Virgil's Aeneid or like sources— literary embellishments that might have been lost on many listeners that resonated with some readers.

Even after fighting had erupted and Boston lay under siege, town leaders acted as a government in exile, so they invited Peter Thacher to give the annual address on March 5, 1776—in Watertown rather than occupied Boston. It would be the only oration delivered outside of town. In 1777 town leaders returned to the original ceremonial ritual, which they continued through 1783—except that they gathered at the First Church (Old Brick) Meeting House rather than Old South. Joseph Warren gave the oration in both 1772 and 1775; no one else spoke more than once. Hancock had his opportunity in 1774; Samuel Adams, for whatever reason, was never selected. The tone shifted as protest moved to revolt, and revolt to revolution. Early speakers expressed a hope for reconciliation, a restoration of peace and harmony in the empire. Those at the end, not surprisingly, emphasized the necessity of a nation freed from British rule. The standing army of Britain had been beaten by a citizen army of Americans, observed Thomas Welsh in his 1783 oration. "Henceforth shall the American wilderness blossom as the rose," he proclaimed, turning to scripture, "and every man shall sit under his vine and under his fig tree, and none shall make him afraid."[114]

James Lovell took the pulpit at Old South to deliver the first oration, on April 2, 1771, a perfect location for preaching a secular sermon on civic duty in the face of tyrannical government. Like his father before him, he went to Harvard before becoming a schoolmaster. His politics, however, were quite different. His father avoided protest against the empire; he embraced it. He became involved with the "patriot party" decried by Francis Bernard, joined the Sons of Liberty and counted John Hancock among his associates. Lovell lingered too long in Boston after the fighting erupted in April 1775 and the British arrested him. He would be taken as a prisoner to Halifax when the British evacuated Boston the following March, on board the same ship that carried his father there as a refugee. Eventually exchanged for a New York loyalist, he served in the Continental Congress and, returning to Boston as the Revolutionary War wound down, he once again immersed himself in town politics.

Given the raw emotions unleashed the year before, Lovell's 1771 oration, which follows, was not as impassioned as it could have been. It is certainly no crowd-stirring harangue, designed to send his listeners into the streets to commit acts of civil disobedience. While lamenting that troops had ever been sent and complaining that they had shed innocent blood, he tried to strike a positive note, expressing hope that "Heaven has yet in store such happiness, for this afflicted town and province, as will in time wear out the memory of our former troubles." And yet, in his call to listeners to reclaim their "birthright" of freedom, he made it difficult to reconcile that birthright with any exercise of crown prerogative or parliamentary legislative authority. As with John Dickinson, the "patriot Farmer" to whom he referred approvingly, there was an implicit threat beneath the surface of his explicit call for mutual understanding.

* * *

YOUR design in the appointment of this ceremony, *my Friends, and Fellow-Townsmen*, cannot fail to be examined in quite different lights at this season of political dissention. From the principles I profess, and in the exercise of my common right to judge with others, I conclude it was *decent, wise, and honorable.*

The certainty of being favoured with your kindest partiality and candor, in a poor attempt to execute the part to which you have invited me, has overcome the objection of my inability to perform it in a proper manner; and I now beg the favor of your animating countenance.

The horrid scene we here commemorate, whatever were the causes which concurred to bring it on that dreadful night, must lead the pious and humane of every order to some suitable reflections. The pious will adore the conduct of that BEING who is unsearchable in all his ways, and without whose knowledge not a single sparrow falls, in permitting an immortal soul to be hurried by the flying ball, the messenger of death, in the twinkling of an eye, to meet the awful Judge of all its secret actions. The humane, from having often thought with pleasing rapture on the endearing scenes of social life, in all its amiable relations, will lament with heart-felt pangs their sudden dissolution by the indiscretion, rage and vengeance of unruly human passions.

But, let us leave that shocking close of one continued course of rancour and dispute from the first moment that the troops arrived in town: that course will now be represented by your own reflexions to much more solid, useful purpose than by any artful language. I hope, however, that Heaven has yet in store such happiness, for this afflicted town and province, as will in time wear out the memory of all our former troubles.

I sincerely rejoice with you in the happy event of your steady and united effort to prevent a second tragedy.

Our fathers left their native land, risqued all the dangers of the sea, and came to this then-savage desart, with that true undaunted courage which is excited by a confidence in GOD. They came that they might here enjoy themselves, and leave to their posterity the best of earthly portions, full *English liberty.* You showed upon the alarming call for tryal that their brave spirit still exists in vigour, tho' their legacy of rights is much impaired. The sympathy and active friendship of some neighboring towns upon that sad occasion commands the highest gratitude of this.

We have seen and felt the ill effects of placing standing forces in the midst of *populous* communities; but those are only what individuals suffer. Your vote directs me to point out the fatal tendency of placing such an order in *free* cities—fatal indeed! *Athens* once was free; a citizen, a favorite of the people, by an artful story gained a trifling guard of fifty men; ambition taught him ways to enlarge the number; he destroyed the commonwealth and made himself the tyrant of the *Athenians*. *Caesar* by the length of his command in *Gaul* got the affections of his army, marched to *Rome*, overthrew the state, and made himself perpetual dictator. By the same instruments, many less republics have been made to fall a prey to the devouring jaws of tyranny—But, this is a subject which should never be dignified with figures; it chuses the plain stile of dissertation.

The true strength and safety of every commonwealth or limited monarchy, is the bravery of its freeholders, its militia. By brave militias they rise to grandeur, and they come to ruin by a mercenary army. This is founded on historical facts; and the same causes will, in similar circumstances, forever produce the same effects. Justice *Blackstone*, in his inimitably clear commentaries, tells us, that "it is extremely dangerous in a land of liberty, to make a distinct order of the profession of arms; that such an order is an object of jealousy; and that *the laws and constitution of England are strangers to it.*" One article of the Bill of Rights is, that the raising or keeping a standing army within the kingdom in a time of peace, unless it can be with consent of parliament, is against law. The present army therefore, tho' called the peace *establishment*, is kept up by one act, and governed by another; both of which expire *annually*. This circumstance is valued as a sufficient *check* upon the army. A less body of troops than is now maintained has, on a time, destroyed a King, and fought under a parliament with great success and glory; but, upon a motion to disband them, they turned their masters out of doors, and fixed up others in their stead. Such wild things are not again to happen, because the parliament have power to stop payment once a year: but, *arma tenenti quis neget?* which may be easily interpreted, "who will bind *Sampson* with his locks on?"[115]

The bill which regulates the army, the same fine author I have mentioned says, "is *in many respects hastily penned*, and reduces the soldier to a state of slavery in the midst of a free nation. This is impolitik: for slaves envy the freedom of others, and take a malicious pleasure in contributing to destroy it."

By this scandalous bill a justice of the peace is empowered to grant, *without a previous oath* from the military officer, a warrant to break open any (freeman's) house, upon *pretence* of searching for deserters.

I must not omit to mention one more bad tendency: 'tis this,—a standing force leads to a total neglect of militias, or tends greatly to discourage them.

You see the danger of a standing army to the cause of freedom. If the *British* Parliament consents from year to year to be exposed, it doubtless has good reasons. But when did *our* assembly pass an act to hazard all the property, the liberty and lives of their constituents? What check have *we* upon a *British* Army? Can *we* disband it? Can *we* stop its pay?

Our own assemblies in *America* can raise an army; and *our* Monarch, George the 3d. by our constitution takes immediate command. This army can *consent* to leave their native provinces. Will the royal chief commander send them to find barracks at *Brunswick* or *Lunenberg*, at *Hanover*, or *the commodious hall of Westminster*? Suppose the last—Suppose this army was informed, nay *thought* the parliament in actual rebellion, or only on the *eve* of one against their King, or against *those who paid and cloathed them*— for there it pinches:—We are *rebels against parliament*;—we adore the King.

Where, in the case I have stated, would it be the value of the boasted *English* Constitution?

Who are a free people? Not those who do not suffer actual oppression; but those who have a *constitutional check upon the power* to oppress.

We are slaves or freemen; if, as we are called, the last, where is our check upon the following powers, *France, Spain*, the *States of Holland*, or *the British Parliament?* Now if any one of these (and it is quite immaterial which) has right to make the two acts in question operate within this province, they have right to give us up to an unlimited army, under the sole direction of one *Saracen* Commander.

Thus I have led your thoughts to *that* upon which I formed my conclusion, that the design of this ceremony was *decent, wise* and *honorable*. Make the bloody 5th of *March* the Era of the resurrection of your birthrights, which have been murdered by the very strength that nursed them in their infancy. I had an eye *solely* to parliamentary supremacy; and I hope you will think every other view beneath your notice in our present most alarming situation.

Chatham, Cambden and others, gods among men, and the *Farmer*, whom you have addressed as the friend of *Americans*, and the common benefactor of mankind; all these have owned that *England* has right to exercise every power over us, but that of taking money out of our pockets without our consent. Tho' it seems almost too bold therefore in us to say "we doubt in every single instance her legal right over this province", yet *we must assert it*. Those I have named are mighty characters, but *they* wanted one advantage providence has given *us*. The *beam* is carried from our eyes by the flowing blood of our fellow citizens, and now we may be allowed to attempt to remove the *mote* from the eyes of our exalted patrons. That mote, we think, is nothing but *our obligation to England first, and afterwards Great-Britain, for constant kind protection of our lives and birthrights against foreign danger*. We acknowledge that protection.

Let us once more look into the early history of this province. We find that our *English* Ancestors disgusted in their native country at a *Legislation*, which they saw was sacrificing all their rights, *left its Jurisdiction*, and sought, like wandering birds of passage, some happier climate. Here at length they settled down. The King of *England* was said to be the royal landlord of this territory; with HIM they entered into mutual sacred compact, by which the prick of tenure and the *rules of management* were fairly started. It is in this compact that we find OUR ONLY TRUE LEGISLATIVE AUTHORITY.

I might here enlarge upon the character of those first settlers, men of whom the world was little worthy; who, for a long course of years, assisted by no earthly power, defended their liberty, their religion and their lives against the greatest inland danger from the savage natives:—but this falls not within my present purpose. They were secure by sea.

In our infancy, when not an over-tempting jewel for the *Bourbon* Crown the very *name* of ENGLAND saved us; afterwards her *fleets and armies*. We wish not to depreciate the worth of that protection. Of our gold, yea of our most fine gold, we will freely *give* a part. Our fathers would have done the same. But, must we fall down and cry "let not a stranger rob and kill me, O my father! let me rather dye by the hand of my brother, and let him *ravish* all my portion?"

It is said that disunited from *Britain* "we should bleed at every vein." I cannot see the consequence. The *States of Holland* do not suffer thus. But grant it true, SENACA, would prefer the LAUNCETS of *France, Spain* or any other power to the BOW-STRING, tho' applied by the fair hand of *Britannia*.

The declarative vote of the *British Parliament* is the death-warrant of *our* birthrights, and wants only a Czarish King to put it into execution. *Here* then a door of salvation is open. *Great Britain* may raise *her* fleets and armies, but it is only *our own* King that can direct their fire down upon our heads. He is gracious, but not omniscient. He is ready to hear our APPEALS in their proper course; and knowing himself, tho' the most powerful prince on earth, yet, a subject under a divine constitution of LAW, that law *will* ask and receive from the twelve Judges of *England*. These will prove that the claim of the *British Parliament* over *us* is not only ILLEGAL IN ITSELF, but a DOWN-RIGHT USURPATION OF HIS PREROGATIVE as KING OF *America*.

A brave nation is always generous. Let us appeal therefore, at the same time, to the generosity of the PEOPLE of *Great-Britain*, before the tribunal of *Europe*, not to envy *us* the full enjoyment of the RIGHTS OF BRETHREN.

And now, *my Friends and Fellow Townsmen*, having declared myself an *American* Son of Liberty of true charter-principles; having shewn the critical and dangerous situation of our birthrights, and the true course for speedy redress; I shall take the freedom to recommend with boldness one previous step.—Let us show we understand the true value of what we are claiming.

The patriot *Farmer* tells us, "the cause of *LIBERTY* is a cause of too much dignity to be sullied by turbulence and tumult.—Anger produces anger; and differences, that might be accommodated by kind and respectful behaviour, may by imprudence be enlarged to an incredible rage. In quarrels—risen to a certain height, the first cause of dissention is no longer remembered, the minds of the parties being wholly engaged in recollecting and resenting the mutual expressions of their dislike. When feuds have reached that fatal point, considerations of reason and equity vanish; and a blind fury governs, or rather confounds all things. A people no longer regard their interest, but a gratification of their wrath."[116]

We know ourselves subjects of common LAW: to that and the worthy *executors* of it let us pay a steady and conscientious regard. Past errors in this point have been written with gall by the pen of MALICE. May our future conduct be such as to make even that vile IMP lay her pen aside.

The *Right* which imposes *Duties* upon us is in dispute: but whether they are managed by a *Surveyor General, a Board of the Commissioners, Turkish Janizaries* or *Russian Cossacks*, let them enjoy, during our time of fair tryal, the common personal protection of the laws of our constitution. Let us shut our eyes, for the present, to their being *executors of claims subversive to our rights*.

Watchful hawkeyed JEALOUSY ever guards the portal of the temple of the GODDESS LIBERTY. This is known to those who frequent her altars. Our whole conduct therefore, I am sure, will meet with the utmost candor of her VOTARIES: but I am wishing we may be able to convert even her basest APOSTATES.

We are SLAVES 'till we obtain such *redress* thro' the justice of our KING as our happy *constitution leads us to expect*. In that condition, let us behave with the propriety and dignity of FREEMEN; and *thus* exhibit to the world a new character of a people which no history describes.

May the allwise and beneficent RULER OF THE UNIVERSE preserve our *lives* and *health*, and prosper all our lawful *endeavours in the glorious cause of* FREEDOM.

A PROBLEMATICAL REMINISCENCE[117]

Professor Alfred Young did something that many historians dream of doing but rarely actually do: he reshaped a historical debate by recovering the all but lost, thereby making the obscure prominent. It began with a serendipitous encounter when he was engaged in research at the Bostonian Society library. It ended with a highly regarded essay, then a book, on George Robert Twelves Hewes, Boston shoemaker, an observer of and participant in the American Revolution.[118]

Hewes had been one of those whose depositions ended up in A Short Narrative. *He testified about an encounter that he claimed to have had with a group of eight or nine British soldiers following the incident on King Street. As he recollected, at near one o'clock in the morning, after he had gone home then back out, the soldiers intercepted him as he made his way toward the town house. One of them asked him "how he fared"; he responded "very badly," seeing that townsmen had been killed by soldiers. He then asked the soldier if this had not been "a dreadful thing." The soldier "swore by God it was a fine thing, and said you shall see more of it." Hewes carried a cane; the sergeant in charge of the detail took it from him. "The deponent further adds" that, earlier in the evening, he had seen a young man knock on the door of the custom house, then pass through it, just before the relief party arrived.*

What else did he see or do that night? The deposition does not say.[119] How reliable is his testimony? No more or less than that of others, most likely. He made his statement to justices of the peace Richard Dana and John Hill less than two weeks after the events he described and yet, even that soon after the fact, was he confused about when he encountered the soldiers and what they said to each other? Would that large a group have been out that late, considering that all had been ordered back to their barracks hours before? Would he have been going to the town house then, when most who were there had already decided to go home?

However plausible his statements in 1770, those he made later were much less so. Hewes added nothing more to the record until over sixty years after the fact, in response to questions put to him by two different interviewers. Both marveled at Hewes's memory, as did Professor Young more recently. But these accounts, the first printed in 1834, the second a year later, only compound the problem of determining reliability.[120] The men who interviewed Hewes mixed his first-hand comments with their third-hand extrapolations and it can be difficult to distinguish Hewes's views from theirs. Hewes tried to respond to specific questions and, given his age—over ninety—those questions may have involved a bit of coaxing, possibly even coaching. The differences between the two accounts are notable and details offered in one are absent from the other.

The excerpt that follows is from the first account. Here, Hewes recalled that he was married at the time of the massacre but he could not remember how many children he had. He gave details about the confrontation between the sentry and the apprentice lacking in earlier accounts, which could indeed be true. But he placed them in a setting that seems to be wrong in far too many particulars. His discrepancies only get worse—about the timing and order of Preston's and the soldiers' trials, about the outcome in the latter, and even about his own role. He recalled testifying in Preston's trial; there is no record of it. His brother Shubael did testify, but in the soldiers' trial, not Preston's.

The primary point in all of this is not that Hewes stands apart as an unreliable witness. Even John Adams and Thomas Jefferson, whose involvement in writing the Declaration of Independence cannot be denied, misremembered their own pasts. Looking back many years later, they thought there had been a signing ceremony on July 4, 1776. They erred.[121] Time can warp memory and it is a risky business to rely on a first-hand account that is offered publicly for the first time after the passage of too many years. But time is not the only, or even the most important, problem with memory, whether it be individual or collective, public or private. Memory is often formed as part of a quest for a usable past, one that teaches lessons. The men who interviewed Hewes were in search of those lessons. Hewes had sought to learn them himself.

* * *

After the conclusion of the French war, as it was called in America, until the differences of the American colonies with Great Britain commenced, he continued at Boston, except the two years absence with his brother.

During that period, said Hewes, when I was at the age of twenty-six, I married the daughter of Benjamin Sumner, of Boston. At the time of our intermarriage, the age of my wife was seventeen. We lived together very happily seventy years. She died at the age of eighty-seven.

At the time when the British troops were first stationed at Boston, we had several children, the exact number I do not recollect. By our industry and mutual efforts we were improving our condition.

An account of the massacre of the citizens of Boston, in the year 1770, on the 5th of March, by some of the British troops, has been committed to the record of our history, as one of those interesting events which lead to the Revolutionary contest that resulted in our independence. When the various histories of that event were published, no one living at that time could have expected that any one of the actors in that tragical scene, considerably advanced in life, would have lived to revive in our recollections facts relating to it, by the rehearsal of them from his own personal knowledge. But while the public mind has no other source from which it can derive its knowledge of that, and many other interesting events relating to our revolutionary contest, Hewes, with a precision of recollection perhaps unprecedented in the history of longevity, rehearses many facts relating to them, from his own personal knowledge.

We have been informed by the historians of the Revolution, that a series of provocations had excited strong prejudices, and inflamed the passion of the British soldiery against our citizens, previous to the commencement of open hostilities; and prepared their minds to burst out into acts of violence on the application of a single spark of additional excitement, and which finally resulted in the unfortunate massacre of a number of our citizens.

On my inquiring of Hewes what knowledge he had of that event, he replied, that he knew nothing from history, as he had never read any thing relating to it from any publication whatever, and can therefore only give the information which I derived from the event of the day upon which the catastrophe happened. On that day, one of the British officers applied to a barber, to be shaved and dressed; the master of the shop, whose name was Pemont, told his apprentice boy he might serve him, and receive the pay himself, while Pemont left the shop. The boy accordingly served him, but the officer, for some reason unknown to me, went away from the shop without paying him for his service. After the officer had been gone some time, the boy went to the house where he was, with his account, to demand payment of his bill, but the sentinel, who was before the door, would not give him admittance, nor permit him to see the officer; and as some angry words were interchanged between the sentinel and the boy, a considerable number of the people from the vicinity, soon gathered at the place where they were, which was in King street, and I was soon on the ground among them. The violent agitation of the citizens, not only on account of the abuse offered to the boy, but other causes of excitement, then fresh in the recollection, was such that the sentinel began to be apprehensive of danger, and knocked at the door of the house, where the officers were, and told the servant who came to the door, that he was afraid of his life, and would quit his post unless he was protected. The officers in the house then sent a messenger to the guard-house, to require Captain Preston to come with a sufficient number of his soldiers to defend them from the threatened violence of the people. On receiving the message, he came immediately with a small guard of grenadiers, and paraded them before the custom-house, where the British officers were shut up. Captain Preston then ordered the people to disperse, but they said they would not, they were in the king's highway, and had as good a right to be there as he had. The captain of the guard then said to them, if you do not disperse, I will fire upon you, and then gave orders to his men to make ready, and immediately after gave them orders to fire. Three of our citizens fell dead on the spot, and two, who were wounded, died the next day; and nine others were also wounded. The persons who were killed I well recollect, said Hewes; they were Gray, a rope maker, Marverick, a young man, Colwell, who was the mate of Captain Colton; Attuck, a mulatto, and Carr, who was an Irishman. Captain Preston then immediately fled with his grenadiers back to the guard-house. The people who were assembled on that occasion, then immediately chose a committee to report to the governor the result of Captain Preston's conduct, and to demand of him satisfaction. The governor told the committee, that if the people would be quiet that night he would give them satisfaction, so far as was in his power; the next morning Captain Preston, and those of his guard who were concerned in the massacre, were accordingly, by order of the governor, given up, and taken into custody the next morning, and committed to prison.

It is not recollected that the offence given to the barber's boy is mentioned by the historians of the revolution; yet there can be no doubt of its correctness. The account of this single one of the exciting causes of the massacre, related by Hewes, at this time, was in answer to the question of his personal knowledge of the event.

A knowledge of the spirit of those times will easily lead us to conceive, that the manner of the British officers application to the barber, was a little too strongly tinctured with the dictatorial hauteur, to conciliate the views of equality, which at that period were supremely predominant in the minds of those of the whig party, even in his humble occupation; and that the disrespectful notice of his loyal customer, in consigning him to the attention of his apprentice boy, and abruptly leaving his shop, was intended to be treated by the officer with contempt, by so underating the services of his apprentice, as to deem any reward for them beneath his attention. The boy too, may be supposed to have imbibed so much of the spirit of which distinguished that period of our history, that he was willing to improve any occasion to contribute his share to the public excitement; to add an additional spark to the fire of political dissention which was enkindling.

When Hewes arrived at the spot where the massacre happened, it appears his attention was principally engaged by the clamours of those who were disposed to aid the boy in avenging the insult offered to him by the British officer, and probably heard nothing, at that time, of any other of the many exciting causes which lead to that disastrous event, though it appeared from his general conversation, his knowledge of them was extensive and accurate.

But to pursue the destiny of Captain Preston, and the guard who fired on the citizens; in about a fortnight after, said Hewes, they were brought to trial and indicted for the crime of murder.

The soldiers were tried first, and acquitted, on the ground that in firing upon the citizens of Boston, they only acted in proper obedience to the captain's orders. When Preston, their captain, was tried, I was called as one of the witnesses, on the part of the government, and testified, that I believed it was the same man, Captain Preston, that ordered his soldiers to make ready, who also ordered them to fire. Mr. John Adams, former president of the United States, was advocate for the prisoners, and denied the fact, that Captain Preston gave orders to his men to fire; and on his cross examination of me, asked whether my position was such, that I could see the captain's lips in motion when the order to fire was given; to which I answered, that I could not. Although the evidence of Preston's having given orders to the soldiers to fire, was thought by the jury sufficient to acquit them, it was not thought to be of weight enough to convict him of a capital offence; he also was acquitted.

This account given to me by Hewes, although obviously from his own recollection and personal knowledge, it accords with the most correct historians of that event. At my request he confined his rehearsal to the most prominent details relating to it. The source from which the recollection is revived, at this time, gives it novelty, and renders it interesting.

DOCUMENT 30

MONUMENT TO THE FALLEN[122]

For many of Boston's historically minded, November 14, 1888, was a momentous day. It marked the dedication of a monument to the massacre, a granite shaft erected on Boston Common that stands over twenty-five feet high. A proud Governor Oliver Ames noted that this was the state's first commemorative edifice to any event in its long and illustrious history. As part of the same project, the remains of the slain, which lay in the unmarked graves where they had originally been buried, were to be reinterred. Their new resting place would eventually be topped by a headstone noting their place in Revolutionary iconography as martyrs in the cause of freedom.

Noted historian John Fiske capped the November 1888 occasion with a speech in Faneuil Hall, venerated locally as the "Cradle of Liberty." Fiske's literary fame would be most lasting for his book, published that same year, on the Constitution and the "critical period" in which it was crafted. Remembered now as one of a generation of so-called "gentleman historians," Fiske did not really fit that patrician mold—an example, perhaps, of the danger of lumping historians into schools of thought because of loosely shared backgrounds. Nonetheless, he was typical of nationalistic historians of his era who moralized unabashedly about the past. They may not have seen themselves as being objective in the sense that "scientific" historians would claim and yet they still believed that the surviving record fully supported their patriot stance.

Fiske spoke for well over an hour; only the closing portion where he focused on the historical significance of the massacre itself is included here. In setting the background he repeated—approvingly, of course—John Adams's claim that on the night of March 5, 1770, "the foundation of American independence was laid." He emphasized the foolishness in both London and Boston that had precipitated the event—the Townshend duties, Governor Bernard's machinations leading to the dispatch of troops, their antagonizing the town, and the people's righteous indignation, all of which the public now knew "smoothed" the way "for the beginnings of an American union."

Fiske did as the planners had hoped; listeners applauded his remarks and most Bostonians there probably went home pleased, their local pride reaffirmed. Fiske had not been the planners' original choice, however. They turned first to Frederick Douglass. "It is meet that your grand old Commonwealth should take the lead in honoring the memory of patriots and heroes, of whatever race and color," Douglass responded, but, no, he was too busy at that moment to prepare and deliver a weighty speech worthy of the occasion.[123] Perhaps, too, he chose not to become embroiled in the dispute over a monument that had stirred divisive feelings just beneath the surface. There were those who felt it inappropriate that the state's first monument to the Revolution celebrated men who may have been agitators of an unruly mob or mere victims of their excess, rather than true patriots committed to the cause of American freedom. Some may have resented the rising expectations of Boston's black community and with it the elevation of Crispus Attucks as hero. Others who feared the growing labor unrest of their own day may have opposed the violent actions of workingmen in an earlier era and did not want to see strikers casting themselves as patriots in a new struggle against tyranny.[124]

They need not have worried about such associations. The irony to this dispute is that the first monument to the massacre is now the last to be visited, if it is visited at all. It is not a stopping point on the Freedom Trail; it stands alone, almost lost in the open space of that part of Boston Common. It is, in a sense, a monument as well to the impermanence of memory, despite all the efforts to insure that people never forget.

*   *   *

Figure 15 (opposite) The Massacre Monument, dedicated in 1888. A walkway connects it to Tremont Street, on one side, and the rest of Boston Common, on the other. The iron railing that once surrounded it has been cut away. The bas relief above the date, facing Tremont, is essentially a bronze recasting of Revere's engraving. On the left are words by Daniel Webster: FROM THAT MOMENT WE MAY DATE THE SEVERANCE OF THE BRITISH EMPIRE. On the right, words by John Adams: ON THAT NIGHT THE FOUNDATION OF AMERICAN INDEPENDENCE WAS LAID. A statue of Liberty in her Phrygian cap stands above, thrusting forward the links of a broken chain in her right hand, with a furled flag in her left. An eagle, spreading its wings, is at her feet, and above her, on the granite column, the names of the five victims are inscribed. Photo by the author.

It was the sacrifice of the lives of Crispus Attucks, Samuel Gray, James Caldwell, Samuel Maverick, and Patrick Carr that brought about this preliminary victory of the American Revolution. Their death effected in a moment what seventeen months of petition and discussion had failed to accomplish. Instead of the king's representatives intimidating the people of Boston, it was the people of Boston that had intimidated the king's representatives. Nature is apt to demand some forfeit in accomplishing great results, and for achieving this particular result the lives of those five men were the forfeit. It is, therefore, historically correct to regard them as the first martyrs to the cause of American independence; as such they have long deserved a monument in the most honorable place that Boston could give for the purpose; and such a place is Boston Common.

If experience did not teach us how full the world is of paradox and looseness of thought, I should deem it incredible that any student of history should ever have doubted so plain and obvious a conclusion. The present generation of historical students is very creditably engaged in attempts to do justice to the motives of the Tories of the Revolution, who have, in many instances, been maligned and misunderstood. Such attempts deserve our warmest sympathy, for it is the duty of the historian to understand the past, and only in so far as he divests himself of partisan prejudice can he understand it. But in order to be fair toward the Tories, it is not necessary to become Tories ourselves. We seem to be in some danger of forgetting this obvious caution.

Some of our scholars seem to have swung round into the Tory view of the events which ushered in the Revolution, and things have been said about the Boston Massacre which one would think fit to make glorious old Samuel Adams turn in his grave. The motives and purposes of the victims have been belittled or aspersed. In truth, we know little or nothing about their motives and purposes; but we may fairly suppose them to have been actuated by the same feelings toward the soldiery that animated Adams and Warren and the patriots of Boston in general. The five victims were obscure men. As we have lately been reminded, they did not belong to our "first families." This, however, did not prevent Doctor Warren from calling them "our slaughtered brethren,"[125] and I do not suppose anybody that heard this phrase from the lips of that high-minded patriot would have attributed it to a seeking after political effect.

The immense concourse of people, including our "first families," that followed them on the 8th of March to their grave in the Old Granary Burying-ground, unquestionably regarded them as victims who had suffered in the common cause. Of their personal history next to nothing is known. Three of them—Caldwell, Carr, and Maverick—would seem to have been by-standers accidentally shot. Of the two who took a prominent part in the affair, Gray was one of the workmen at the ropewalk; Attucks was a stranger to Boston. He was a sailor employed on Captain Folger's whaleship from Nantucket, which was lying in Boston harbor. He was described as a mulatto, and may very probably have been the slave Crispus, six feet two inches in height, who ran away from his master, William Browne, of Framingham, in the fall of 1750, and was duly advertised in the "Boston Gazette" of November 20, in that year. If that be the case, he was about forty-six years old at the time of his death. It has also been argued that he may have been a Natick Indian, since the name Attucks is certainly an Indian name signifying "deer." Quite likely he had both Indian and African blood in his veins; such a thing was not unusual in the country about Framingham. At the time of his death his home is said to have been in the Island of Nassau, and he was apparently embarked for North Carolina, working his way, perhaps, towards his home. From this time until independence was won, there was hardly a struggle in which brave men of his race and color did not nobly acquit themselves.

Such was the famous "Boston Massacre." The excellent British historian, Mr. [William] Lecky, observes that "there are many dreadful massacres recorded in the pages of history,—the massacre of the Danes by the Saxons, the Massacre of the Sicilian Vespers, the Massacre of St. Bartholomew,— but it may be questioned whether any of them produced such torrents of indignant eloquence as this affair." (Hist. Eng. III, 367.) In commenting upon the very gentle sarcasm here implied, I would remind Mr. Lecky that it will not do to try to measure history with a foot-rule. Lord Sherbrooke —better known as Robert Lowe—declared a few years ago, in a speech on the uses of a classical education, that the Battle of Marathon was really of less account than a modern colliery-explosion, because only one hundred and ninety-two of the Greek army lost their lives.

From such a point of view, one might argue that the "Boston Massacre" was an event of far less importance than an ordinary free fight among Colorado gamblers. It is needless to say that this is not the historical point of view. Historically, the "Boston Massacre" is not only important from the fresh impetus it gave to the nascent revolutionary feeling among the Americans at that time, but it furnishes an instructive illustration of the high state of civilization that had been attained by the people among whom it happened,—by the oppressors as well as those whom it was sought to oppress. The quartering of troops in a peaceful town is something that has in most ages been regarded with horror. Under the senatorial govern- ment of Rome, it used to be said that the quartering of troops, even upon a friendly province and for the purpose of protecting it, was a visitation only less to be dreaded than an inroad of hostile barbarians. When we reflect that the British regiments were encamped in Boston during seventeen months, among a population to whom they were thoroughly odious, the fact that only half a dozen persons lost their lives, and that otherwise no really grave crimes seem to have been committed, is a fact highly creditable both to the discipline of the soldiers and to the moderation of the people.

In most ages and countries the shooting of half a dozen citizens under such circumstances would either have produced but a slight impression, or, on the other hand, would perhaps have resulted on the spot in a wholesale slaughter of the offending soldiers. The fact that so profound an impression was made in Boston and throughout the country, while at the same time the guilty parties were left to be dealt with in the ordinary course of law, is a striking commentary upon the general peacefulness and decorum of American life; and it shows how high and severe was the standard by which our forefathers judged all lawless proceedings.

And here it may not be irrelevant to add that, throughout the constitutional struggles which led to the Revolution, the American standard of political right and wrong was so high that contemporary European politicians found it sometimes difficult to understand it. And for a like reason, even the most far-minded modern English historians sometimes fail to see why the Americans should have been so quick to take offence at acts of the British Government which doubtless were not meant to be oppressive. If George III. had been a bloodthirsty despot, like Phillip II., of Spain; if General Gage had been like the Duke of Alva; if American citizens by the hundred had been burned alive or broken on the wheel in New York and Boston; if towns such as Providence and Hartford had been given up to the cruelty and lust of a beastly soldiery,—then no one would ever have found it hard to understand why the Americans should have exhibited a rebellious temper.

But it is one signal characteristic of the progress of political civilization, that the part played by sheer brute force in a barbarous age is fully equalled by the part played by a mere covert threat of injustice in a more advanced age. The effect which a blow in the face would produce upon a barbarian will be wrought upon a civilized man by an assertion of some far-reaching legal principle, which only in a subtle and ultimate analysis includes the possibility of a blow in the face. From this point of view, the quickness with which such acts as those of Charles Townshend were comprehended in their remotest bearings is the most striking proof one could wish of the high grade of political culture which our forefathers had reached through their system of perpetual free discussion in town-meeting. They had, moreover, reached a point where any manifestation of simple brute force in the course of a political dispute was exceedingly disgusting and shocking to them. To their minds the careless or wanton slaughter of five citizens conveyed just as much meaning as a St. Bartholomew's massacre would have conveyed to the minds of men in a lower stage of political development.

It was not strange, therefore, that Samuel Adams and his friends should have been ready to make the "Boston Massacre" the occasion of a moral lesson to their contemporaries. As far as the offending soldiers were concerned, they were most honorably dealt with. There was no attempt to wreak a paltry vengeance on them. Brought to trial on a charge of murder, after a judicious delay of seven months, they were ably defended by John Adams and Josiah Quincy, and all were acquitted save Montgomery and Kilroy, who were convicted of manslaughter, and branded in the hand. There were some hot-heads who grumbled at the verdict, but the people of Boston generally acquiesced in it, as they showed by choosing John Adams for their representative in the Assembly.

At the same time, such an event as the "Boston Massacre" could not fail for a long time to point a moral among a people so unused to violence and bloodshed. Paul Revere, who was one of the earliest American engravers, published a quaint colored engraving of the scene in King street, which for a long time was widely circulated, though it has now become very scarce. Below the picture are the following verses, written in the rhymed ten-syllable couplets which the eighteenth century was so fond of turning out by the yard:—

> "Unhappy Boston! see thy sons deplore
> Thy hallowed walks besmeared with guiltless gore,
> While faithless P—n and his savage bands
> With murderous rancour stretch their bloody hands,
> Like fierce barbarians grinning o'er their prey
> Approve the carnage and enjoy the day.
> If scalding drops from rage, from anguish, wrung,
> If speechless sorrows labouring for a tongue,
> Or if a weeping world can aught appease
> The plaintive ghosts of victims such as these,
> The patriot's copious tears for each are shed,
> A glorious tribute which embalms the dead.
> But know! Fate summons to that awful goal,
> Where Justice strips the murderer of his soul;
> Should venal c—ts, the scandal of the land,
> Snatch the relentless villain from her hand,
> Keen execrations on this plate inscribed
> Shall reach a Judge who never can be bribed."

These last lines give expression to the feelings of those who condemned the verdict of the court, and they show how intense was the indignation over the bloodshed and the sympathy for the victims. The self-restraint shown by the people, while under the influence of such feelings, is in the highest degree creditable to Boston, and the moral lessons of the story are such as ought never to be forgotten. Adams and Warren, and their patriot friends, were right in deciding that the fatal 5th of March should be solemnly commemorated each year by an oration to be delivered in the Old South Meeting-house, and this custom was kept up until the recognition of American Independence in 1783, when the day for the oration was changed to the 4th of July.

At the very first annual March [town] meeting after the massacre, it was proposed to erect a monument to commemorate it. The form of the proposal shows that the character of the event was understood by town-people at that time as I have endeavored to set it forth to-day. In dedicating this memorial on Boston Common after the lapse of more than a century, we are but performing an act of justice too long delayed. There let it stand for future generations to contemplate as a monument of the wickedness and folly of all attempts to employ brute force in compelling the obedience of the people to laws which they have had no voice in making.

DOCUMENT **31**

A MORE BALANCED VIEW[126]

Boston's "Freedom Trail" brings together public and private agencies, the taxpayer's obligatory payment combined with the donor's voluntary contribution—supplemented by the proceeds from what tourists buy and take home as mementos. Of course, for the Freedom Trail to work as intended, visitors from around the U.S. need to feel that they have come back to their roots, that no matter what part of the country they call home, they are connected to the past that is celebrated along this two-and-half-mile-long walk. It is, as one scholar put it, "one of the key public history venues in the country," a "wonderfully confusing collection of public buildings, churches, museums and historic markers."[127]

The walk used to be shorter and marked by a foot-wide, bright red line from start to finish. Subtly colored reddish bricks have replaced the more garish paint along some stretches, but not all. The Bunker Hill monument and the U.S.S. Constitution, berthed at the navy yard, caused Charlestown to be added to the route, increasing its length by a mile. In earlier years there were nearly thirty marked points along the trail; now there are just under twenty. Collectively they are all supposed to tell the same story and stand as memorials to the American past, even though they range from the Colonial Era to decades past the Revolution. They have their individual characteristics as well, from the U.S.S. Constitution and its embodiment of the idea of invincibility as "Old Ironsides" to the Old South Meeting House and its association with free speech and patriot orators.

And then there are the two stopping points associated with the events of that long-ago March 5 evening: the martyrs' grave in the Granary Burying Ground and the star set within a spoked wheel of stones commemorating "The

Figure 16 The Old State House—known as the town house to the Revolutionary generation—is an eighteenth-century architectural island in a twentieth-century skyscraper sea. The staircase and door leading to the floor below the balcony were removed long ago. The Bostonian Society collections are housed inside on the topmost floor, with exhibits and a gift shop below. The streets outside were reconfigured so that the intersection outside bears little resemblance to the 1770 setting, and the circle of paving stones commemorating the massacre on the traffic island is impossibly close to the building. The modern structure to the left is built over the onetime site of the guard house. The National Park Service's visitors' center is located on the ground floor. Photo by the author.

Massacre"—this, even though the star does not mark the actual site, despite claims that it does. Tourists who step off the curb by the Old State House to reach it need to be careful as they cross over to what is a traffic island in a busy intersection.

The National Park Service became involved with the Trail in the 1970s, using federal funds to help create the Boston National Historical Park. The Trail thus became part of the Park Service's larger effort to provide "sources of inspiration, where people come to be refreshed and recharged, physically and spiritually."[128] Boston's National Historical Park acts as an umbrella for the various organizations involved in the Freedom Trail, which had been only loosely joined for some twenty years before that. The Park Service visitor center in downtown Boston is adjacent to the Old State House—located near the spot of the main guard house where Preston fatefully sallied forth.

The Park Service publishes guides to various historical sites, including one for Revolutionary Boston, which uses the Freedom Trail as a convenient locator. Barbara Clark Smith, a Yale Ph.D. in American Studies and longtime curator at the Smithsonian, wrote the text for the Park Service Revolutionary Boston pamphlet. Her discussion of the massacre, included below, shows how the desire to be even-handed and fair-minded can be effectively combined with an acceptance of the historian's limited ability to reconstruct the past. Others have taken a balanced approach as well. Even more profusely illustrated and lightly written tour guides for the Trail, which present Boston as the home of freedom and equality, celebrate American heroes without denigrating British villains.[129] Still, attempts at historical consciousness-raising—in Boston as at nearby Plimoth Plantation or faraway Colonial Williamsburg—often raise eyebrows because of their ties to those who commercialize and sentimentalize the past.[130]

* * *

For more than two centuries, Paul Revere's print of the Boston Massacre of March 5, 1770, has shaped Americans' idea of that dramatic event. Revere copied (without permission) from a work by Henry Pelham. Rushed into print, Revere's image made a strong and timely political point. Judged by evidence given at the soldiers' trials and by other eyewitnesses, Revere's version distorted the event in several respects. He depicted unarmed townspeople, well-dressed and peaceable. He portrayed the soldiers drawn up in an orderly line, firing into the crowd at the command of their captain. A Boston jury found that the redcoats had fired their weapons in a confused manner, not on any officer's orders. Besides, the crowd was distinctly less-well-to-do than Pelham and Revere showed it to be. It was composed of working people, some of whom carried clubs and pelted the soldiers with rocks and snowballs. The patriot depiction misrepresented events to win sympathy and support from people outside Boston. Even at the time, not everyone accepted the patriot view. John Adams, who served as a defense lawyer for the soldiers, dismissed the crowd in King Street as a "motley rabble of saucy boys, negroes and molattoes, Irish teagues and outlandish jack tarrs." Historians note that the massacre followed on the heels of seemingly petty disputes. A few days earlier, ropewalk workers had brawled with soldiers in the streets. On March 5, a fracas arose when a wigmaker's apprentice taunted a British captain over a disputed barber bill. Patriots might have seen the resulting encounter as a grievous case of British oppression, but from another view it seemed a tragic but petty incident. Many 18th-century Americans found it impossible to separate the two views. Daily conflicts were just what they expected when government stations an armed force amidst a civilian population. Over the centuries, Englishmen had struggled to ensure that no monarch would rule them with a standing army. Bostonians knew that the ministry currently ruled and taxed Ireland by an armed force. In fact, two of the four regiments sent to Boston in 1768 came directly from Irish duty. Although violence might break out over seemingly small matters, there was nothing trivial about the fundamental issue in the minds of many Bostonians: would colonists in British America be reduced to the oppressed position of the Irish or retain the status of free English subjects? The massacre raised questions that were fundamental to the Revolution. The Declaration of Independence had no less than four clauses touching on the dangers of "standing armies." The Constitution and Bill of Rights enshrine civilian supremacy over the military, the right to a fair trial, and freedom of assembly. America's founding documents were profoundly influenced by the bloody conflict of March 5, 1770.

NOTES

INTRODUCTION

1 John Adams to Matthew Robinson, March 2, 1786, in Charles Francis Adams, ed., *The Works of John Adams*, 10 vols. (Boston: Little, Brown, and Co., 1850–1856), 8:384.

2 L. H. Butterfield, et al., eds., *Diary and Autobiography of John Adams*, 4 vols. (Cambridge, MA: The Belknap Press of Harvard University Press), 2:79, diary entry for March 5, 1773.

3 The "child independence" (in reference to the 1761 writs of assistance controversy), in a letter from Adams to William Tudor, March 29, 1817, and first colonies allusion in Adams's letter to William Keteltas, November 25, 1812, in Adams, ed., *Works*, 10:248 and 23, resp.

4 See Adams to Jedediah Morse, January 5, 1816, in ibid., 10:203.

5 For which see David B. Quinn and Alison M. Quinn, eds., *Discourse of Western Planting* (London: The Hakluyt Society, 1993).

6 Lawrence Harper, *The English Navigation Laws* (New York: Columbia University Press, 1939) and *England's Commercial and Colonial Policy*, the last volume in Charles M. Andrews, *The Colonial Period in American History*, 4 vols. (New Haven: Yale University Press, 1934–1938), remain excellent starting points on the subject. Jack P. Greene, *Peripheries and Center* (Athens: University of Georgia Press, 1986) placed the navigation system within a political and constitutional context.

7 Viola Barnes's *The Dominion of New England* (New Haven: Yale University Press, 1923) is dated but still useful; also see David S. Lovejoy, *The Glorious Revolution in America* (New York: Harper & Row, 1972); Richard R. Johnson, *Adjustment to Empire* (Leicester: Leicester University Press, 1981); and J. M. Sosin, *English America*, 3 vols. (Lincoln: University of Nebraska Press, 1980–1985).

8 Danby Pickering, ed., *The Statutes at Large*, 46 vols. (Cambridge: Joseph Bentham et al., 1762–1807), 12 Charles II c. 18, with the most important elaborations in 25 Charles II c. 7 (in 1673) and 7 & 8 William and Mary c. 22 (1696) at 7:452–460, 8:397–400, and 9:428–436, resp.

9 Oliver M. Dickerson, *The Navigation Acts and the American Revolution* (Philadelphia: University of Pennsylvania Press, 1951) and Thomas C. Barrow, *Trade and Empire* (Cambridge, MA: Harvard University Press, 1967) offer very different views of the extent and significance of smuggling in the pre-1763 empire.

10 See the overview in Carl Ubbelohde, *Vice-Admiralty Courts and the American Revolution* (Chapel Hill: University of North Carolina Press, 1961).

11 Letter from Charles Gravier, Comte de Vergennes, as printed in [John Lind], *Three Letters to Dr. Price* (London: T. Payne, 1776), 138n.

12 As quoted from Clarence Walford Alvord and Clarence Edwin Carter, eds., *The Critical Period, 1763–1765* (Springfield: Illinois State Historical Society, 1915), 7. Also see the discussion in John Shy, *Toward Lexington* (Princeton: Princeton University Press, 1961), 52–80, and what Shy called "the first step toward Lexington", 68–69.

13 1 William and Mary, 2 sess. C. 2, in Pickering, ed., *Statutes*, 9:69 (original in italics).

14 John Phillip Reid, *In Defiance of the Law* (University Park: Pennsylvania State University Press, 1981) examines the legal/constitutional distinction and, equally important, explains how imperial administrators and protesting colonists made use of "forensic evidence" in making their respective cases.

15 Douglas Edward Leach, *Roots of Conflict* (Chapel Hill: University of North Carolina Press, 1986), "hostility or indifference" on 11; "bloodless coup" on 7.

16 Contrast Stephen Saunders Webb, *The Governors-General* (Chapel Hill: University of North Carolina Press, 1979) with Richard Johnson, "Charles McLean Andrews and the Invention of Colonial American History" *William and Mary Quarterly*, 3rd series 43 (1986):519–541, and the exchange between Webb and Johnson on 408–459 of that same volume.

17 See Neil R. Stout, *The Royal Navy in America, 1760–1775* (Annapolis: Naval Institute Press, 1973), and, for the army, Shy, *Toward Lexington*, passim.

18 James Munro and Almeric W. Fitzroy, eds., *Acts of the Privy Council of England. Colonial Series*, 6 vols. (London: Her Majesty's Stationery Office, 1908–1912), 4:569.

19 Britain's postwar financial woes are discussed in John Bullion, *A Great and Necessary Measure* (Columbia: University of Missouri Press, 1982) and put into the large context of Britain's growing "fiscal military state" in John Brewer, *The Sinews of Power* (New York: Alfred A. Knopf, 1989).

20 P. D. G. Thomas reviewed British postwar policies in a detailed trilogy: *British Politics and the Stamp Act Crisis* (Oxford: Clarendon Press, 1975); *The Townshend Duties Crisis, 1767–1773* (Oxford: Clarendon Press, 1987); and *Tea Party to Independence* (Oxford: Clarendon Press, 1991).

21 The Declaratory Act can be found in Pickering, ed., *Statutes*, 27:19–20, at 6 George III c. 12.

22 The three key elements of Townshend's program are in Pickering, ed., *Statutes*, 7 George III c. 41 (customs commissioners), c. 46 (new duties), and 8 George III c. 22 (vice-admiralty courts) at 27:447–449, 505–512, and 28:70–71, resp., with details for the latter laid out in Munro and Fitzroy, eds., *Privy Council. Col. Ser.*, 5:151–153.

23 Henry Hulton, "Some account of the Proceedings of the People in New England from the Establishment of a Board of Customs in America, to the breaking out of the Rebellion in 1775," unpublished manuscript, Andre De Coppet Collection, Princeton University Library, 26.

24 Legal scholar John Phillip Reid focuses on the affair to show how local control of the law could be used to negate claims of imperial authority. See his *In a Rebellious Spirit* (University Park: Pennsylvania State University Press, 1979).

25 These development are discussed in Joseph Tiedemann, *Reluctant Revolutionaries* (Ithaca: Cornell University Press, 1997).

26 The "letters" were first serialized in newspapers and then printed in pamphlet form, including the one quoted here: [John Dickinson], *Letters from a Farmer in Pennsylvania* (Philadelphia: David Hall and William Sellers, 1768), from Letter II, 10.

27 For conspiratorial fears as they grabbed hold of protesting colonists, see Bernard Bailyn, *The Ideological Origins of the American Revolution* (Cambridge, MA: The Belknap Press of the Harvard University Press, 1967).

28 [Dickinson], *Letters*, "inflammatory measures" on 6, "dreadful stroke" on 5 (both in Letter I).

29 See Documents 1 and 2.

30 G. B. Warden, *Boston, 1689–1776* (Boston: Little, Brown, and Co., 1970) is incisive on Boston's peculiar place in the crisis of empire. See too William Pencak, *War, Politics, & Revolution in Massachusetts* (Boston: Northeastern University Press, 1981); and John W. Tyler, *Smugglers and Patriots* (Boston: Northeastern University Press, 1986). Hiller B. Zobel, *The Boston Massacre* (New York: W. W. Norton & Company, 1970) also has much on Boston, opening with events in 1760 and carrying through the massacre and trials. Adroitly mixing legal with political history, it well deserves its reputation as a classic in the field.

31 See Document 3.

32 Colin Nicolson, *The 'Infamas Govener'* (Boston: Northeastern University Press, 2001) reviews Bernard's stormy career. Bernard's letter to Hillsborough of June 18, 1768, in The National

Archives (TNA), Public Record Office (PRO), Colonial Office (CO) 5/757, is indicative of the tone the Governor took in his reports to London. There he claimed that the Sons of Liberty's resistance to imperial authority was so complete and unthinking that it verged on "Madness."

33 For the provisions of the act, see 5 George III c. 33, in Pickering, ed., *Statutes*, 16:305–318.

34 Franklin in the House of Commons, February 13, 1766, printed in Leonard Labaree, et al., eds., *The Papers of Benjamin Franklin*, 39 vols. (New Haven: Yale University Press, 1959–), 13:142.

35 Pauline Maier, *From Resistance to Revolution* (New York: Alfred A. Knopf, 1972) has a good deal on the Sons of Liberty in Boston.

36 Known now as the Old State House.

37 See Document 4.

38 From the "Journal of the Times," as collected in Oliver Morton Dickerson, ed., *Boston under Military Rule* (Boston: Chapman & Grimes, 1936), 16, entry for October 28, 1768. Items for the "Journal" were composed—by whom, precisely, it is not clear—in Boston, sent to papers in other colonies where they were printed and then turned around and reprinted in sympathetic Boston newspapers.

39 Message from the lower House to Bernard of May 31, 1769, printed in *Speeches of the Governors of Massachusetts, From 1765 to 1775* (Boston: Russell and Gardner, 1818), 167. See too the formal House resolution of June 29, 1769 in Document 6, which was prompted by the parliamentary resolutions passed the previous February—transcribed as Document 5.

40 In *The Acts and Resolves, Public and Private, of the Province of Massachusetts Bay*, 21 vols. (Boston: Wright & Potter, 1869–1922), 3:544–546; and Pickering, ed., *Statutes*, 13:142–146, at 1 George I Stat. 2 c. 5, resp.

41 See Lieutenant Alexander Ross's deposition, printed as Document 7.

42 See the account printed in the *Boston Gazette*, February 26, 1770, transcribed as Document 8. Zobel, *Boston Massacre*, reviews this incident on 164–179.

43 Testimony about what supposedly occurred at the ropewalk is included in Documents 19 and 20. At the very least this March 2 incident would include the soldiers Warren, Carrol, and Kilroy, and the slain civilian Gray.

44 Zobel, *Boston Massacre*, 180–205 chose to tell the massacre tale in story form, though Zobel's endnotes discussed the many unanswered—even unanswerable—questions resulting from the surviving record.

45 See the *Boston Gazette*, March 12, 1770 account, included as Document 9.

46 Jurists took as their guide William Hawkins, *A Treatise of the Pleas of the Crown*, 2nd ed., 2 vols. (London: J. Walthoe, 1724–1726), 1:69–87, for the distinctions separating justifiable homicide, excusable homicide, manslaughter, and murder; and the more recent William Blackstone, *Commentaries on the Laws of England*, 4 vols. (Oxford: Clarendon Press, 1765–1769), 4:176–204 (Book IV, Chap. 14), which generally agreed with Hawkins.

47 Hutchinson noted this in his diary, now in the Egerton Mss. 2666, British Library (BL), fos. 70–71, sentiments incorporated into his *The History of the Province of Massachusetts-Bay*, 3 vols. (Cambridge, MA: The Belknap Press of the Harvard University Press, 1936; edited by Lawrence Mayo), 3:196.

48 See Document 11.

49 *A Report of the Record Commissioners of the City of Boston, Containing the Selectman's Minutes from 1769 through April 1775* (Boston: Rockwell and Churchill, 1893), 58.

50 Hutchinson to Francis Bernard, March 30, 1770, Mass. Archives XXVI:467, from the Massachusetts Historical Society (MHS) typescript, 1015.

51 Hutchinson to Hillsborough, March 1770, Mass. Archives XXVI:454–455, from the MHS typescript, 989, for the "authority statement"; Hutchinson to Hillsborough, April 27, 1770, TNA PRO/CO/5/768, fos. 116–124 for the "Shadow of Power."

52 See Documents 13 and 14.

53 See Documents 12 and 15.

54 He in fact pulled this off with Ebenezer Richardson, who was convicted by a Suffolk County jury in April of murder for killing Christopher Seider. Richardson was held in jail for two years without the Court pronouncing sentence. After receiving a royal pardon he slipped out of the colony.

55 Hillsborough to Hutchinson, April 26, 1770, TNA PRO/CO/5/165, fos. 93–96.

56 "Wilfully and feloniously" from the inquest into the death of Michael Johnson (Crispus Attucks), reproduced as Document 17. Preston was identified as giving the order to fire in the Samuel Gray inquest, at Ch.M.1.8.206, Boston Public Library (BPL) mss. The coroners' reports for Caldwell (Ch.M.1.8.186), Carr (Ch.M.1.8.123), and Maverick (Ch.B.12.10) are also at the BPL. For one example of testimony provided at these inquests, see Robert Goddard's deposition, transcribed as Document 16.

57 *Boston Gazette*, March 12, 1770; *Boston Evening-Post*, March 12, 1770; and Edward Lillie Pierce, ed., *Letters and Diary of John Rowe* (Boston: W. B. Clarke, 1903), 19.

58 *Boston Evening-Post*, March 19, 1770; Pierce, ed., *Letters and Diary of John Rowe*, 199.

59 See Document 18.

60 See Document 9 for the text of the original *Boston Gazette*, March 12, 1770 report, and Figure 5 for the Revere engraving.

61 See Document 19.

62 Hutchinson to John Pownall, March 21, 1770, Mass. Archives XXVI:464, from the MHS typescript, 1007.

63 *A Short Narrative of The horrid Massacre in Boston* (Boston: Edes & Gill, 1770), 80.

64 *Additional Observations to a Short Narrative of the Horrid Massacre in Boston* (Boston, 1770), 3n.

65 *Short Narrative*, 87. See the Bowdoin-Temple Papers (reel 47), part of the Winthrop Papers, MHS, for the original of James Bowdoin's letter to Richmond, with the list of intended *Short Narrative* recipients in Britain, and Bowdoin's letter to William Bollan of March 27, 1770, showing Bowdoin's anger over the "horrid massacre" *and* Hutchinson's counter-efforts in assembling his own of depositions. Also see Document 14.

66 See Document 20.

67 See Document 21.

68 Notice of the bonds for three of the four in the BPL collections: Ch.F.10.90 (Edward Manwaring), Ch.A.2.7 (Hammond Green), and Ch.A.3.112 (John Munroe).

69 See Document 23.

70 Hutchinson to Hillsborough, October 30, 1770, TNA PRO/CO/5/759, fo. 61.

71 Josiah Quincy Jr. to Josiah Quincy, March 26, 1770, as quoted from Josiah Quincy, *Memoir of the Life of Josiah Quincy, Junior*, 3rd ed. (Boston: Little, Brown, and Co., 1875), 28. Also see Adams's recollections, in Butterfield, et al., eds., *Diary and Autobiography*, 3:292–293.

72 See note 1 above.

73 John Hodgson, ed., *The Trial of William Wemms . . .* (Boston: J. Fleeming, 1770), 9.

74 Ibid., 54–68, for Quincy's closing argument, with his reference to Kilroy on 57 and homicide on 68.

75 Ibid., 153.

76 Trowbridge's instructions are included as Document 25.

77 Hutchinson to Hillsborough, December 5, 1770, TNA PRO/CO/5/759, fos. 759–761.

78 The punishment, as noted in Blackstone, *Commentaries*, 3:360 (Book IV, Chap. 28).

79 Although it appears that the juries in both trials were predisposed to be lenient and were perhaps in some sense stacked, though not illegally or invisibly to town leaders. See Zobel, *Boston Massacre*, 244–247 and 270–271.

80 And Montgomery, at least, was hardly innocent if he did indeed say, after safely away from Boston, that he joined the mob in calling out "fire" before he discharged his musket. See Hutchinson's at best secondhand claim to this effect in Catherine Barton Mayo, ed., "Additions to Thomas Hutchinson's 'History of Massachusetts'" *American Antiquarian Society. Proceedings* 59 (1949):33.

81 See, again, Josiah Quincy Jr. to his father, March 26, 1770, in Quincy, *Memoir*, 28. For Quincy's desire to indict the town, see Hutchinson diary, Egerton Mss. 2666 (BL), fo. 75.

82 Pownall letter of May 1770, Ms. 791 BPL.

83 Hutchinson, *History*, 3:237, echoing his diary entry, Egerton Mss. 2666 (BL), fo. 76. Zobel, *Boston Massacre*, 221, agreed. I disagree.

84 See Document 22.

85 Mayo, ed., "Additions," 34.

86 See J. Wright, *Sir Henry Cavendish's Debates of the House of Commons*, 2 vols. (London: Longman, Brown, Green & Longmans, 1842), 2:138, for Edmund Burke's failed May 1770 motion. Richmond likewise failed in the House of Lords. Upset as Rockinghamites (like

Burke) and Pittites were about troops having been sent to Boston in 1768, they disliked mobs—as did John Adams, for that matter. The massacre had merely provided the impetus for the opposition's call for an inquiry, a move in the works many months before. Even though the Privy Council would determine in July that "there is much reason to apprehend that there was a premeditated design to seek occasion of such quarrels for forcing the Regiments to leave the Town" (TNA PRO/CO/5/765, fo. 159; also Munro and Fitzroy, eds., *Privy Council. Col. Ser.*, 5:246–264), there would be no official parliamentary inquiry—just continued frustration. By then Hillsborough felt that something decisive needed to be done to prevent Massachusetts from using the event as a first step toward independence. See his letter to Hutchinson of October 3, 1770, in TNA PRO/CO/5/765, fo. 185.

87 This trial received scant attention. All that can pass for a transcript is in Hodgson, ed., *Trial*, Appendix, 211–217. There are also brief notes in the *Massachusetts Gazette*, December 13, 1770; the *Boston Evening-Post*, December 17, 1770; and the *Boston Gazette*, December 17 and 24, 1770, March 18 and 25, and April 1, 1771. A fragment of what is apparently the testimony of Charles Bourgatte, Manwaring's servant, is in the BPL ms., Ch.M.1.8.217. Manwaring made some comments in his petition of August 4, 1771 to the Treasury (T) for compensation, found in TNA PRO/T1/486. See too Hutchinson's post-mortem to Hillsborough of December 12, 1770, TNA PRO/CO/5/758, fos. 180–181, and Hillsborough's general satisfaction with the trials in letters of December 11, 1770 and February 12, 1771, TNA PRO/CO/5/765, fos. 194 and 199, resp.

88 See Documents 24 and 29 for examples of problems in the record.

89 See *Report of the Record Commissioners*, 74, in a note from the selectmen to the town clerk of December 28, 1770.

90 See Documents 26 and 27.

91 See Document 28 for the first of the annual massacre orations, on March 5, 1771.

92 Labaree, et al., eds., *Papers of Franklin*, 13:150.

93 Larry Rivers with Arnold Weinstein, *What Did I Do?* (New York: HarperCollins, 1992), 476.

94 Hodgson, ed., *Trial*, "mad behaviour" and "rabble of Negroes" on 176; "Irish teagues" and "molattoes" on 174.

95 Ibid., 125.

96 For the larger context, see Gordon S. Wood, "A Note on Mobs in the American Revolution" *William and Mary Quarterly*, 3rd series 23 (1966):635–642; Pauline Maier, "Popular Uprisings and Civil Authority in Eighteenth-Century America" ibid., 3rd series 27 (1970):3–35; Richard Maxwell Brown, "Violence and the American Revolution" in Stephen G. Kurtz, ed., *Essays on the American Revolution* (Chapel Hill: University of North Carolina Press, 1973); Dirk Hoerder, *Crowd Action in Revolutionary Massachusetts* (New York: Academic Press, 1977); Russell Bourne, *Cradle of Violence* (New York: John Wiley & Sons, 2006); and Benjamin L. Carp, *Rebels Rising* (Oxford: Oxford University Press, 2007).

97 Adams to Benjamin Hichborn, January 27, 1817, in Adams, ed., *Works*, 9:551.

98 Butterfield, et al., eds., *Diary and Autobiography*, 3:292.

99 *A Memorial of Crispus Attucks, Samuel Maverick, James Caldwell, Samuel Gray and Patrick Carr From The City of Boston* (Boston, 1888) contains the program of November 14, 1888 dedication, including John Fiske's speech at Faneuil Hall (see Document 30). Boston was still not united on the appropriateness of the memorial, however, and the division carried into the Massachusetts Historical Society, which opposed the proposal. See Louis Leonard Tucker, *The Massachusetts Historical Society: A Bicentennial History* (Boston: The Massachusetts Historical Society, 1995), 155–157; and, for deeper background, Stephen Kantrowitz, "A Place for 'Colored Patriots': Crispus Attucks among the Abolitionists, 1842–1863" *Massachusetts Historical Review*, 11 (2009):97–118.

100 *Message of His Honor the Mayor Concerning the Proposed Tablet to be Placed Over the Tomb in Which were Interred the Victims of the Boston Massacre of March 5th 1770* (Boston: Rockwell and Churchill, 1890). The stone marker proposed in 1890 would have had the massacre victims commemorated on one side, and Seider (Snider) on the other. The actual marker, put in place in 1906, joins them on the same side, for passers-by to see.

101 Thus reads the inscription on the headstone. The victims of the massacre and Seider had been linked in a 1772 broadside, *A Monumental Inscription on the Fifth of March*, prompted by Ebenezer Richardson's not yet being sentenced. That Preston and six soldiers had escaped punishment altogether, with the two being convicted being found guilty only of manslaughter

and Richardson still not having answered for his crime, such miscarriages of justice should "be told to Posterity" and passed down "'Till Time shall be no more," so that "AMERICA" would "be preserved" from tyrants.

102 Clarence S. Brigham, *Paul Revere's Engravings* (New York: Atheneum, 1969), 52–78 remains the best starting place. Also see the illustrations interspersed in the text by Paul Revere, John Bufford, Alonzo Chappel, and Howard Pyle.

103 See, for example, his (with Donald MacRaild) handbook for those learning the historian's craft, *Studying History*, 3rd ed. (Houndmills: Palgrave Macmillan, 2007), and his cautions to those who already practice it in *War: Past, Present & Future* (New York: St. Martin's Press, 2000).

104 Benjamin Woods Labaree, *The Boston Tea Party* (New York: Oxford University Press, 1964), 256.

DOCUMENTS

1 *Journals of the House of Representatives of Massachusetts*, 55 vols. (Boston: Massachusetts Historical Society, 1919–1990), 44:20–23 (Appendix).

2 *The Glorious Ninety-Two* (Boston: Massachusetts General Court, 1949).

3 Dennys Deberdt was employed by the Massachusetts House, not the governor, so, technically speaking, he did not represent the colony. Like other lobbyists—Benjamin Franklin, perhaps most famously—he depended on sympathetic Members of Parliament or those who had the king's ear to make his case for the repeal of unpopular navigation acts. Michael Kammen examines their difficult position when it came to influencing imperial policy in *A Rope of Sand* (Ithaca: Cornell University Press, 1968).

4 From the copy sent to Governor Henry Moore of New York, printed in E. B. O'Callaghan, ed., *Documents Relative to the Colonial History of the State of New-York*, 15 vols. (Albany: Weed, Parsons and Company, 1853–1857), 8:58–59.

5 As seen in his letter of January 23, 1768 to Governor Moore, printed in ibid., 8:7.

6 From a generally friendly sketch, the "Memoirs of the Right Honourable the Earl of Hillsborough" *The London Magazine*, 50 (August 1781):356.

7 The post of secretary of state for the southern department dated from the early seventeenth century, as did its counterpart in the northern department. Both dealt with domestic as well as foreign affairs, and they shared some duties with the Board of Trade, which dated from 1696. The overlap created friction. Technically the secretaries were policy advisors; effectively, because the men who served as secretaries all sat in Parliament and the secretaryships were cabinet-level posts, they made policy as well. The American secretary had oversight of North America and the West Indies, plus Senegal and Gambia.

8 Chesterfield to the Earl of Dartmouth—who would succeed Hillsborough—in a letter of May 24, 1766, printed in the Historical Manuscripts Commission, *The Manuscripts of the Earl of Dartmouth*, 3 vols. (London: Eyre and Spottiswoode, 1887–1896), 3:182.

9 From the Francis Bernard Papers, 6:280–288, Ms. Sparks 4, Houghton Library, Harvard University; also printed, with slight differences, in *Letters to the Ministry* (Boston: Edes & Gill, 1769), 12–17.

10 Pencak, *War, Politics & Revolution*, 160.

11 Nicolson, *The 'Infamas Govener,'* 7.

12 See Francis Bernard's *Select Letters on the Trade and Government of America* (London: W. Bowyer and J. Nichols, 1774).

13 Bernard to Lord Barrington, November 23, 1765, in Edward Channing and Archibald Cary Coolidge, eds., *The Barrington–Bernard Correspondence* (Cambridge, MA: Harvard University Press, 1912), 96.

14 Bernard addressed this letter to the Earl of Shelburne, secretary of state for the southern department. He did not yet know that, as of January, Hillsborough headed the new American department and that he would be reporting to him instead.

15 John Temple as the exception.

16 The *Boston Gazette and Country Journal*, December 5, 1768, the first of four essays written under that nom de plume for the paper that month. He apparently wrote an equal number for the *Gazette* as "Candidus," on the same subject over the same period.

17 The best introduction to the real Adams as opposed to the Adams of hackneyed tradition remains Pauline Maier's essay on him in *The Old Revolutionaries* (New York: Alfred A. Knopf, 1980), 3–50.

18 *Journals of the House of Commons*, 32:185–186. As approved by Parliament on February 9, 1769. The small number of revisions made by the Commons, which were accepted by the Lords, have been inserted without noting the original language.

19 For Pitt and the disputes revolving around taxation versus legislation, and so-called "internal" taxes versus "external" taxes, see my "When Words Fail: William Pitt, Benjamin Franklin, and the Imperial Crisis of 1766" *Parliamentary History*, 28 (2009):341–374.

20 See Introduction note 86.

21 *Journals of the House of Representatives*, 45:168–172, passed on June 29, 1769.

22 The Massachusetts Government Act, which can be found in Pickering, ed., *Statutes*, 30:381–390 (14 George III c. 45).

23 A decision not to pursue prosecution.

24 TNA PRO/CO/5/88, fos. 179–180. I added indentations for paragraphs and made minor changes in the punctuation. Zobel, *Boston Massacre*, puts Ross's case into context in a chapter on "Soldiers and the Law," 132–144; see too Hoerder, *Crowd Action*, 212–215.

25 Essentially a bench warrant, ordering an arrest or detention in jail.

26 From the account in the *Boston Gazette*, February 26, 1770. Contrast this version of events with that reported in the *Boston Evening-Post*, February 26, 1770, which included more details and less invective, and the administration-friendly *Massachusetts Gazette*, March 1, 1770, which attempted to be even more dispassionate.

27 See L. Kinvin Wroth and Hiller B. Zobel, eds., *Legal Papers of John Adams*, 3 vols. (Cambridge, MA: The Belknap Press of the Harvard University Press, 1965), 2:396–411 for a fine discussion of how the Richardson case unfolded.

28 J. L. Bell, "From Saucy Boys to Sons of Liberty: Politicizing Youth in Pre-Revolutionary Boston" in James Marten, ed., *Childhood in Colonial America* (New York: New York University Press, 2007), 204–216.

29 William Allen was one of those slain by British soldiers during the riots at St. George's Fields in 1768, itself an extension of the Wilkeite agitation then sweeping London.

30 *Boston Gazette*, March 12, 1770.

31 The most detailed study remains Mary Ann Yodelis, "Boston's Second Major Paper War: Economics, Politics, and the Theory and Practice of Political Expression in the Press, 1763–1775," Ph.D. dissertation, University of Wisconsin, 1971. Although dated, Arthur M. Schlesinger's *Prelude to Independence: The Newspaper War on Britain, 1764–1776* (New York: Alfred A. Knopf, 1958) remains valuable.

32 *Boston Chronicle*, March 8, 1770.

33 *Boston Evening-Post*, March 12, 1770.

34 From the March 12 issue, just after notes on the martyrs' funeral four days earlier.

35 Esther Forbes, *Paul Revere and the World He Lived in* (Boston: Houghton Mifflin, 1942), 472, n19.

36 Unpublished notes sent to the author by Charles Bahne.

37 Thomas Hutchinson to Thomas Gage, March 6, 1770, TNA PRO/CO/5/759, fos. 61–62.

38 William H. Nelson's discussion of Hutchinson in *The American Tory* (Oxford: Oxford University Press, 1961), 21–39 is a good starting point. Bernard Bailyn, *The Ordeal of Thomas Hutchinson* (Cambridge, MA: The Belknap Press of Harvard University Press, 1974) and William Pencak, *America's Burke* (Lanham: University of America Press, 1982) show how far later historians have run with the themes suggested there.

39 Gathered most conveniently in John Phillip Reid, ed., *The Briefs of the American Revolution* (New York: New York University Press, 1981).

40 That is to say, the Earl of Hillsborough, the American secretary.

41 Thomas Gage to the Earl of Hillsborough, April 10, 1770, TNA PRO/CO/5/88, fos. 55–58.

42 See, for example, his letter of May 10, 1768 to Lord Barrington, in Clarence Edwin Carter, ed., *The Correspondence of General Thomas Gage*, 2 vols. (New Haven: Yale University Press, 1931–1933), 2:450.

43 Gage to Hillsborough, September 26, 1768, in ibid., 1:196.

44 In New York, where he kept his headquarters.

45 Thomas Preston to William Pitt, Earl of Chatham, March 17, 1770, in the Pitt Papers, TNA

PRO 30/8/97, part I, fos. 109–114. Preston sometimes used dashes instead of periods to end sentences; likewise, apparently, to indicate new paragraphs. In those instances I substituted periods and indented for paragraphs. Preston wrote in a fairly continuous stream, so I also formed new paragraphs to ease the reading.

46 He is repeating here what Justice Dana said at the hearing related by Lieut. Alexander Ross (see Document 7).

47 The town meeting to Chatham, March 23, 1770, TNA PRO 30/8/97, part I, fos. 115–117.

48 Gordon E. Kershaw, *James Bowdoin: Patriot and Man of the Enlightenment* (Brunswick: Bowdoin College Museum of Art, 1976), 1.

49 Thomas Gage to William Dalrymple, April 28, 1770, Thomas Gage Papers, William L. Clements Library, University of Michigan.

50 See Introduction note 38.

51 Robert Goddard deposition, Ch.M.18.184, BPL mss.

52 From the transcript that Hutchinson sent to London, in TNA PRO/CO/5/759, fo. 358.

53 The word "dead" followed "laying," but was scratched out.

54 Attucks's name was written above "Michael Johnson," which had a line drawn through it.

55 For "*note bene*"—note well.

56 Verdict of the Coroner's Jury Upon Body of Michael Johnson [Crispus Attucks], March 6, 1770, 1891.0056.005, The Bostonian Society and Old State House Museum, Boston.

57 Benjamin Quarles, *The Negro in the American Revolution* (Chapel Hill: University of North Carolina Press, 1961), 3–9 remains the best starting point for Attucks. Also see Kantrowitz, "A Place for 'Colored Patriots'" at Introduction note 99; and, online, J. L. Bell, "On the Trail of Crispus Attucks" *Readex eNewsletter* 4 (February 2009).

58 See John Bell's discussion of Attucks's identity in his blog, "Boston 1775," February 24 and 25, 2008, and in his "On the Trail of Crispus Attucks."

59 Ch.M.1.8.224, BPL mss. The indictment came close to being punctuation free; I added most of the commas.

60 Blackstone, *Commentaries*, 4:342 (Book IV, Chap. 27).

61 See the discussion in William E. Nelson, *Americanization of the Common Law* (Cambridge, MA: Harvard University Press, 1975), 18–35.

62 Hiller B. Zobel, "Law Under Pressure, 1769–1771" in George Athan Billias, ed., *Law and Authority in Colonial America* (Barre.: Barre Publishers, 1965), 202.

63 The "Esquire" was added later, by another hand.

64 *A Short Narrative of The horrid Massacre in Boston* (Boston: Edes & Gill, 1770), 5–32.

65 From the town meeting minutes of March 13, 1770, in A Report of the Record Commissioners of the City of Boston, *Boston Town Records, 1770 Through 1777* (Boston: Rockwell and Churchill, 1887), 13. See *A Short Narrative*, 17, for Bartholomew Kneeland's deposition to Richard Dana and John Hill, dated March 12.

66 *A Narrative, of the Excursion and Ravages of the King's Troops* (Worcester: Isaiah Thomas, 1775).

67 The Merchants of Boston, *Observations on Several Acts of Parliament* (Boston: Edes & Gill, 1769).

68 The editors/committee members added this note: "Since writing this narrative, several depositions have appeared, which make it clear that the sentry was first in fault. He overheard a barber's boy saying, that a captain of the 14th (who had just passed by) was so mean a fellow as not to pay his barber for shaving him. Upon this the sentry left his post and followed the boy into the middle of the street, where he told him to show his face. The boy replied, 'I am not ashamed to show my face to any man.' Upon this the sentry gave him a sweeping strike on the head with his musket, which made him reel and stagger, and cry much. A fellow-apprentice asked the sentry what he meant by this abuse? He replied, 'Damn your blood, if you do not get out of the way I will give you something;' and then fixed his bayonet and pushed at the lads, who both ran out of his way. This dispute collected a few person about the boy, near the Custom House. Presently after this, the party of above-mentioned came into kingstreet, which was a further occasion of drawing people thither, as above related."

69 *A Fair Account of the Late Unhappy Disturbance at Boston in New England* (London: B. White, 1770), 5–28. The first five pages were printed as a single paragraph, so I added paragraph breaks to ease the reader's task. I also eliminated references to specific deposition numbers, either in what followed here or in the *Short Narrative* with which the *Fair Account* took issue.

With but one exception, all of the depositions were dated between March 12 and 16. That exception—included as no. 97, the first in order—was dated April 22 and was therefore sent to London well after Robinson left Boston.

70 The reference here is to a 1352 law, still in effect in Britain at that time, at 25 Edward III c. 2 in Pickering, ed., *Statutes*, 2:50–53. Massachusetts had its own treason statute, passed in 1696, that essentially repeated the words of the 1352 law and applied them to the colony.

71 Which appears as no. 110 in *A Fair Account*, Appendix, 10–11.

72 They appeared as nos. 11 and 38, resp., in *A Short Narrative*, Appendix, 7–8 and 23–25.

73 No. 23 in *A Short Narrative*, Appendix, 13.

74 Dalrymple commanded the 14th Regiment, Carr the 29th; Dalrymple was also overall commander.

75 No. 9 in *A Short Narrative*, Appendix, 5–6.

76 No. 104, in *A Fair Account*, Appendix, 7.

77 No. 100, in ibid., Appendix, 3–4.

78 No. 46 in *A Short Narrative*, Appendix, 31–32.

79 No. 55 in ibid., Appendix, 42.

80 No. 53 in ibid., 38–40 and no. 112 in *A Fair Account*, Appendix, 13–14.

81 Hickling's deposition is no. 73 and Greenwood's is no. 96—the last—in *A Short Narrative*, Appendix, at 59–60 and 75–77, resp. Town leaders considered Greenwood's deposition tainted and regretted its inclusion (go to their note at ibid., 75n). See their letter to Franklin of July 13, 1770, in Document 22. Both Greenwood and Hammond Green, whose deposition (no. 95) comes just before Greenwood's in *A Short Narrative*, would be indicted within days of giving their statements to two justices of the peace.

82 No. 54 in *A Short Narrative*, Appendix, 40–41.

83 Benjamin Andrews, whose deposition was no. 93 in ibid., Appendix, 72.

84 Charles Bourgatte, in other sources.

85 No. 58 in *A Short Narrative*, Appendix, 44–47. He may have been illiterate, since he made his mark rather than wrote his signature on this deposition.

86 No. 95 in ibid., Appendix, 73–74.

87 No. 123 in *A Fair Account*, Appendix, 21–22.

88 *Additional Observations to a Short Narrative of the Horrid Massacre in Boston* (1770). I excluded the two long footnotes printed with the text. The first is a statement by town clerk William Cooper explaining the need for this additional information. The second is a discussion of the value of exports from Britain to the colonies, and the value of colonial exports to Britain. In projecting an increased value of colonial exports to Britain over the next century, and a population increase where Americans would (implicitly) surpass Britons in number, the town leaders were bolstering their argument for a less trade-restrictive navigation system.

89 A Latin phrase presumably familiar to many at the time: "with force and arms."

90 Town committee to Franklin, July 13, 1770, in Labaree, et al., eds., *Papers of Franklin*, 17:186–193.

91 Ch.P.24, BPL mss.

92 Sylvia Frey, *The British Soldier in America* (Austin: University of Texas Press, 1981), 53.

93 John Adams to Jedediah Morse, January 5, 1816, in Adams, ed., *Works*, 10:201.

94 For interesting comments on Langford and the town watch in general, see J. L. Bell, "'I Never Used to Go out with a Weapon': Law Enforcement on the Streets of Prerevolutionary Boston" in *Life on the Streets and Commons, 1600 to the Present* (Boston: Dublin Seminar for New England Folklife Annual Proceedings, 2005), 41–55.

95 Hodgson, *Trial*, 19.

96 TNA PRO/CO/5/759, fo. 382.

97 From "Vindex" in the *Boston Gazette*, January 28, 1771.

98 Judge Edmund Trowbridge, in Hodgson, *Trial*, 178–197. I have deleted Trowbridge's numerous footnote references to legal history or case law, almost all of which were drawn from treatises by English jurists, most notably Matthew Hale and William Blackstone. I kept references to statutes that Trowbridge mentioned aloud and changed them to the more familiar forms from the shorthand used by the printer. I also created more paragraphs because Trowbridge's instructions could be ponderous in their detail.

99 See Professor Coquillette's introductory essay to "The Law Commonplace Book" in Daniel R. Coquillette and Neil Longley York, eds., *Portrait of a Patriot: The Major Political and Legal*

Papers of Josiah Quincy Junior, 5 vols. (Boston: The Colonial Society of Massachusetts, 2005–2009), 2:3–77.

100 In this context, Trowbridge meant "any." He uses "either" this way a number of times.
101 A common Latin phrase; in essence, "for an even stronger reason."
102 Another instance of the usage identified in Documents note 100. More follow.
103 In this context, he meant "not any." He would use it that way again.
104 Self-defense, in the context of a sudden, unprovoked attack.
105 From the *Boston Gazette*, December 17, 1770, which can also be found in Harry Alonzo Cushing, ed., *The Writings of Samuel Adams*, 4 vols. (New York: G. P. Putnam's Sons, 1904–1908), 2:83–89.
106 From the January 21, 1771 installment; also printed in Cushing, *Writings*, 2:142 and 143, resp.
107 Anger as brief madness.
108 Another familiar Latin phrase: "enemy of all mankind."
109 From the *Boston Evening-Post*, December 24, 1770.
110 For the breakdown of this world as both cause and consequence of the Revolutionary movement, see Gordon S. Wood, *The Radicalism of the American Revolution* (New York: Alfred A. Knopf, 1992).
111 Carol Berkin, *Jonathan Sewall: Odyssey of an American Loyalist* (New York: Columbia University Press, 1974), 46.
112 James Lovell, *An Oration Delivered April 2d, 1771* (Boston: Edes & Gill, 1771). Lovell's address was reprinted, along with all of the rest given between 1771 and 1783, in *Orations Delivered at the Request of the Inhabitants of the Town of Boston, to Commemorate the Evening of the Fifth of March, 1770*, 2nd ed. (Boston: Wm. T. Clap, 1807).
113 From the town meeting minutes of March 13, 1770, in *Boston Town Records*, 14.
114 From Micah 4:4, in the Old Testament.
115 Lovell noted that he was quoting the English essayist Sir John Trenchard, who was alluding to the Old Testament tale of Samson in Judges 13–17.
116 Lovell is quoting from Dickinson's *Letters*, Letter III, 15 and 17.
117 From A Citizen of New-York [James Hawkes], *A Retrospect of the Boston Tea-Party, with a Memoir of George R. T. Hewes* (New York: S. S. Bliss, 1834), 27–33.
118 Alfred Young's "George Robert Twelves Hewes (1742–1840): A Boston Shoemaker and the Memory of the American Revolution" *William and Mary Quarterly*, 3rd series 38 (1981):561–623 acted as a précis to *The Shoemaker and the Tea Party* (Boston: Beacon Press, 1999).
119 No. 75 in *A Short Narrative*, Appendix, 90.
120 James Hawkes's account was followed by that of Benjamin Bussey Thatcher, printed as: By A Bostonian, *Traits of the Tea Party; Being a Memoir of George R. T. Hewes* (New York: Harper & Brothers, 1835). There are reasons to suspect the reminiscences offered many years after the fact in Rhode Island's most famous Revolutionary Era incident as well. See my "The Uses of Law and the *Gaspee* Affair" *Rhode Island History*, 50 (1992):3–21. By contrast, Joseph Plumb Martin's reminiscences of his years as a Connecticut soldier in the Revolutionary War, though also offered over a half century after the fact, are accepted as far more reliable. See them in George F. Scheer, ed., *Private Yankee Doodle* (Boston: Little, Brown, and Co., 1962).
121 See the discussions in Charles Warren, "Fourth of July Myths" *William and Mary Quarterly*, 3rd series 2 (1945):237–272; and Garry Wills, *Inventing America* (New York: Doubleday, 1978), 337–344.
122 John Fiske, "Address" in *A Memorial of Crispus Attucks, Samuel Maverick, James Caldwell, Samuel Gray and Patrick Carr* (Boston, 1889), 81–89. I have inserted paragraph breaks that Fiske or the printers chose not to make.
123 Ibid., 94.
124 To get some sense of these fears, see A. C. Goodell, Jr., "The Boston Massacre," first printed in the *Boston Daily Advertiser*, June 3, 1887, then reissued as a pamphlet.
125 Fiske was quoting from Warren's March 5, 1772 commemorative speech, reprinted in *Orations*, 20 (see note 112 above). Warren also gave the fourth anniversary oration, on March 6, 1775. He would be slain at the Battle of Bunker Hill a few months later.
126 Barbara Clark Smith, "A Revolutionary Era" in *Boston and the American Revolution* (Washington, D.C.: National Park Service, 1998), 40–41.
127 Nina Zannieri, "Report from the Field: Not the Same Old Freedom Trail—A View from the

Paul Revere House" *The Public Historian*, 25 (Spring 2003):43. Also see Alfred Young's comments on his involvement with the Trail as a historical consultant in "The Freedom Trail: Walking the Revolution" in *Liberty Tree* (New York: New York University Press, 2006), 296–324.

128 From a statement by Bill Mott, Jr., NPS director, 1985–1989, printed in Horace M. Albright, Russell E. Dickenson, and William Penn Mott, Jr., *National Park Service: The Story Behind the Scenery* (Las Vegas: K. C. Publications, 2007), 93.

129 An excellent example of the type being Blanche M. G. Linden (author) and Steve Dunwell (photographer), *Boston Freedom Trail* (Boston: Back Bay Press, 1996).

130 For the problem in general, see David Lowenthal, *Possessed by the Past* (New York: Free Press, 1996); and at Colonial Williamsburg in particular, Richard Handler and Eric Gable, *The New History in an Old Museum* (Durham: Duke University Press, 1997).

SUGGESTED READING

Virtually all of the manuscript documents associated with the Boston Massacre can be found in four locations: in Boston at the Boston Public Library, the Massachusetts State Archives, and the Massachusetts Historical Society; and near London at the National Archives in Kew. All of the contemporaneous published pamphlets and court proceedings are included in the Early American Imprint Series, now online and text searchable. All of the Boston newspapers printed at the time of the massacre were reproduced on microfilm years ago and will no doubt be available in digitized, online text-searchable formats in the not too distant future. At least some of the unpublished material will eventually be digitized and put online as well. There is, notably, a plan in the offing to do just that with the Colonial Office Papers at the National Archives. Those papers contain much of the official correspondence between London and Boston, most notably letters to and from Gage, Hillsborough, and Hutchinson. They also include transcripts of testimony in the soldiers' trial which differ from the printed version in Hodgson. See Wroth and Zobel's edition of John Adams's legal papers, and Zobel's book on the massacre for a discussion of this and other sources.

Both the basic printed sources and the leading secondary sources are listed below. Robert Allison's brief book is an excellent starting point and Richard Archer's recent study offers interesting insights, but Hiller Zobel's much more involved examination remains the standard account. Zobel's book sparked criticism at the time, most notably by Jesse Lemisch and Pauline Maier, but no rival full-length study until Archer's some forty years later. See the books by Robert Tucker and David Henderickson, and Theodore Draper for the larger Revolutionary Era context. Ian Christie and Benjamin W. Labaree's British/American dialogue remains an interesting way to approach the problems of empire that led to revolution. Peter Thomas's book provides excellent insight into British policies over the years framing the massacre. John Shy's account of the British army and the issue of soldiers among colonial civilians in peacetime is unsurpassed. See too the studies by John Phillip Reid on this issue and on the contest between local and imperial law.

A Fair Account of the Late Unhappy Disturbance at Boston in New England. London: B. White, 1770.

A Short Narrative of The horrid Massacre in Boston. Boston: Edes & Gill, 1770.

Adams, Randolph G. "New Light on the Boston Massacre." *American Antiquarian Society. Proceedings* 47 (1937):259–354.

Additional Observations to a Short Narrative of the Horrid Massacre in Boston. Boston, 1770.

Allison, Robert J. *The Boston Massacre.* Beverly: Commonwealth Editions, 2006.

Archer, Richard. *As If an Enemy's Country.* New York: Oxford University Press, 2010.

Bailyn, Bernard. *The Ordeal of Thomas Hutchinson.* Cambridge, MA: The Belknap Press of the Harvard University Press, 1974.

Bourne, Russell. *Cradle of Violence*. Hoboken: John Wiley & Sons, 2006.

Carp, Benjamin L. *Rebels Rising*. Oxford: Oxford University Press, 2007.

Christie, Ian, and Labaree, Benjamin W. *Empire or Independence, 1760–1776*. New York: W. W. Norton, 1976.

Dickerson, Oliver, ed., *Boston under Military Rule, 1768–1769*. Boston: Chapman & Grimes, 1936.

Draper, Theodore. *A Struggle for Power*. New York: Times Books, 1996.

Hodgson, John. *The Trial of William Wemms . . . .* Boston: J. Fleeming, 1770.

Hoerder, Dirk. *Crowd Action in Revolutionary Massachusetts, 1765–1780*. New York: Academic Press, 1977.

Lemisch, Jesse. "Radical Plot in Boston (1770): A Study of the Use of Evidence." *Harvard Law Review* 84 (1970):485–504.

Maier, Pauline. "Revolutionary Violence and the Relevance of History." *Journal of Interdisciplinary History* 2 (1971):119–135.

——. *From Resistance to Revolution*. New York: Alfred A. Knopf, 1972.

——. "A New Englander as Revolutionary: Samuel Adams." In Pauline Maier, *The Old Revolutionaries*. New York: Alfred A. Knopf, 1980:3–50.

Pencak, William. *War, Politics, & Revolution in Provincial Massachusetts*. Boston: Northeastern University Press, 1981.

Reid, John Phillip. *In a Defiant Stance*. University Park: Pennsylvania State University Press, 1977.

——. *In a Rebellious Spirit*. University Park: Pennsylvania State University Press, 1979.

——. *In Defiance of the Law*. Chapel Hill: University of North Carolina Press, 1981.

Shy, John. *Toward Lexington*. Princeton: Princeton University Press, 1965.

Thomas, Peter D. G. *The Townshend Duties Crisis*. Oxford: Clarendon Press, 1987.

Tucker, Robert W., and Hendrickson, David C. *The Fall of the First British Empire*. Baltimore: Johns Hopkins University Press, 1982.

Warden, G. B. *Boston, 1689–1776*. Boston: Little, Brown, and Co., 1970.

Wroth, L. Kinvin, and Zobel, Hiller B., eds. *Legal Papers of John Adams*. 3 vols. Cambridge, MA: The Belknap Press of the Harvard University Press, 1965.

York, Neil L. "Rival Truths, Political Accommodation, and the Boston 'Massacre.'" *Massachusetts Historical Review* 11 (2009):57–95.

Zobel, Hiller, "Law Under Pressure: Boston, 1769–1771." In George Athan Billias, ed., *Law and Authority in Colonial America*. Barre.: Barre Publishers, 1965:187–205.

——. "Newer Light on the Boston Massacre." *American Antiquarian Society. Proceedings* 78 (1968):119–128.

——. *The Boston Massacre*. New York: W. W. Norton, 1970.

INDEX

Related titles from Routledge

Revolutionary America
1763–1815:
A Documentary Reader
By Francis D. Cogliano and Kirsten E. Phimister

Primary sources are an integral part of any historical period, and represent the backbone of historical record. *Revolutionary America, 1763–1815: A Documentary Reader* was designed in parallel with *A Political History*, and includes excerpts from vital works from the era that shaped The Untied States. With each document framed by editors Francis D. Cogliano and Kirsten E. Phimister, students and instructors can be guided through this great conflict by the voices and texts that first set the course for the War for Independence.

To provide further reading and learning opportunities, *Revolutionary America* also has a vast companion website, featuring extended versions of the documents from the reader, as well as study tools for students and additional resources for instructors. These tools are perfect for either the classroom or the independent scholar, whether used on its own, or as a companion to *A Political History*.

Versatile and crucial to a complete understanding of the era, *Revolutionary America, 1763–1815: A Documentary Reader* is the ideal guide to the changing landscape of the early republic.

ISBN 10: 0-415-99711-9 (hbk)
ISBN 10: 0-415-99712-7 (pbk)

ISBN 13: 978-0-415-99711-9 (hbk)
ISBN 13: 978-0-415-99712-6 (pbk)

Available at all good bookshops
For ordering and further information please visit:
www.routledge.com

Related titles from Routledge

Revolutionary America, 1763–1815
A Political History
By Francis D. Cogliano

Revolutionary America explains the crucial events in the history of the
United States between 1763 and 1815, when settlers of North America
rebelled against British rule, won their independence in a long and
bloody struggle, and created an enduring republic.

Now in its second edition, *Revolutionary America* has been completely
revised, updating the strengths of the previous edition. New features
include:

- New introduction for the second edition
- New chapter on Native Americans
- Revised and expanded bibliographic essay
- Updated historiography throughout the text
- Companion Website with study aids, maps, and documentary
  resources

Revolutionary America also examines those who were excluded from
the immediate benefits and rights secured by the creation of the new
republic. In particular, Cogliano describes the experiences of women,
Native Americans, and African Americans, each of whose experiences
challenged the principle that "all men are created equal," which lay at
the heart of the American Revolution.

Placing the political revolution at the core of the story, *Revolutionary
America* presents a clear history of the War of Independence, and
lays a distinctive foundation for students and scholars of the Early
Republic.

ISBN 10: 0-415-96485-7 (hbk)
ISBN 10: 0-415-96486-5 (pbk)

ISBN 13: 978-0-415-96485-2 (hbk)
ISBN 13: 978-0-415-96486-9 (pbk)

Available at all good bookshops
For ordering and further information please visit:
www.routledge.com